Commandments
of the
Bhagavad
Gita

J.P. Vaswani

Compiled & edited by
Prabha Sampath & Krishna Kumari

JAICO PUBLISHING HOUSE
Ahmedabad Bangalore Bhopal Bhubaneswar Chennai
Delhi Hyderabad Kolkata Lucknow Mumbai

Published by Jaico Publishing House
A-2 Jash Chambers, 7-A Sir Phirozshah Mehta Road
Fort, Mumbai - 400 001
jaicopub@jaicobooks.com
www.jaicobooks.com

THE SEVEN COMMANDMENTS OF
THE BHAGAVAD GITA
ISBN 978-81-8495-083-0

First Jaico Impression: 2010
Fourth Jaico Impression: 2012

Printed by
Repro India Limited
Plot No. 50/2, T.T.C. MIDC Industrial Area
Mahape, Navi Mumbai - 400 710.

Contents

1   Sri Krishna – The Master and His Message   1

2   The Mahabharata   5

3   The Composition of the Epic   7

4   The Bhagavad Gita: Its Background   19
Why the Kurukshetra War Was Fought

5   The Significance of the Gita   31

6   The Essence of the Gita   37

7   Sadhu Vaswani and the Gita   67

8   The Gita: A Universal Scripture   77

9   The Three-fold Path of the Gita   83

10   The Symbolism of the Gita   113

11   The First Commandment: 119
'Thou Shalt Not Identify Thyself with the Body'

12   The Second Commandment: 161
'Thou shalt not fail to do thy duty'

13   The Third Commandment: 201
'Thou Shalt Do Thy Duty and a Little More'

14 The Fourth Commandment: 233
   'Thou Shalt Not Miss Thy Daily
   Appointment with God'

15 The Fifth Commandment: 263
   'Whatever Thou Doest, Do It for the
   Love of God'

16 The Sixth Commandment: 279
   'Thou Shalt Seek the Lowest Place'

17 The Seventh Commandment: 307
   'Thou Shalt Rejoice in Everything that the
   Will of God Brings to Thee'

Appendix 1 335

Appendix 2 369

Glossary 371

Sri Krishna
The Master and His Message

He came here upon this earth long ago! Tradition tells us that Sri Krishna came here 5000 years ago. He came with bewitching beauty. He came with the matchless music of His magical flute. And, even as He played upon the flute, so our *puranas* tell us, the very winds thrilled, the trees swayed, the rivers resonated, the buzzing bees and the cooing *koel* stopped to listen, and the stars and moon stood still, and many hearts were hushed as divine melody poured forth from the flute!

Who was He? Nameless — for a thousand names are not enough to name Him aright. Who was He?
The purest of the pure was He, spotless, stainless; in Him was the light that casts no shadow. Who was He? The *gopas* and the *gopis*, the simple cowherds and milkmaids who had the good fortune to have Him grow up amidst them, whose rare privilege and blessing it was to have beheld His beautiful face, with whom He played games and indulged in a thousand divine *leelas* — the *gopas* and *gopis* exclaimed when they saw Him face to face: "We have seen the light of love in His face! We have seen the rapture of love! We have seen the ecstasy of love! We have seen the face of *ananda* — the bliss that no ending knows!"

Who was He? The light of God shone in His eyes, the smile of divinity was on His lips, the wonder of the infinite was in His gaze, and the fragrance of the spring breeze was in His wondrous words.

Born on a dark and rainy night when His parents were incarcerated in the dungeon of a tyrant, He had two mothers who doted upon Him — Devki who gave birth to Him, and Yashoda who had the privilege of bringing Him up. He grew up in the salubrious environs of Brindaban, on the banks of the blessed Jamuna river. Out in the open He lived; He felt close to nature; He tended the cows, and consorted with the simple and innocent *gwalas* of Govardhan. He listened to the mystic voice of nature and He heard too, the voice of the inner realm of the spirit. In due course, this cowherd, this mystic flute player, became the greatest teacher of men, the Master of spiritual wisdom. And those who heard Him speak, exclaimed: "Never has man spoken as He!"

On the battlefield of Kurukshetra, in the midst of ranged armies ready for battle, He gave utterance to that great wisdom which the centuries have revered as the *Bhagavad Gita*. Since then, kingdoms have come and gone; empires have been built and crumbled to their fall; civilizations have been born, and like bubbles floating on the surface of a stream, civilisations have burst — but the *Gita* lives on.

Innumerable relics of ancient arts and memorials of kings and emperors have vanished, perished with the onslaught of time. But the *Gita* lives on!

The *Gita* lives on! It has moved, inspired, illumined the soul of India for over fifty centuries — and the day is close at hand when it will move and inspire all of humanity. For I verily believe, as Sadhu Vaswani said, that the *Gita* is a Bible of humanity.

Though the message was given on the sacred soil of *Bharat Varsha*, it is meant not only for India, but for all humanity! Though the message was given to us fifty centuries ago, it has so much to teach the world even today — especially those of us who are the sons and daughters of this excited, agitated, stressed age.

2

The Mahabharata

The *Mahabharata* is the greater in size of the two great epics of India. Scholars tell us that it is more than eight times the size of Homer's Iliad and Odyssey put together. It contains over 1,00,000 stanzas, and is therefore called *Satasahasri*. It consists of eighteen *Parvas* or chapters, with a nineteenth section which forms a sort of appendix to the whole. It is the world's longest poem, and its unique feature is that it contains within itself, the *Bhagavad Gita* which is the ultimate world scripture.

The *Mahabharata* may be regarded as a veritable discourse on *dharma* or righteousness. Written by *Rishi* Ved Vyasa who is thought to have compiled the *Vedas*, the *Mahabharata* is often referred to as the fifth *Veda*, for its myriad stories and incidents bring out every truth that is embedded in the *Vedas*. 'Yata Dharma Stato Jaya', where there is righteousness, there is victory, may be said to be the central theme of this encyclopaedic epic. It celebrates the ultimate and unfailing triumph of good over evil, and the story brings home to us eternal, universal truths that can teach us to aspire to the best life here and hereafter.

Rishi Ved Vyasa tells us:

> '*Yadihaasti tadanyatra*
> *Yannehaasti na kutrachit*'

> That which is here can be seen elsewhere; but
> that which is not found here, cannot be seen
> anywhere else.

This is just an indication of the comprehensive nature of
the epic, and all the aspects of human life and human
nature that it deals with. The lofty heights and the
deplorable depths to which men can rise and fall – the
glory, the greed, the whole extent of the eternal conflict
between *dharma* and *adharma* is captured in this great saga
of love and hatred, good and evil, war and peace. It is
sanctified and ennobled by the presence of Sri Krishna, a
dearly beloved *avatara* of Lord Vishnu, who participates in
the action of the epic.

The Composition
of the Epic

There is a very interesting story that concerns the composition of this epic. When *Rishi* Ved Vyasa undertook its composition, he realized that it would be a monumental task, well beyond human abilities. At this point, Brahma appeared before him and instructed him to invoke Lord Ganesha to assist him in the task. Lord Ganesha readily agreed to write down all that the rishi dictated. But he insisted on one condition: the dictation had to go on and on, without a break. If ever there was a break, Lord Ganesha would give up and leave.

Ved Vyasa was nonplussed. How could he dictate such a massive and complex work without a break? On the other hand, without Lord Ganesha's help, he could never ever hope to complete it! He thought for a moment, and then agreed to the condition. But he too, laid a condition before his divine stenographer: Ganesha should not write down anything, the full significance of which he had not understood.

The conditions were mutually accepted and the monumental task began. As he had anticipated, Ved Vyasa often needed time to compose those stanzas which embodied complex ideas and situations. At such stages, he would deliberately dictate a difficult stanza, and Lord Ganesha was forced to slow down, or even stop his writing, to try and decipher the meaning of what he had just heard. This gave Ved Vyasa the gap he needed to compose further.

This beautiful story only goes to show that the *Mahabharata* is a work of great complexity and profundity.

Bhishma

The events of the epic take place in the *Dwapara yuga*. The kingdom of Hastinapur was ruled by a noble king named Shantanu. He fell in love with a beautiful fisherwoman called Satyavati and wished to marry her. Her father insisted that his daughter would only marry him on the assurance that *her* children would inherit the throne. Shantanu was reluctant to accept this, for he had a noble and valiant son, who was also wise and virtuous, called Devavrata. When Devavrata heard of his father's predicament, he voluntarily took a vow of celibacy, renounced his right to the crown, and requested the fisherwoman to become his father's wife. Devavrata, from then on, became known as Bhishma.

Dhritarashtra and Pandu

Founded on the supreme sacrifice of Bhishma, this strange marriage produced two sons, Chitrangada and Vichitravirya, who ruled one after the other. The latter had two sons – Dhritarashtra, who was born blind; and Pandu, who was born with a pale complexion. When they grew up, Bhishma got them both married. Dhritarashtra married

Gandhari, who, out of a feeling of devotion to her blind husband, decided to blindfold herself for the rest of her life.

Pandu took two wives, Kunti and Madri. Kunti had, in the past, given birth to a son, while she was unmarried. The child, named Karna, an offspring of *Surya*, the Sun God, was abandoned and brought up by a humble folk. He grew up to be a valiant soldier, though no one ever suspected his origins. Between Kunti and Madri, Pandu had five sons – Yudhishtira, Bhima, Arjuna, Nakula and Sahadeva – known as the Pandavas. When Pandu died, Madri decided to sacrifice herself on his funeral pyre, and Kunti was left with the task of bringing up the five princes.

The Kauravas and the Pandavas

Dhritarashtra had one hundred sons, known as the Kauravas, the eldest of whom was Duryodhana. Now the cousins, the Kauravas and the Pandavas, were brought up together, but Duryodhana developed a strong hatred and ill-will towards his cousins.

The princes were trained under a great Brahmin guru, Dronacharya. Arjuna emerged as the champion warrior out of this training. When his supremacy was challenged by Karna, he refused to compete with Karna on the ground that he was of a lower caste, the son of a charioteer. Enraged at the refusal, Duryodhana made Karna the ruler of a province called Anga, thus conferring upon him a status equal to that of Arjuna. Deeply moved by this gesture, Karna became Duryodhana's most trusted and loyal friend, until his death.

The Palace of Wax

Dhritarashtra was a weak and biased ruler. He was disturbed by the growing popularity of the Pandavas, as against his sons. Gandhari's brother Shakuni, plotted and conspired with his nephews to do away with their cousins. A palace of wax was constructed at Shakuni's behest, and Kunti and the Pandavas were invited to stay there. Suspicious of this, the Pandavas dug a tunnel out of the palace and escaped to safety, even as the palace was set afire.

Realizing that their lives were in danger at the hands of the ruthless Kauravas, Kunti and her sons disguised themselves as mendicant Brahmins and travelled from place to place. Thus they reached the Kingdom of Drupada where the beautiful princess Draupadi was to marry the most skilful archer who would emerge as a winner in a contest of valour.

Several princes and noblemen were all set to compete for the hand of the beautiful maiden. But none could pass the tough test of skill in archery. Karna, now the King of Anga, came to attend the meet. But Draupadi insulted him, and he was turned away. Arjuna, disguised as a young Brahmin, took the test and emerged successful. The king gave the princess's hand to the young stranger and they went to the humble dwelling where they now lived with their mother. They called out to her to come and see what they had brought back for her that day.

Kunti, who thought that they were referring to the alms they had received, told them, 'Whatever it may be, divide it equally among the five of you.'

The Marriage of Draupadi

The words were spoken; the dice were cast, and there would be no going back now. Draupadi was to become the wife of the five Pandava brothers! The wedding was celebrated in style, and now that the Pandavas's whereabouts became known, Dhritarashtra was constrained to invite them back to Hastinapur, and set up Yudhishtira as the ruler of their share of the kingdom. Here, under the guidance of Lord Krishna, they ruled wisely and well. They built a beautiful city called Indraprastha, with a magnificent palace, where Yudhishtira performed the *Rajasuya Yagna*. Kings and princes came to attend the event, and were full of praise for the Pandavas. The Kauravas had also been invited. Duryodhana's clumsy gait in the magnificent halls of the palace amused Draupadi who laughed at his mistakes. Duryodhana was so enraged at her behaviour, that when he returned to Hastinapur, he plotted and connived with Shakuni and Dushasana, one of his brothers, to strip the Pandavas of their kingdom, power, and wealth, and to drive them out of hearth and home.

The Game of Dice

The Kauravas issued an invitation to the Pandavas to play a game of dice, a royal custom which a prince could not refuse. Shakuni used loaded dice which he could cast in his own favour, and the Pandavas lost heavily at every throw. It was unfortunate that Yudhishtira could not bring himself to stop, for he was very fond of the game. As the game progressed, the Pandavas lost everything they had, including their kingdom and their crown, and even their freedom. In a last desperate gamble, prompted by the evil

Shakuni, Yudhishtira offered Draupadi as the wager, and she too, was lost to the false dice. The Pandavas and their wife were all now the slaves of the Kauravas.

Draupadi *Vastraharan*

In a fit of vengeful malice, Duryodhana ordered Dushasana to drag Draupadi by her hair to the court. Even as she protested vehemently, he told Dushasana to strip her of her clothes. The elders of the Kuru dynasty, Bhishma, Dhritarashtra and their guru, Dronacharya, were mute spectators to the outrage being perpetrated. Draupadi's five husbands simply hung their heads in shame and grief. Only Vidhura, the blind king's half-brother, dared to protest, but to no avail.

Dushasana began the terrible deed that would bring everlasting shame to his family. In her utter despair and misery, Draupadi prayed to Lord Krishna, who came to her aid instantly, and she was saved from outrage. No matter how long and hard he pulled, Dushasana could not disrobe her, for she was now under the Lord's protection – and her garment turned into an endless stretch of fabric which issued forth continuously and protected her honour and virtue. The Kauravas were left in shame and ignominy, unable to accomplish the dastardly deed they set out to perform.

Too late, King Dhritarashtra woke up to the horror of the events taking place in his court. He used his sovereign power to set the Pandavas and Draupadi free – but one condition remained. As losers in the game, they would be forced to spend twelve years in the forest, and the thirteenth year incognito, before they could reclaim their lost kingdom. If they were detected, the whole cycle of exile would have to be repeated.

Enraged at the humiliation meted out to them, Bhima and Arjuna swore vengeance against the Kauravas. They would have taken on their cousins then and there, but they were restrained by Yudhishtira who warned them that they would have to bide by the rules of the game they had lost, even though their opponents had defrauded them.

The Pandavas in Exile

Twelve long years did the Pandavas spend in the depth of the forests. Their one source of joy and comfort was the constant, never-failing support and friendship of Lord Sri Krishna, who was Kunti's nephew, and their maternal cousin. (Kunti and Vasudeva, Sri Krishna's father, were brother and sister, although Kunti had been given in adoption.)

Many were the adventures they faced, myriad events befell them, and numerous friends and well-wishers they gained, during those twelve long years. When the thirteenth year began, they decided to take their abode at the court of King Virata, all of them suitably disguised to prevent detection.

Yudhishtira became a dice-player to entertain the king. Arjuna donned female garb to become the dance and music teacher to Princess Uttara. Bhima became the royal cook. Nakula and Sahadeva took charge of the stables. Draupadi was appointed the queen's maid-in-waiting, calling herself Sairandhari.

The End of Keechaka

The queen's brother, Keechaka, was a strong and powerful man in the court of Virata. He began to make improper advances to the beautiful Sairandhari. Unable to put up with his harassment, she complained to Bhima. One night, Bhima lured him out to a secret encounter and thrashed him to death in an unarmed combat. Of course, no one suspected that the palace cook could have accomplished such a feat!

However, Keechaka's presence had been a restraining factor against Virata's enemies, for the kingdom was rich in cattle-wealth and often attacked by marauders. Now that Keechaka was out of the way, Duryodhana launched an attack on the kingdom. King Virata ordered his young son, Prince Uttar, to defend the country. Yudhishtira, in the disguise of Kanka, persuaded the king to let Arjuna (Brihannala, as he was known) to accompany the prince as his charioteer. When they confronted Duryodhana's army, Uttar's courage failed him and he was about to flee from the field, but Arjuna calmed him down. Recovering the Pandava weapons that he had hidden, he fought a fierce battle in which the Kauravas were routed and forced to flee for their lives.

The Pandavas Are Revealed

But the Kauravas hit back in an unexpected way. Suspecting that none other than Arjuna could have fought so fierce a battle, they proclaimed that they had detected the Pandavas before the thirteenth year was complete, and so they would have to resume the cycle of exile.

However, the Pandavas came out of their disguise and claimed their kingdom. They had paid the full penalty for their defeat in the game of dice, spending twelve years in exile, and the thirteenth year incognito, as per the conditions laid. Acting as their emissary, Sri Krishna went to the Kauravas and demanded that the Pandavas' kingdom should be returned to them forthwith. Duryodhana refused the request. Yudhishtira was willing to compromise in the interest of peace, and offered that he would be willing to accept five villages in lieu of their kingdom. But the adamant Duryodhana would not pay heed to the plea. Now, a battle would become the only option by which the dispute could be settled.

At this juncture, Kunti revealed to Karna the secret of his birth and urged him to join his natural brothers and become their king, as the eldest. But his loyalty and love for Duryodhana would not allow Karna to fulfill his mother's wish, even though he was overwrought with emotion at the discovery of his true identity.

The Battle of Kurukshetra

Thus the stage was set for the battle between the Pandavas and the Kauravas at Kurukshetra. Kings and their armies from all over the land took sides to join one of the camps and participate in the ensuing battle. Though Sri Krishna would not take sides or fight in the battle, he graciously consented to become Arjuna's charioteer. Bhishma was declared the chief of the Kauravas, while Draupadi's brother Drishtadhyumna, was the leader of the Pandavas.

The *Bhagavad Gita*

As the gongs sounded and conches were blown to signal the start of the war, Arjuna fell into deep distress and despair at the sight of his kinsmen and friends ranged against one another, ready to kill and be killed, for the sake of land. He laid down his bow, and declared that he could not fight such a ruthless battle.

At this juncture, Sri Krishna, acting as his true friend, guide and guardian, counselled him on his duty, and on the ideal attitude to life and action that a man should adopt. It is this advice which is enshrined in the *Bhagavad Gita*, which many of us revere today as the ultimate scripture.

The Ravages of War

Consoled and comforted by divine guidance, Arjuna fought bravely, as indeed, did the others. One by one, leaders and elders and generals lost their lives on both sides. Bhishma's body was riddled with arrows shot by his favourite nephew Arjuna. Drona was slain by Draupadi's brother, to settle an old dispute. On their part, the Pandavas lost Arjuna's brave young son Abhimanyu. Karna was slain by Arjuna.

Bhima single-handedly killed ninety-eight of the Kaurava brothers. To fulfill Draupadi's vow of revenge, he killed Dushasana, and with the blood of his entrails, tied up Draupadi's hair, which she had left loose and undressed since the indignity she had suffered at the Kuru court. Finally, he killed Duryodhana in a one-to-one combat. The

Kauravas were utterly and totally destroyed.

All that remained of the once-great dynasty were the five Pandava brothers. Every one of their sons had been killed in a midnight attack on their camp by Ashwathama, acting in revenge for the death of his father Drona. The only heir to the once-proud clan was now in the womb of Uttara, who had been married to Abhimanyu, son of Arjuna and Shubadhra, Lord Krishna's sister. Bhishma passed away; and the Pandavas's triumphant entry into Hastinapur was a desolate event, for the kingdom was full of wailing widows.

Yudhishtira began to rule the kingdom, and he also took care of the older members of the family — Dhritarashtra, Gandhari, and Kunti. Soon, the three grief-stricken old people renounced worldly life and entered the *tapovana* (forest of meditation), where they were killed in a fire. In time, Uttara's and Abhimanyu's son Parikshit was crowned the king, and the Pandava brothers and Draupadi left on their final journey Godwards.

4

The Bhagavad Gita:
Its Background

Why the Kurukshetra War Was Fought

For thirteen long years, the Pandavas had lived in exile, untraced by the Kauravas, while the kingdom which was theirs by right, was ruled by the wicked Duryodhana. For thirteen long years, the Pandavas had withstood the harassments and troubles meted out to them at the instigation of the Kauravas; and they successfully spent the last year – the thirteenth year – *incognito*, in concealment, unrecognised by the rest of the world.

Having successfully completed the thirteen years of exile imposed on them by the Kauravas, the Pandavas finally came out to claim their share of the kingdom, with their own city, Indraprastha, as its capital. Lord Sri Krishna, who was not only their maternal cousin, but their friend, philosopher, guide, and spiritual mentor, willingly undertook the role of their emissary, and approached the Kauravas with a request to hand over half the empire to the Pandavas as promised.

Duryodhana, blinded by ego and malice, was adamant. He would not return half the kingdom as his father had promised; he would not give five towns or five villages to his five cousins; he would not even give away as much land as *the point of a needle* to the Pandavas.

Sri Krishna returned to the Pandavas and advised them that they should now prepare to fight for their rights, for Duryodhana was deaf and blind to all that was good and right and just in this world.

The Pandavas and the Kauravas had already started gathering their forces; several allies and friends also offered their armies to the two sides. Both sides decided to seek the help of Sri Krishna, for He was the lord of the powerful *Narayan Sena* which consisted of thousands and thousands of strong and valiant soldiers. So Duryodhana and Arjuna travelled to Dwaraka to meet Sri Krishna.

When they arrived at the palace of the Yadavas, Sri Krishna was asleep on a couch in His chamber. The cousins were asked to enter the chamber and take their seats. In his deep humility and piety, Arjuna sat near the feet of the Lord – the lotus-feet that were dear to him. In his pride and arrogance, Duryodhana, who considered himself the Lord's equal, took a seat near the head of the couch. When the Lord opened His eyes, He naturally saw Arjuna first. Only later did He see Duryodhana.

Sri Krishna welcomed the two cousins, and enquired of them the purpose of their visit. When He realised that both of them had come to seek His help, He decided that He would offer the first choice to Arjuna, for it was Arjuna whom He had seen first. This angered Duryodhana, but he had to consent to the proposal.

The Lord turned to Arjuna and said: "You are here to seek

my help in the war, and I offer you the first choice. You can either have me on your side – unarmed – or you can choose my strong and valiant *Narayan Sena* to fight for you. But I must warn you, I will only be a witness to this war. For I am bound by a vow not to take up arms. So you may choose."

Arjuna did not hesitate even for a minute. "My dear Lord, I want You, and nothing and no one else, besides You."

Sri Krishna turned to Duryodhana, who was delighted by what he thought to be Arjuna's utter folly. With alacrity, he expressed his wish to have the powerful *Narayan Sena* on his side.

Thus it was that the Lord became Arjuna's charioteer in the war between the Kauravas and the Pandavas. The *Mahabharata* gives us the detailed description of this holy war. It is said to have lasted in full force for eighteen days, by which time most of the armies on both sides were destroyed. There followed a bitterly fought mace-duel, in which Bhima killed Duryodhana. Angered by the humiliation, Ashwathama killed Draupadi's children and set fire to the Pandava camp. Innumerable kings, great spiritual leaders and gurus, countless warriors and common soldiers sacrificed their lives, so that justice, goodness, and *dharma* could be vindicated.

The *Gita* is but a section, a part of the great epic *Mahabharata*. But it is worth its weight in rubies and gold.

Ved Vyasa, the great *rishi* who wrote the *Mahabharata* was indeed divinely inspired when he composed it. The whole work is charged with a lofty idealism and has several passages of unparallelled depth and profundity. These are inspired by *gnana* (wisdom), *dhyana* (meditation), and *karma* (action). They are radiant with purity and wisdom.

In the centre of this magnificent epic is set the crowning jewel of the *Gita* – the 'Song of Life', the 'Song Supreme', as Sadhu Vaswani describes it. It is known as the *Srimad Bhagavad Gita*, the Lord's song or the song divine. The song was uttered by Sri Krishna on the battlefield of Kurukshetra.

On the Kurukshetra, we read, was the *Gita* delivered by the Lord. Kurukshetra literally means 'area of action' or 'field of work'. The *Gita* gives us a noble message of work; it is a gospel of action.

The *Gita* is often spoken of as *Gitopanishad*, as the 'milk of the scriptures' and, the 'essence of the *shastras*'.

'The *Gita*,' writes Mahatma Gandhi, "is not a historical discourse. A physical illustration is often needed to drive home a spiritual truth." Thus, Gandhi tells us, what happened on the *dharmakshetra* of Kurukshetra, was not just a war between the cousins – the Pandavas and the Kauravas. It is the war that has taken place, is taking place, and will continue to take place in the mind within man, now and forever. It is the eternal, universal strife between good and evil.

The Opening of the Gita

The Kauravas's father Dhritarashtra is physically as well as morally blind. His great love for his hundred sons blinds him to all sense of justice and morality. Even when he could have intervened to save the situation and avoid the battle by returning the Pandavas's share of the kingdom back to them, he allows himself to be led – misled – by his blind love for his sons. When he hears that his uncle, Bhishma Pitamaha, has been fatally injured in battle and is lying on his deathbed of arrows, awaiting the auspicious hour of his death, he is profoundly moved, and requests Sanjaya to narrate to him the details of the war, as it has happened up to that time.

Thus it is through Sanjaya's narrative to Dhritarashtra that the Kurukshetra war and the *Bhagavad Gita* are reported to us.

The *Bhagavad Gita* actually opens with the words of Sanjaya's narration to Dhritarashtra . . .

The Pandavas and the Kauravas had arranged their respective armies on the battlefield. Duryodhana beheld the mighty army of the Pandavas, which was led by Drishtadhyumna, brother of Draupadi, and brother-in-law of the Pandavas. Ranged on the side of the Pandavas were the valiant Arjuna, the mighty Bhima, as well as distinguished kings and noble warriors like Satyaki, Virata, Dhrupada, and Kuntibhoja, and the young and brave Abhimanyu. The Kaurava army was led by Bhishma; this army had the presence of the great guru of the Kauravas and Pandavas, Dronacharya. There was also Kripacharya, the *Rajguru* of the Kauravas; Karna, Ashwathama, Vikarna, and the brave and loyal brothers of Duryodhana.

At this point Lord Krishna arrived on the battlefield with Arjuna, driving the magnificent chariot which had been presented to Arjuna by *Agni*, the God of Fire. This chariot was drawn by white horses, which were also a divine gift. The flag on the chariot had an emblem of Hanuman, the heroic devotee of Sri Rama.

It was Bhishma who first blew his mighty conch, following which the roar of conches, kettledrums, tabors, tambourines and cornets arose from all leaders on the Kauravas's side, creating a thunderous effect.

On the Pandavas's side, Sri Krishna blew his divine conch, Panchajanya. Arjuna blew his conch named Devadatta. Bhima blew his heavy, large conch, called Paundra. Yudhishtira blew his conch called Anantvijaya. Nakula and Sahadeva blew their conches, Sughosta and Manipushpaka. Then all the mighty warriors on the Pandavas's side, blew their conches together, and the combined sound created a terrible fear in the hearts of Dhritarashtra's sons. The sounds of the mighty conches echoed and re-echoed from the earth and the sky, on the battlefield of Kurukshetra.

Arjuna's Dilemma

'Dharmakshetre kurukshetre samaveta yuyutsavaha...'

On the holy plain, the field of the righteousness, the field of the Kurus, gathered together, eager for battle...

Let us note – the very first word of the *Gita*, the opening word of this magnificent scripture is *dharma*, the great word of ancient India. Just as Beauty was dear to Greece and Power was dear to Rome, *dharma* was close to the soul of India. Our ancient *rishis* exhorted us to 'build our life in *dharma*'.

Dharma is derived from *dhru* which means 'hold'. *Dharma* is the power, the force, the *jivan shakti* which holds life. *Kshetra* means 'field'.

Let us therefore, ask ourselves: "What am I sowing in the field of life — *dharma* or *adharma*?" If you are one of the blessed souls who are sowing the seeds of *dharma*, your life becomes a song, a *Gita* of the Lord!

Thousands of researchers have delved into the specifics of the war fought in Kurukshetra. Even today, when trains stop at modern Kurukshetra on the Delhi-Shimla route, people strain their necks to see outside, even alighting from the train to 'get the feel' of the site where the great battle took place. Hundreds of learned volumes have been written about the battle itself.

However, for the true seeker, the *jignasu* who wishes to tread the spiritual path, the *Gita* belongs to a different dimension, which transcends the geographical and historical setting. True, the conflict between the Pandavas and the Kauravas is the central theme of the great epic. But this war between kinsmen is symbolic of the good fight that each man must fight — the war between good and evil, the war within. A particularly compelling aspect of this fight is the clash between conflicting duties.

Amidst the noise of conches, kettledrums, tabors and horns which herald the beginning of the battle, Arjuna, *Partha*, requests his divine charioteer, *Parthasarathi*, to drive his chariot between the two armies, so that he might see those who have assembled to fight for the evil-minded Duryodhana.

The Lord drives the chariot forward and says to His
devoted disciple and dear friend, "Arjuna, behold all the
Kurus gathered together."

What does Arjuna see?

> Then saw Arjuna standing there, uncles and
> grandfathers, teachers, mother's brothers, sons
> and grandsons, cousins and comrades, fathers-in-
> law, and friends in both armies. Seeing all these
> kinsmen, Arjuna was deeply moved to pity.
>
> I: 26-28

It is necessary that we understand Arjuna and his
predicament here. He is no ordinary man; he is a great
hero; Dronacharya's greatest disciple, and a friend of Lord
Sri Krishna.

Arjuna then, is a great soul, but utterly confounded by the
grave situation that he faces now. He has come to the
battlefield, prepared to fight, but at the moment of
decisive action, he is confounded.

The first *adhyaya* of the *Gita*, as Sadhu Vaswani pointed
out, is a section on depression, *Arjuna Vishada Yoga*. Indeed,
the first step in spiritual life is *vishada* (darkness of the
soul).

Is it not true that when we set out in quest of the life
spiritual, we pass through a period characterized as
"darkness of the soul"? At the very first step that we take
on the spiritual path, we cry out in sorrow, "What is the
meaning of life? What does it all mean? Why are we here?
Whither do we go from here?"

Even Jesus cried out, 'My God! My God! Why hast Thou forsaken me?'

Did not Draupadi too, experience this darkness of the soul when she cried out, "All have left me, my kinsmen, my brothers, my father – even You, O Krishna!"

All of us must pass through a period of loneliness and internal conflict before we can enter into self-knowledge, true awareness of the Self. It is in this loneliness that we can shed our ego, and realise that we are not alone.

And so, Arjuna, the great hero, the brave warrior, stands confounded on the field of Kurukshetra.

> 'My limbs fail, my mouth is parched, my body quivers, my hair stands on end. My Gandiva bow slips from my hand and my skin burns all over; I am not able to stand steady; my brain is reeling.'
>
> I: 29-30

Arjuna is sad and lonely. His mind is agitated; his consciousness is clouded. This hero of a hundred fights suddenly begins to suffer from nervous fright. This has happened to men and women again and again. Renunciation, turning our back on life and action, running away from it all, seems a very easy option. In Arjuna's case, he is moved by pity, and pity opens the door to weakness. "Can I slay my kinsmen and be happy?" he asks.

> 'I desire not victory, O Krishna, nor kingdom, nor pleasures. What is kingdom to us, O Krishna, or enjoyment or even life itself?'
>
> I: 32

Arjuna is well aware that the Pandavas have every chance of winning, because their cause is just, and above all, because Krishna is with them. It is not the possibility of defeat or victory that agitates Arjuna. His mind is torn by doubts and fears and anxieties.

Is it not a crime to murder one's kinsmen and annihilate a whole race?

Is it not *adharma* to kill the ancient traditions of a whole family?

Is it right to fight and kill one's kinsmen just because they happen to be on the wrong side? Would it not be the right thing to do to spare the lives of his cousins, his guru, and his dearly loved grandfather?

Let us note here that Duryodhana is not in the least bothered by such worries. Never, ever does he reflect upon the injustice or *adharma* of his cause. He simply does not differentiate between good and evil.

But then, the *Gita* is not addressed to Duryodhana. It is addressed to Arjuna who, in this great war between good and evil, stands firmly on the side of *dharma*. He has made the choice between good and evil long ago, but now, he is torn asunder by a seemingly irresolvable conflict. Arjuna, like so many of us, is bewildered by the choice he has to make. He is in the grip of uncertainty. He faces the classic dilemma − to act or not to act.

It is only honest, conscientious people who are forced to confront such perplexing situations. As for selfish, unscrupulous men, they are guided and motivated only by their own desires and narrow interests.

Truly has it been said, by innumerable commentators, that the 'battle' here is not a fight between armies, but a *war within a soul*. They tell us that the chariot symbolizes the body, in which the mind (Arjuna) is seated, along with Sri Krishna, the *Atman*, the *Self*. The horses symbolize the five senses. And Kurukshetra is the plane of action, the plane of friction, the world of strife and contradictions, that we inhabit. Therefore have the wise ones taught us that life on earth is a battle, and all of us must fight the good fight, for the just cause. True, when we fight others, we hurt them, we harm them, we inflict violence on them. And even when we conquer our near and dear ones, we lose! But when we choose to fight all that is base and weak and selfish and petty within us, we cannot help but win!

It was Swami Ramdas who said, "There is no greater victory in the life of a human being than victory over the mind. The true soldier is he who fights not the external, but the internal foes."

Fortunately for Arjuna, Sri Krishna holds the reins of the chariot, for God is always on man's side in the fight against evil. So when Arjuna says, "I will not fight", and sinks into silence and despair, Sri Krishna is at hand to guide him with words of wisdom.

"Weep not," the Master tells His dear, devoted disciple, "but be a man, a master-man! Abandon weakness! Stand up in courage! Stand up and fight!"

Sadhu Vaswani emphasized the heroic note in the *Gita*. He called the *Gita*, the 'Song of Strength', the 'Song of *Shakti*'.

'*Uttishta! Paramtapa!*' Stand up, Arjuna! Each one of us is called upon to fulfill our task in life. To fight the good fight, as I have said repeatedly. Evil is within us, evil is outside us. Everywhere, there are wrongs to be righted, weaknesses to be fought and conquered. We cannot say, 'I will not fight!'

The Lord tells us, even as he tells Arjuna: "Stand up and fight! For life is a battlefield." Stand up and fight evil! Stand up and fight injustice! Conquer the ego! Vanquish your weaknesses!

The message of the *Gita* is the message of courage, heroism and *atmashakti*. The *Gita* teaches us that weakness is a sin, while *shakti* is a spiritual virtue.

5

The Significance of the Gita

The *Gita* is a holy scripture, a song celestial, a thought-provoking discourse, a sacred gospel, the word of God – and a profound, powerful poem. It is also a deeply significant spiritual work, and a unique philosophical treatise. The speaker of the *Gita* is none other than the Lord, Sri Krishna himself.

Amazingly, He delivered this divine discourse in the unusual environment of a terrible war that was set to change the whole history of this ancient land.

How was this possible?

Records tell us that the *Gita* has been translated into at least thirty-six languages. Sadhu Vaswani rightly referred to it as a 'world scripture', and a 'Bible of humanity'. Sri Adi Shankara himself wrote one of the most respected and authoritative commentaries on the *Gita*. Other distinguished spiritual luminaries like Sri Ramanuja, Sri Madhavacharya, Sri Vallabhacharya, and Sri Jnaneshwar have added valuable insights to their respective *bhashyas*. In modern times, Lokmanya Tilak, Mahatma Gandhi, and Sri Aurobindo have written about the *Gita*. As for me, I was privileged to be the disciple, devotee, and nephew of a

great-souled saint, whom many regarded as a 'living Gita'
– Sadhu Vaswani. This book draws greatly on his extensive
teachings, discourses, and writings on the *Gita*.

Every single *shloka*, indeed every line, every word of the *Gita*
unveils such profound truths and deep spiritual vistas,
that books and commentaries have been written on single
chapters of the *Gita*, single concepts from the *Gita* – nay,
single lines of the *Gita*.

There is another interesting fact revealed to us in the
Anugita Parva of the *Mahabharata*. Here, a war-weary and
dejected Arjuna asks his Divine Mentor, Sri Krishna, to
repeat the teachings of the *Gita* to him. The Lord's reply is
significant:

'I am unable to repeat in its entirety, the philosophy of the
Supreme *Brahman* which I had told you while in a state of
deep yoga'.

This should answer the question I raised earlier.

The *Gita* is no ordinary conversation (*samvada*) between
two ordinary beings on one of the many battlefields of the
world. No! The *Gita* is an extraordinary scripture – the
record of an extraordinary discourse between two
extraordinary men – one, the Lord Himself in human
incarnation. His *vishvarupa* would be revealed to His
extraordinary listener, the most valiant archer on the
battlefield of Kurukshetra.

For those of us who are interested in certain precise details
like the how and why and when of it all, let me also add –
the battle of Kurukshetra was regarded as a *dharma yuddha*, a
righteous war which was fought according to precise rules.

With the grand old Bhishma, the epitome of nobility on
one side, and Yudhishtira, the embodiment of
righteousness on the other side, the battle would follow
precisely laid down norms and principles. When the battle
was about to start, we saw that Arjuna had thrown down
his weapons. This meant that he was not ready to engage
in the battle. Under such circumstances, no one from the
opposite side would have attacked him, or indeed
commenced the war, when the *Gita samvada* was in progress.

It is a sad fact, however, that in the later stages of this war,
the bitter rivalry between the two factions led them to
disregard rules and commit terrible atrocities, such as the
murder of Abhimanyu. There is yet another significant
fact that we may note. It is often thought that the divine
religious teachings of Hinduism, the *Vedas* and the
Upanishads, originated in the *tapovana* or the forest of
meditation. The *Gita*, which contains the essence of the
Upanishads was, on the contrary, delivered on the battleground. The symbolical inference we must draw is this: the
great Hindu teachings are not just meant for renunciates
who have withdrawn from the world; they are dynamic,
vital; they represent the science of action, no less than the
science of reflection and contemplation. The *Gita*'s
message is not for meditation alone; it is for deeds of daily
life; it is for action; it is for you and me.

The *Gita*'s universal relevance and timeless appeal are
emphasized by its total avoidance of dogma and bigotry;
and so Sri Krishna tells us:

> 'However men approach Me, even so do I greet
> them. For the path men take from every side is
> Mine, O Arjuna!'
>
> IV: 11

The *Mahabharata* features Sri Krishna and Arjuna as incarnations of two ancient *rishis*, Narayana and Nara. Thus the *Gita* flows out of this beautiful, symbolic Nara-Narayana relationship, which embodies the principle of *jivatma* and *paramatma*. As the *jivatma* learns to rise above the miseries and delusions of this world, it moves closer to the *paramatma*, and finds its sins and miseries washed away.

Why does Arjuna fall a prey to such confusion, despair, and dejection? He has been the hero of many battles, and until this point, has not felt any doubts or reservations about this war, which he has resolved to face as a sacred duty and obligation, as a fight against evil and unrighteousness.

We are told that before they prepared for battle that morning, Yudhishtira had his own fears and reservations about the mighty Kaurava forces. In fact, it was he who had asked Arjuna, "How can victory be ours in the face of such an army?" And Arjuna had allayed his fears by quoting an ancient saying:

'Those who are desirous of victory, conquer not so much by might and prowess, as by truth, compassion, piety, and virtue.'

He adds, emphatically: 'Victory is sure to be where Krishna is.'

Until the crucial moment when Arjuna asks his Divine Charioteer to drive him to the middle space between the two armies, Arjuna was firm in his resolve, steadfast in his determination, unshakeable in his faith.

Even modern management practitioners advise us in

similar terms: when you find it difficult to take a decision, when you are not sure that this is the course of right action for you in any given situation, consider the pros and cons carefully and judiciously. Observe dispassionately and judge between the opposing possibilities.

This is what Arjuna does, too. The blowing of the conch-shells by the warriors on both the sides seems to have reminded him, in a flash, of the severity of the test he faces. And his view of the objective reality of the situation makes his inner predicament far more acute. Arjuna is no coward; nor is he foolish, unwise. From social, ethical, as well as the narrow worldly point of view, he marshals his arguments to prove that the battle he is about to fight is not really worthwhile.

Arjuna is not suffering from momentary weakness or fear. He is, in fact, passing through a deep spiritual crisis caused by the realisation that the social, moral, religious, and ethical values that he had always cherished as precious and dear to his heart, are suddenly crumbling down all around him. The fundamental principles of his life are challenged by the disturbing reality of the situation he finds himself in.

Such a crisis can come only to noble souls. The unthinking, insensitive, average person does not face such despair or indecision. It only happens to a person whose faith in his values is threatened. Do we really have to be in a state of such utter despair and dejection before we attain wisdom?

Arjuna's despair is no ordinary despair – it is not for nothing that it is called *Vishada Yoga*, or the yoga of despair. To feel such acute despair is also a step in the process of yogic achievement. It is not a state of *tamas* (slothful inaction) leading to utter frustration. It is the yoga of despondency which develops into a deep spiritual quest for the truth. It is an awakening of the consciousness that the mind must evolve beyond its narrow confines and expand its consciousness.

Sri Krishna, therefore, finds His dear, devoted disciple in an apt frame of mind to receive His supreme wisdom. He then puts Arjuna to the test:

1. He first makes sure that Arjuna is not motivated by narrow concerns of egoism.

2. Then He cleanses Arjuna's thoughts by removing unwanted illusions.

3. Next, He determines the merit and worth of the aspirant, and proceeds to put him through spiritual discipline.

The corresponding stages in the *Gita* are:

1. Sri Krishna's gentle reproach to Arjuna

2. His mild accusation of Arjuna's 'high-sounding words of wisdom'

3. His ever-merciful, ever-compassionate response to Arjuna's submission to better wisdom: 'I am Your disciple. Please teach me; I have sought refuge in You.'

Again and again, on the battlefield of our life, we will find ourselves in the same situation as Arjuna. The Lord may not be with us in person, but His grace and mercy are ever-abiding in our lives. If we surrender ourselves at His lotus-feet, He is sure to show us the way, even as He guided Arjuna out of despair.

6

The Essence of
the Gita

The *Mahabharata* has eighteen books; the great battle of Kurukshetra in which the Kauravas were all killed, lasted eighteen days. The *Bhagavad Gita* too, contains eighteen chapters – and this is of great significance.

The great Kurukshetra war was not merely symbolic. But it is highly significant that the Krishna-Arjuna *samvada* is set against the background of this war. In other words, while the war in the *Mahabharata* is real, it assumes a deeply symbolical significance as the context of the *Gita*. In fact, many scholars and lay readers find the Krishna and the Arjuna of the *Gita*, to be very different from the Krishna and the Arjuna whom they meet elsewhere in the *Mahabharata*.

Some scholars even go to the extent of suggesting that, in order to enter the spiritual world of the *Bhagavad Gita*, we must forget the larger context of the *Mahabharata* and its bitter family strife. In fact, the *Mahabharata* is seen as a vast temple or a theatre in which the *Gita* is a very special, very sacred, shrine. Entering this shrine, we grow in awareness of the life of the spirit; and the war in this context becomes for us a spiritual struggle. It is the battle for the kingdom of heaven, the kingdom of the soul. It is the battle between the forces of darkness and the forces of light *within* us.

It is so easy for us to withdraw from this battle, to decide *not* to fight! Thus Arjuna symbolizes the human soul, and Krishna, the charioteer of the soul.

Scholars also point out that the image of the chariot which we have come to associate with the *Gita*, has been used with deep symbolic significance in the *Upanishads*, in Plato, in the Buddha's teachings as well as in later writers. In Buddhist teaching, the chariot is described as 'He that runs in silence'; the wheels of the chariot are *Right Effort*; the charioteer is *dhamma*, or Truth. The chariot is there to lead us on to *nirvana*, the kingdom of Heaven, which is 'the land free from fear'.

Sadhu Vaswani emphasized the fact that the *Gita* was given by Sri Krishna to Arjuna: Arjuna, who was young in years, rich in idealism and strong in the powers of concentration, symbolizing the best of the spirit of the youth. He was also a young man of culture and character, of *shakti* and *bhakti*, and *sattvic* aspiration.

And the *Gita* was delivered on the battlefield, the field of action. The *Gita* is thus the gospel of action – action without aggression, action without passion, devoid of selfishness, and free from desire. Such action grows out of *tapasya* (self-discipline), not out of the desire to dominate or to reap the fruit.

Karma or action is but one aspect of the *Gita*'s message. The other two are *gnana* (knowledge) and *bhakti* (devotion). Very often, the great interpreters of the *Gita* in the past have emphasized one or the other of these aspects — the *karma marga*, the *gnana marga*, or the *bhakti marga*. Perhaps these three *margas* relate to the cycle of human evolution — the three stages of the evolution of the individual.

The first stage is that of *karma* or action. After action comes *gnana* or knowledge. Not content with action, we begin to question; we want to know, to understand more and more. Then comes the third stage of *bhakti* or devotion. After we have acted, worked, and tried to know, we realize that love of God is ultimate fulfillment. In God is the fulfillment of life, the perfection of all powers, the realisation of the Self.

People often separate *karma*, *gnana*, and *bhakti*, one from the other. But the *Gita*, as Sadhu Vaswani described it, is a scripture of synthesis. And all three *margas*, I believe, are but three steps on the One Way which we might well call the *mukti marga* or the Way of Liberation. This is the triple path too, of purification, illumination, and union.

Thus the *Gita* begins with the sound of hundreds of conches and drums. These are stirring sounds of a great impending battle, a battle for inner victory. But one soul is afraid to enter the battle lines; it is ready to give up the struggle, for it is afraid of death, the death of its passions and desires! Perhaps it also fears the death of the body, for death seems to be the end of everything! (Chapter 1)

Then we hear the eternal voice speaking: it comforts the trembling, fear-filled soul. It talks to us of our own immortality, the divinity of the soul within us. (Chapte 2)

Then there is the call to action—not action in time, but action in Eternity, *karma yoga*. (Chapter 3)

Then is unfolded to us the secret doctrine whereby we may perceive inaction in action and action in inaction. (Chapter 4)

We are taught to distinguish too, between renunciation of action (*karma sanyasa*) and right performance of action (*karma yoga*). The assurance given to us is that both can lead to supreme bliss, but without *karma yoga* (the Way of Action), renunciation is difficult to attain. (Chapter 5)

Now we are told about the Path of Meditation, the power of prayer. This teaches us the yoga of equanimity – the yoga that enables us to perceive the One in All and the All in One. (Chapter 6)

The divine teacher then tells us of the cycle of manifestation, declaring the meaning of knowledge and wisdom (*vignana* and *gnana*). To know God is to know all there is to know. (Chapter 7)

We are then told about the Path of Light that will lead us to God, to the supreme eternal state of peace and blessedness. (Chapter 8)

The sacred Truth of the Lord's divine mystery is now unfolded to us: God pervades all the universe; all things are rooted in Him, but He is not rooted in them. He transcends the universe. He is the Eternal, Universal *Atman* that pervades creation. By fixing our minds on Him, by worshipping Him, we can reach Him. (Chapter 9)

The Lord's revelation of Himself continues: He is the Transcendent and Immanent One. He alone abides. (Chapter 10)

We are then told of the Lord's transfiguration, revealed to His dear, devoted disciple. Arjuna, who is able to see His *Vishwarupa Darshana*. (Chapter 11)

We hear now about the Path of Devotion, and the true *bhakta* who is beloved of the Lord. (Chapter 12)

We also learn the Philosophy of Life according to the Lord, which can help us in our quest after the Perfect Life. (Chapter 13)

The supreme wisdom regarding the conquest of the three gunas — *sattva*, *rajas*, and *tamas* is now declared to us. (Chapter 14)

We learn too, of the cosmic World-Tree, which must be cut down by the weapon of non-attachment. (Chapter 15)

We are taught to recognize the divine and the demoniac qualities in human beings, so that we may cultivate those divine qualities that are beloved of the Lord. (Chapter 16)

We are also told of the three kinds of faith, and the true faith that we must inculcate in ourselves to reach the Lord. (Chapter 17)

And then, finally, the various strands of the magnificent symphony are brought together in the one ultimate message that is the Lord's sacred promise to all of us: 'Come to Me for thy moksha.' (Chapter 18)

The *Bhagavad Gita*, literally, *The Song of the Lord*, is essentially
a song of life. It shows us how the *jivatma*, who lives the
life of separation here on earth, may be united with his
divine source, the *paramatma*. It shows us the path which
we must take to reach our homeland. But this way is to be
trodden, not merely spoken about. Step by step must man
move on the path, until the wanderer reaches his true
home!

Chapter I of the Gita is entitled *Arjuna Vishada* – the
despondency, the depression or the loneliness of Arjuna. It
is significant that the very first chapter of the *Gita* begins
with *vishada yoga,* a deep depression, the dark night of the
soul. Arjuna's heroism and courage crumble, giving way to
utter confusion and confoundment. How can he
participate in the terrible carnage that is about to ensue?
How can he take up arms against his own kinsmen and
elders, grandfathers, teachers, grandsons, cousins, uncles,
and friends? How could he set out to destroy his own
relatives and friends for the sake of a kingdom? Can there
be any pleasure in kingship that is obtained at such a
terrible price? Is it not wisdom to turn away from such a
terrible sin that will destroy all the ancient traditions of
the family? Surely, the better option would be for himself
(Arjuna) to be unresisting and unarmed, allowing the
enemies, the sons of Dhritarashtra, to slay him.

Seeing the armies arrayed at Kurukshetra, Arjuna's
question to Sri Krishna is this: "How can I fight those I
love?" Indeed, it may be said that this opening chapter is
largely in the questioning or interrogatory mode. As
Arjuna sees the situation, his spiritual dilemma intensifies.
His inner predicament assumes terrible proportions. He

marshals several arguments – social, ethical, moral, and spiritual – to state that the ensuing war would be a terrible act of sin, and informs Sri Krishna that he will not fight in such a war.

Arjuna is indeed sincere, but his mind is under a cloud. His words are uttered in agony and attachment (*moha*). He has yet to learn the lesson of desireless action. His *vairagya* is not true determination, it is born out of illusion and attachment. He says, "I will not fight," and sinks into silence.

> 'Having spoken thus, on the battlefield, Arjuna sank down on his chariot-seat, casting away his bow and arrow, his mind overwhelmed by grief.'
>
> I: 47

With Chapter II, the Lord's teaching begins. This chapter is entitled *Sankhya Yoga* or the yoga of knowledge. The Lord tries to stir Arjuna out of his sudden faint-heartedness by appealing to his reason and his intelligence. Until now, He has listened to Arjuna in silence, allowing him to express his anguish and agony. Now, it is time for Him to dispel Arjuna's doubts – indeed, to dispel the ignorance of all humanity – with the brilliant message of the *Gita*.

It would be fair to say that the great spiritual truths revealed in this chapter form, as it were, the foundation on which the *Gita*'s teachings are built.
While the Lord enunciates very profound and therefore, somewhat difficult concepts, He allows Arjuna to interrupt Him several times with his questions and his doubts, so that he may be convinced by the teachings. Thus the Lord proves to be a wonderful teacher.

Three great truths are declared in this chapter:

1. The *Atman*, the Real, is deathless. It cannot be destroyed. Death is an experience, not of the *Atman*, but of the body.

2. The body is subject to change, disease, old age, and death. It has to be cast off like a worn-out garment, so that the *Atman* may assume other embodiments. For death is certain for the born, as is birth for the dead. Thus grieving over death is futile.

3. The enlightened aspirant must realise that his right is to work, and work alone. The fruits, the results of the work, should never be his concern.

When we do not desire anything, when we do not expect anything, we will always enjoy peace and contentment. The man who realizes that he is but an instrument of God, acts dispassionately, desirelessly. Such a one is the *stithaprajna*, the man of steady wisdom.

> 'He whose mind is free from anxiety amid pains,
> indifferent amid pleasures, loosed from passion,
> fear and rage, he is called a seer illumined.'
>
> II: 56

Such a man of stable mind conquers the senses, the passions and emotions, attains to true peace. He becomes one with *Brahman*.

> This is the divine state (*brahmistithi*), O Arjuna!
> Having attained thereto, none is ever bewildered.
> Whoso, even at the end (the hour of death), is

established in that state, he goeth to *brahma-nirvana*, the bliss of God.'

II: 72

Chapter III, entitled *Karma Yoga,* outlines for us the Path of Action.

Arjuna is thrilled by the picture of the illumined *stitha-prajna,* and wants to know why he should take up any action at all, when the superior way of knowledge or *gnana* is open to him.

In answer to Arjuna's query, Sri Krishna unfolds His doctrine of action. The ideal of *karma yoga* is desireless action. This state cannot be reached by giving up all action. What is demanded is not renunciation of work, but renunciation of selfish desire.

Action *(karma)* is inevitable. Inactivity is physically impossible: even the mere maintenance of the body requires action. But the sad fact is that the world is in bondage to work. Therefore, work must be done as *yagna,* offering to the Lord. This is *nishkama karma* at its best, action as worship of God. No work is incumbent upon the Lord, yet He continually works, so that He may inspire us by His own example.

> 'Surrendering all actions unto Me, with thy thoughts resting on the Self Supreme, from desire and egoism freed, and of mental fever cured, fight thou, O Arjuna!'

III: 30

The Lord insists that we *must* act. Arjuna *must* fight, for it is his duty as a warrior.

> 'Better is one's own duty (or path or law,
> *swadharma*), though imperfectly done, than the
> duty (or law) of another, well discharged. Better
> death in the discharge of one's own duty. To
> follow another's duty is full of danger.'
>
> III: 35

Surrender everything to God, and act in a spirit of non-attachment, even like the *Rajayogi*, King Janaka. Act! For without action, life will fail, the Lord urges us:

> 'Thus knowing Him (the Self) as greater than
> the *buddhi*, steadying the lower self by the Self,
> slay, O Arjuna, the enemy in the form of desire,
> so difficult to overcome.'
>
> III: 43

Chapter IV, entitled *Gnana Yoga*, unfolds to us the secret doctrine of Divine Wisdom. If we have ever wondered how and why great saviours of the human race appear amongst us at certain specific times and contexts, if we wonder with Emperor Akbar as to why the Lord should manifest Himself in human incarnations upon this earth, Sri Krishna has the answer to our query:

> 'Whenever there is a decay of *dharma* (righteous-
> ness), O Arjuna, and there is exaltation of
> *adharma* (unrighteousness), then I project
> Myself.'
>
> IV: 7

Dharma is a very important concept in Hinduism. *Dharma* is

right conduct, right mode of behaviour, right observance,
which holds, sustains life. In its widest sense, *dharma* is
righteousness that leads us towards God.

The Lord descends among us as an *avatara*, when *dharma*
declines. He comes to help and heal, to protect the world,
to save sinking humanity.

> 'For the protection of the good, for the
> destruction of the wicked, for the sake of
> establishing righteousness, I come into birth
> from age to age.'
>
> IV: 8

This is something we should know — that God comes
among us to help us ascend towards Him. We can
approach Him in any way, He will meet us even on that
way. The Lord acts too; but actions stain Him not. His
actions are born of grace and compassion. From His
example we should learn what kind of actions we should
perform, and what kind of actions we must avoid.

> 'What is action (*karma*)? And what is inaction
> (*akarma*)? Even the wise men are herein bewil-
> dered. Therefore, I will declare to thee what
> action is, knowing which thou shalt be delivered
> from evil.'
>
> IV: 16

It is important that we must avoid *vikarma* or wrong action.
Do not reject action, the Lord tells us. What binds us is
not action, but egotism. What binds us is selfishness. Act,
but make your action a *yagna*, an offering to the Lord, and
you are no longer bound.

'Thus many kinds of sacrifice are spread out
before the Eternal, they are the means of
reaching God. Know thou that all these are born
of action. Knowing this thou shalt be free.'

IV: 32

This is spiritual wisdom at its best. It reveals the fact of
unity – the unity of all creatures in the *Atman*, the Self, the
Spirit, in Krishna. This is both self-realisation and God-
realisation.

'And having known this wisdom (*gnana*), thou, O
Arjuna, shall not again fall into this confusion.
For, by this wisdom, thou wilt see all beings,
without exception, in the *Atman* (the Self), and
thus in Me!'

IV: 35

Such wisdom (*gnana*) burns up all our accumulated, as well
as future, *karmas*. When this synthesis of *gnana* and *karma*
(wisdom and action) is achieved, we act in the spirit of
sacrifice to God. Then, nothing can bind us.

'Therefore, cleave asunder with the sword of
wisdom this doubt in thy heart, born of
ignorance, be established in yoga, and stand up,
O Arjuna!'

IV: 42

Chapter V, entitled *Karma Sanyasa Yoga* tells us about the
Path of Renunciation. *Karma Sanyasa* is renunciation of
action. Sri Krishna has praised right action, as well as
renunciation of action. So Arjuna wants to know which is
better. Should he renounce his *karma* as a warrior and

follow the path of *sanyasa*? Or should he follow his *karma* as a *kshatriya* and fight to the finish?

Let us understand clearly that *sanyasa* is renunciation of action while *karma yoga* is engaging in action without concern or desire for the fruits of the action.

The Lord assures Arjuna that *both* of these lead to the highest goal of God-realisation, but the *yoga* of action, he says, is superior to the renunciation of action.

What are we to understand by this? For those of us who are still struggling towards attainment, *karma yoga* is far better, because desireless action, steadfast dedication to one's duty is the best way to eliminate negative qualities and purify the mind. But when we have evolved and attained to realisation, we will realize that there is no difference between action and renunciation. Thus *karma yoga* is like the ladder we use to climb on to the top of a house, but once we have got there, the ladder becomes unnecessary.

It is pointless to take to renunciation, while one is still restless with passions and desires. Action, especially desireless action, can purify and still the mind. In the true spirit of *karma yoga*, a man performs acts of selfless service, dedicating all action to the Lord, for the Lord is the assimilation of all *yagna* and *tapas* (sacrifice and austerity).

> 'And having known Me as the enjoyer of sacrifices and austerities, as the mighty ruler of all the worlds, as the lover of all that lives, he (the sage) goeth to peace.'
>
> V: 29

Chapter VI, *Dhyana Yoga*, enlightens us about the Path of Meditation. Thus far, we have learnt about the value of *karma yoga* by which we renounce not actions themselves, but the fruits of the actions. This kind of desireless action, we have been told, brings about purity of mind. In this chapter we are taught to appreciate the value of a purified mind, and how we may attain to God by meditating effectively on Him with a pure mind. For when we renounce selfish purpose, when we walk the way of disinterested action, we allow the Divine Will to work through us.

> 'For the sage who wishes to attain to yoga, action
> is said to be the means; for the same sage, when
> he has attained to yoga, serenity is said to be the
> means.'
>
> VI:3

How may we attain to this state of serenity? Sri Krishna actually explains to Arjuna, a little of the technique of meditation:

1. Choose a pure, quiet place.

2. Choose a stable and not too high seat.

3. Restrain the mind and senses: the mind must be free from lower desires if you wish to meditate and go into inward stillness.

4. Sit motionless, with body, head, and neck held erect with a fixed gaze focussed on the tip of the nose.

5. With a heart serene and fearless, hold your mind from its restless roaming, and lose your thoughts, and your self in the immensity of the Lord's being.

The object of *dhyana yoga* is to meditate on Him, the Lord, the beloved of the soul, and so to attain union with Him. He who would attain to meditation must walk the middle path. He must be temperate in all his activities; he must adopt the golden mean between the extremes of asceticism and indulgence. Such a man lives in the world, but is detached from the world. His focus, his goal, his joy is in God-realisation.

He renounces desires; he restrains his senses; he eliminates fear, and rests his mind in the *Atman*. He develops *samadrishti* — that the One *Atman* which resides within him, resides also in all things, all creatures, all forms of life. He realises that he can never purchase happiness for himself with the suffering of others.

Arjuna observes that the fickle, turbulent, strong, and obstinate mind is very difficult to control. How then, can we attain to the yoga of equanimity? The Lord offers two ways:

1. *Abhyasa* or constant practice

2. *Vairagya* or dispassion, absence of desire;

> Yoga is hard to attain by one who is not self-controlled.
> 'But by the self-controlled it is attainable by striving through proper means. Such is My conviction.'
>
> VI: 36

What of the man who strives, but does not succeed? The Lord assures us that no man who is a sincere seeker can come to an evil end. We need never despair, for the Lord is all love and compassion, and will not let our sincere efforts go in vain. We will rise, step by step, to realisation. Thus the *Gita* holds out to every seeker the hope, nay, the promise, that though he falls a hundred times, he will rise again! His failures are only temporary.

The *tapasvi* (ascetic) inflicts severe penances on his body; the *gnani* (knower of the *Vedas*) is learned and wise; the *karmi* (man of activity) is hardworking and sincere. But greater than them all is the true *yogi*. And the best of *yogis*, according to the *Gita*, is he who offers to the Lord his love and devotion, and worships Him in faith.

> 'And, of all *yogis*, he who, full of faith adoreth
> Me, with his Self abiding in Me, he is deemed by
> Me to be the most completely harmonised (the
> most devoted).'
>
> VI: 47

In Chapter VII, entitled *Gnana Vignana Yoga*, the Lord gives us an explanation of His manifested state. In short, it is thus: all that exists is nothing but the manifestation of the Lord Himself. He is the cause of the appearance of the universe and all things in it. The earth, water, fire, air, ether, mind, intellect, and ego – the lower *prakriti* – make up His eight-fold nature. His is also the life-element which upholds and sustains the universe and makes it active.

> 'There is naught whatsoever higher than I, O
> Arjuna! All that is here is threaded on Me as
> rows of pearls are threaded on a single string.'
>
> VII: 7

He is in all creation, yet *beyond* all creation. He is the fresh taste in the waters; He is the light in the moon and sun; He is the *shabda* in all the *Vedas*; He is the fragrance of the earth; He is the life in all that lives; He is the wisdom of the wise, and the splendour in all that is splendid. Alas, the world, deluded by the three *gunas*, fails to see His divine manifestation in all that is!

We are also told of four types of *bhaktas* who worship the Lord for different reasons — to seek protection in distress; to seek illumination; to seek success; and lastly, those who seek Him, and Him *alone*. These are the *gnani bhaktas*, who are truly beloved of the Lord. To them, the Lord makes this promise.

> 'Those who know Me as the One that underlies the elements (*adhibuta*), and the gods (*adhidaiva*), and all sacrifice (*adhiyagna*), they, harmonized in mind, know Me even in the hour of death.'
>
> VII: 30

Chapter VIII, entitled *Aksharabrahman Yoga*, shows us the Path of Light that will take us Godward. Arjuna begs the Lord to enlighten him on that yoga which one may practise even in *antakala* (the hour of death) and so attain to the Supreme. The Lord's reply is succinct:

> 'He, who, casting off the body, goeth forth, meditating upon Me alone, at the hour of death, he attaineth to My State (*madbhavam*). Doubt that not!
>
> VIII: 5

Think of the Lord and do your duty! When these two are

linked together, we are sure to reach the Lord.

> 'Arjuna, he who constantly thinketh upon Me
> with a mind that regardeth none else, he, the *yogi*,
> *nityayuktah* (ever harmonized, always absorbed in
> Me), he easily attaineth Me.'
>
> VIII: 14

This then is the secret of yoga – to remember God
constantly. The universe has come into being, and
dissolved through several *yugas*. Several such time-cycles
have come and gone. There is no end to the process of
birth, death, and rebirth, until we attain to the Eternal.
He, the Highest, may be reached by unswerving devotion.

> 'Having known all this, the *yogi* passes beyond all
> merit that comes from the study of the *Vedas*,
> from sacrifices (*yagna*), from austerities (*tapas*)
> and holy gifts (*dana*), and goeth to the supreme
> eternal state of peace and blessedness.
>
> VIII: 28

Chapter IX, entitled *Rajavidya Rajaguhya Yoga*, outlines for
us the supreme mystery of the yoga of sovereign science
and sovereign secret. Arjuna's devotion, his earnest
questioning, and his genuine aspiration to learn the truth
have all proved that he is the true disciple. And therefore,
the Lord now declares to him the great secret, or the
'secret truth'.

> 'By Me the whole universe is pervaded in My
> unmanifest aspect. All beings have root in Me,
> but I am not rooted in them.

And yet the beings have no root in Me. Behold
My divine mystery, My Self creates all,
sustaineth all, yet is not rooted in them.'

IX: 4-5

Alas, those of us who are ignorant, do not recognize the
Lord's supreme nature. Evolved, enlightened souls, on the
other hand, realize that He is the One behind the All, and
worship Him with a fixed mind and unceasing devotion.
Such men, who have sought their ultimate refuge in the
Lord, are taken care of in every respect. What is the kind
of devotion that pleases the Lord? In one of the most
beautiful and most quoted verses of the *Gita*, the Lord
tells us:

'Whatever thou doest, whatever thou eatest,
whatever thou offerest, whatever thou givest
away, whatever austerities thou dost practise, let
it all be done, O Arjuna, as an offering unto Me.'

IX: 27

When all our actions, thoughts, and words are offered to
God as *Krishna Arpanam*, we are freed from the bonds of
karma. Therefore, the way is clear:

'Fix thy mind on Me; be devoted to Me; worship
Me; bow down to Me. Thus having controlled
thyself, and making Me thy goal supreme, thou
shalt come unto Me.'

IX: 34

Chapter X is entitled *Vibhuti Yoga*, or the yoga of divine
manifestation. Here, the Lord in His divine magnanimity,
very kindly reiterates for Krishna the divine secrets that

He has thus far unfolded to him.

'Hear again, O Arjuna, My supreme word. From
a desire to do thee good, I will declare it to thee,
for thou art My beloved.'

                                                    X: 1

All the qualities – wisdom, forgiveness, non-delusion,
truth, *ahimsa*, equanimity, contentment, austerity, and
charity – arise from the Lord. He is the root and essence
of everything. The word used by the Lord is *vibhuti*,
meaning glory or sovereignty; and also suggesting an idea
of all-pervasion and immanence. In other words, the whole
universe, in all its splendour and magnificence, is but a
fragment of the Lord's Divine Self.

'But of what use to thee, O Arjuna, is this
detailed knowledge? I sustain this whole
universe, pervading it with but one fragment of
Myself: and I abide!'

                                                    X: 42

Chapter XI, entitled *Vishwarupa Darshana Yoga,* is, indeed,
special, for during this part of the divine discourse, the
Lord reveals His cosmic form to His dear, devoted
disciple, Arjuna. Having heard the Lord's glories from the
Lord Himself, Arjuna now asks his divine charioteer to
reveal to him His cosmic form. With devotion and
reverence and deep humility, he says:

'If Thou thinkest, O Lord, that by me It can be
seen, then reveal to me, O Lord of yoga
(Krishna), Thine imperishable self.'

                                                    XI: 4

The Lord grants Arjuna his wish; He also makes it
possible for Arjuna to behold His *vishwarupa* with his inner,
divine eye. This is how Sanjaya describes that ecstatic
vision that Arjuna beheld, which, in turn, it was also
Sanjaya's privilege to behold, with the special perception
granted to him by Ved Vyasa.

> 'Could but a thousand suns blaze forth all at
> once in the sky, it would be like the splendour of
> that exalted Being.'
>
> XI: 12

The vision is uplifting, wonderful and truly awe-inspiring.
Arjuna sees the vast universe existing and resting in the
Lord. He sees indeed, that the Lord is without any
beginning, middle, or end, an infinite power, with endless
forms. He sees creation and destruction taking place
simultaneously. He sees divine radiance that is limitless.
He prostrates before the divine vision, and salutes the
Lord in all His Glory.

The Lord instils in Arjuna the incontrovertible fact that
the destruction of his enemies will come about whether or
not Arjuna takes part in the war, for such is the will of the
Lord. Therefore, Arjuna must stand up and fight.

> 'Arise thou, then! Obtain renown!
> Fight thou thy foes!
> The kingdom awaits thee.
> By Me, not thee, they all are slain: seem thou to
> slay!
> Be thou My instrument!
> But strike, O knight!'
>
> XI: 33

Arjuna is thrilled, but also overawed, for he 'hath seen That which none hath seen before'. But to comfort him and allay his fear, Sri Krishna resumes His familiar, gentle human form, so that Arjuna may be reassured.

Rare and hard indeed, is it for ordinary mortals to behold the Form that Arjuna has thus far beheld. No amount of scriptural study or sacrifices or by gifts or austerity, can one be entitled to behold the Form Supreme. What is required is pure and simple-minded devotion.

'But by devotion to Me alone, devotion undivided, may I thus be known and seen in essence, and entered into, O Arjuna!

> Who doeth work for Me, who maketh Me his
> supreme goal, he, My devotee, freed from
> attachment, without ill-will towards any creature,
> he cometh unto Me, O Arjuna!'
>
> XI: 54-55

Rightly did Sri Shankaracharya call this last *sloka*, 'the essence of the whole *Gita*'.

Chapter XII is perhaps the most well-known and most discussed section in the *Gita*. Entitled *Bhakti Yoga*, it shows us the Path of Devotion which each one of us can choose to walk, if we so aspire.

Which is better, Arjuna wonders: to worship Krishna with *bhakti*, as the Lord manifest, or to concentrate on the unmanifest? In the worship of Krishna, both devotion and work can be offered to the Lord (that is, *bhakti* and *seva*). But in the worship of the unmanifest, there is only contemplation. Which is the better way of attainment for the aspirant? The Lord avers that *Gnana Yoga* is more difficult than *Bhakti Yoga*.

> 'Greater is the toil of those whose minds are set on the unmanifested; for the path of the unmanifested is hard for the embodied to attain.'
>
> XII: 5

But there is hope for all of us; the path of *bhakti* (devotion) is open to us. All it requires is that we focus unswervingly on the Lord, fix our minds on Him, consecrate all our actions to Him, and remember Him constantly. If this is not possible, we must simply choose to serve Him in all our actions. If this, too, is difficult, we can simply surrender all our actions to the Lord, renouncing all fruits of action.

The Lord then gives us the attributes and qualities which makes a devotee dear to Him. These are outlined in the last eight verses of this chapter, which are described as the *Gita Amritashtam* (the nectar of the *Gita*) in eight *slokas*. Before the evening *satsang* in the Sadhu Vaswani Mission, we hear these eight *slokas* in the divine, melodious, mellifluous voice of Sadhu Vaswani.

What are the qualities of the true *bhakta* who is dear to the Lord?

- He is free from ill will and egoism. He bears no ill will to any creature; he is forgiving, and is poised in pain and pleasure.

- He is content and ever in harmony, his mind and understanding dedicated to the Lord.

- He does not disturb the world, nor is he disturbed by the world.

- He is without ambition, and free from passion and fear.

- He does not rejoice, grieve, or crave for anything.

- He is the same to foe and friend. He is the same in honour and dishonour; he is free from attachment.

- He takes praise and blame alike. He is satisfied with whatever the Lord is pleased to grant him.

> 'They, verily, who worship this *dharma* (law) of immortality, as taught herein, and, endowed with faith, believe in Me as the Supreme, they, My *bhaktas*, are My beloved.'
>
> XII: 20

Chapter XIII, entitled *Kshetra Kshetragna Vibhaga Yoga*, offers us a philosophy of life and the universe, by drawing our attention to the distinction between *prakriti* and *purusha* (nature and the spirit), the field and the knower of the field that is, *kshetra*, the body, or the scene of activity; and *kshetragna* or consciousness.

Whatever we see around us is a combination of *purusha* and *prakriti*, spirit and matter, soul and body. The Lord Himself is the Knower of the body, who dwells in all bodies. He who realizes that the body is the field, and the indweller in the body is the Lord, has attained real wisdom. The fields are different, but the Knower of the field is one. The individual souls (*jivatmas*) are different but the Supreme Soul (*paramatma*) is one only.

The constituents of the field (*kshetra*) are twenty-four principles:

1. the *avyakta* or the unmanifest;

2. the *ahankara* or the ego;

3. *buddhi* or reason;

4. *manas* or mind — the discursive reason;

5-14. the ten *indriyas*, that is, the five senses and their five domains (eyes — sight; ears — hearing; nose — smell, etc.);

20-24. the five gross elements, that is, earth, fire, water, air, and ether.

Vikaras (modifications) arise in the *kshetra*, because our *jiva* is associated with *maya*. These *vikaras* are desire, aversion, pleasure and pain, association, cognition and constancy.

In human nature, there are two forces at work — one leading the soul towards God, and the other towards ignorance. The individual soul, who is ignorant of the *Atman* or *purusha*, identifies himself with the body, and is subject to the three *gunas*. But one who is aware of the Spirit Supreme, dedicates his life to the Lord and attains liberation.

Freedom and immortality are assured to us when we realize that the One Imperishable Spirit dwells equally in all perishable forms. In this awareness, we perceive that *prakriti* is responsible for all activities, while the *Atman* is actionless.

'They who, by the eye of wisdom, see this
distinction between the field and the Knower of
the field, and who understand how beings may
be released from *prakriti*, liberated from matter,
they verily, go to the Supreme.'

XIII: 34

Chapter XIV, entitled the *Gunatraya Vibhaga Yoga*, teaches us
to differentiate between the three *gunas*, and tells us that
we must conquer the three *gunas* to attain liberation.

Having learnt that nature (*prakriti*) is the field through
which the Supreme Self (*purusha*) gives expression to itself,
we now learn a little more about the qualities (*gunas*) of
nature — what they are, how they bind man, how they
operate and how we may rise above them. The three *gunas*
are *sattva*, *rajas*, and *tamas* — purity, passion and inertia. All
of them bind us through attachment.

Of these, *tamas*, born of ignorance, can be conquered by
karma yoga or right action; *rajas*, the source of which is
thirst for sensual pleasure, can be cured by dedication to
one's own duty (*swadharma*); *sattva*, which is itself stainless
and pure, nevertheless binds us to happiness, must be
conquered by desireless detachment.

The *gunatita* (one who has conquered the three *gunas*) is
firmly rooted in the Supreme Self. He is desireless, he is
unaffected by praise or blame; he is the same to friend and
enemy; he sees God in all, and regards himself as the
instrument of the Lord.

'He who serveth Me with unswerving devotion,
passes beyond the *gunas* and becomes one with

Brahman. For I am the abode of *Brahman,* the inexhaustible nectar of immortality: I am the ground of eternal righteousness and the source of unending bliss.'

XIV: 26-27

Chapter XV is entitled *Purushottama Yoga,* and talks to us of the World-Tree, the tree of *prakriti.* All trees have their roots down in the earth, but this remarkable tree of *samsara* (creation) has its roots *above* in the Supreme Self. The trunk and branches of this tree grow downwards, nourished by the *gunas;* sense-objects are its buds; its secondary roots stretch down below, binding it to worldly action.

Alas, not many of us understand the real form of this tree – neither its origin, nor its end, nor its foundation. The Lord urges us to cut the tree down, by the weapon of non-attachment. This tree is called the *ashvatta,*meaning, 'not stable', 'in a flux' – that which is constantly subject to change, even as everything in this world is subject to decay and death.

In this cosmic tree of *prakriti* appear *jivas* or individuals. The *Purushottama* or the Supreme Self, pervades all; He is indestructible and is known as the Supreme Person. He who knows the Lord as *Purushottama,* knoweth all and he worships the Lord with all his soul.

'Thus have I told thee the most secret teaching, Arjuna! He who knoweth this, he is illuminated and his labours are finished, O Arjuna!'

XV: 20

Chapter XVI, entitled *Daivasura Sampad Vibhaga Yoga*, teaches us the distinction between the divine and the demoniac. Here, the Lord classifies two distinct sets of qualities which are opposed to each other — he urges us to root out our evil traits, and cultivate divine qualities. Both are to be found in human beings, for in all of us is a mixture of the three *gunas*.

Fearlessness, purity of mind, sacrifice and service, compassion and humility, characterize the divine being while hypocrisy, arrogance, delusion, anger, and ignorance characterise the demonical being. The divine qualities lead us Godward; as for the demoniac qualities, they open up the triple gateway of hell: lust, wrath, and greed. Unless we are released from these three gates, we cannot proceed towards our highest goal.

> 'Therefore, let the holy law be thy rule in determining what should be done or what should not be done. Knowing what hath been declared by the holy law, do thou, O Arjuna, thy work in this world.'
>
> XVI: 24

Chapter XVII, entitled *Shraddhatraya Vibhaga Yoga*, enlightens us on the three kinds of faith which are inherent in human nature — *sattvic, rajasic,* and *tamasic*.

The *guna* which dominates in us, also determines the kind of faith we develop: if we are *sattvic*, our faith is pure; if *rajas* dominates in us, our faith is clouded by worldly intentions; and if *tamas* is dominant, our faith is selfish, impure, and dark.

The *gunas*, in turn, are determined by the food we eat, which also determines our activities, such as the kind of sacrifices, austerities, and charity that we practise. There is no need to renounce actions, sacrifices, austerities, and charity in order to attain the Lord.

All that is required is that we surrender *all* these actions to Him; we must perform all these activities as worship of God, in the spirit of *arpanam* and surrender, which is done by uttering the *vedic mantra*, 'Om Tat Sat'. This means that all our actions are done for His sake; we do not expect to gain anything from them; all that we wish is for God to accept them. Thus are all our activities purified and sanctified and made acceptable to the Lord.

Om Tat Sat is the *Gita's mantra*; its repetition is a sacramental act which opens the doors of grace to us. It is the *mantra* of faith.

> 'Whatsoever is done without faith, whether it be offering in sacrifice, gift, or austerity, or anything else, is called *asat*, O Arjuna! Such work is of no value hereafter or here.'
>
> XVII: 28

Chapter XVIII, the final word in the *Gita*, is entitled *Moksha Sanyasa Yoga*, the yoga of Liberation by Renunciation.

The conclusion of the Song Supreme, encapsulates the whole message of the *Gita*. In a brief, masterly summary, the divine teacher ensures that His dear, devoted disciple achieves self-mastery and enlightenment.

The ultimate message of the *Gita* is this: by doing our *swadharma*, we can attain liberation. The only requisite is that we should surrender all our actions to the Lord, and give up attachment, egoism, selfishness, and desire. When we offer our duty as worship of God, we obtain His grace, and attain to Him.

The *Gita* is essentially a call to action, this is why Sri Krishna urges us not to renounce action, but to renounce its fruits and attachment to results instead. This is the ideal of *nishkama karma* (desireless action).

Arjuna, at the beginning of the discourse, had failed to understand this ideal as a warrior; he was unwilling to do his duty, because he found it disagreeable and unpleasant to kill his own kinsmen. This was, of course, ignorance. Now, he is enlightened, and exclaims joyfully:

> 'Destroyed is my delusion. I have gained recognition through Thy grace, O Krishna! I am firm, my doubts have fled. I shall act according to Thy word.'
>
> XVIII: 73

Arjuna is resolved to act now, in full, firm faith, and devotion. So can we all, for the Lord's assurance is for all of us too:

> 'Abandoning all duties, come unto Me alone for shelter. Grieve not! I shall liberate thee from all sins. Of this, have no doubt.'
>
> XVIII: 66

7

Sadhu Vaswani and the Gita

The *Bhagavad Gita* is the most beloved scripture of the Indian people. For over fifty centuries, some of the holiest, noblest, and best of India's men and women, have turned to the *Gita* for inspiration and guidance in daily living. As I have said, the great thinkers of India, the great *acharyas* have paid reverent homage of their hearts to this ancient scripture, as to no other book in the world. Indeed, the *Gita* has given comfort and consolation to the untold millions who have aspired to a life of freedom and fulfillment.

Truly, the *Gita* has devotees and admirers all over the world. It has been translated into several languages. Some of the world's greatest thinkers have paid glowing tributes to the *Gita*. Emerson always had a copy of the *Gita* on his table. He referred to it as 'an empire of thought'. Schlegel, on reading the *Gita*, broke into a rapture of ecstasy and exclaimed, 'Hail to Thee, author of the mighty poem, whose oracles lift up the soul, in joy ineffable, toward all that is sublime, eternal, divine! Full of veneration, I salute thee above all singers, and I worship unceasingly the trace of thy footsteps!'

Romain Rolland, the Irish poet A.E. (George Russel), Dr.

Humboldt, and Mary Owens from Maryland have paid rich tributes to the *Gita*. Count Keyserling regarded the *Gita* as the greatest philosophic poem in the world's literature. To Sadhu Vaswani, the *Gita* was much more than a 'philosophic poem'. Philosophy, he said, cannot plumb the depths that are within. Philosophy cannot satisfy the deepest longing of the human soul. Philosophy cannot take you to God. Sadhu Vaswani first learnt of the *Gita* when he was studying in school, out of the lips of one of his teachers. He heard the words of the wonderful *sloka* in Chapter 18:

> *'Sarvadharman Parityajya Maamekam Saranam Vraja!'*

> 'Renouncing all rites and writ duties, come unto
> Me, O Arjuna, for single refuge! I shall liberate
> you from all bondage to sin and suffering. Of
> this have no doubt!'
>
> (XVIII: 66)

When Sadhu Vaswani heard these words, he was thrilled, fascinated. He was irresistibly drawn to the *Gita* and began to study it and meditate upon it, *sloka* by *sloka*. For years together, he studied the *Gita*, interpreted the teachings of the *Gita*, and reflected on its sublime thoughts. Indeed, he became one with the *Gita*. To many of us, indeed, he was a living *Gita*. Many people who met him, exclaimed, "Here is a living embodiment of the *Gita*!" Sadhu Vaswani spoke on the *Gita*; he wrote much on the *Gita*. His Sindhi translation of the *Gita* is truly beautiful. And his interpretation of the *Gita* is so lucid and profound that even the beginner on the path can relate to the great scripture.

It has been my blessing and privilege to compile several of his manuscripts on the *Gita* into books. Many of these books have run into several editions, and continue to be sought-after; to mention just a few of them: *Gita: A Bible of Humanity; The Heart of the Gita; Gita Meditations; The Bhagavad Gita: An Outline;* and *The Bhagavad Gita: The Song of Life.*

Some years ago, a professor from an American University met me. He mentioned that he had studied several commentaries on the *Gita*, but not until he had read Sadhu Vaswani's commentary could he understand every *sloka* of the *Gita* clearly. This indeed is the typical reaction of all who read his interpretation of the *Gita*. There is nothing abstract about it, it appeals directly to your heart, it relates to life; it inspires you to be a witness to Sri Krishna's message in deeds of daily life!

Sadhu Vaswani called the *Gita* 'the scripture for the New Age'. To him, it represented not merely the essence of Hinduism, but also the heart and soul of religion and philosophy in their purest form. He believed that its message of *karma* and *dharma* could transform the most savage men into gentle disciples and committed seekers of the Truth. He described the *Gita* as 'a text-book of spiritual culture'. He felt that it could teach us the detachment and dispassion that are essential to spiritual action, for the only life worth living is the life of the spirit. It emphasizes the great truth that wisdom is conquest – conquest of desires, conquest of *trishna*.

He called the *Gita* 'a scripture of synthesis'. He felt that it combined the objective yoga of the *Vedas* and the subjective yoga of the *Upanishads*. He asserted that the *Gita* grew out of a vision of 'supreme synthesis'.

He described the *Gita* as 'a gospel of action'. He emphasized what he called 'the heroic note' in the *Gita*, for it teaches us that weakness is a sin, while *shakti* is a spiritual virtue. 'The message of the *Gita* is one of courage', he wrote. 'Life is a battlefield of values, and your temple, O children of the *rishis*, is on the battlefield! March on! Nor beat retreat!'

The emphasis in the teaching of the *Gita*, he insisted, is on *life*, not words. Do not merely chant the *slokas* of the *Gita*, he urged us, but be a witness to its great teachings in deeds of daily living. The model man of the *Gita* beholds the light shining in the heart within, but not on that account does he withdraw himself from the world. Rather, he devotes himself to a life of duty — the duty of his daily task, the duty he owes to his family, community, country, humanity, the duty he owes to birds and animals, for he realizes too, that birds and animals are man's younger brothers and sisters in the one family of creation. Such a man does his duty in love; he does his work in a spirit of detachment. He lives in the world, but strips himself of all attachment. In the beautiful words of a Sufi singer:

'Penance and pilgrimage,
Fasting and rituals,
Learning and scholarship
Avail little!
The goal is attained
When the two streams
Of love and renunciation
Mingle, flowing together
Into the sea!'

Truly, from the mingling of love and renunciation arises

inward light. It leads the seeker on!

However, Sadhu Vaswani taught us that true renunciation
is inner. We are not asked to renounce the world and dwell
in the depths of the *tapovana* (the forest of meditation), or
on the lonely peak of a hill. Live in the world, he urged us,
but be not of the world! Live in the world, but be attached
to no form, no finite thing. Live in a spirit of detachment,
knowing that no one, nothing, belongs to you, that you
belong to God. Do your daily work, attend to your daily
tasks, but do not forget God for a single moment. Again it
was a Sufi mystic who said, "The true saint goes in and
out amongst the people and eats and sleeps with them, and
buys and sells in the market, and marries and takes part in
social intercourse, and never forgets God for a single
moment."

The man of renunciation having rid himself of 'self' lives
for others. His heart flows in a ceaseless stream of
sympathy to the poor and broken ones, to the forsaken and
forlorn, to birds and animals. He lives to serve, beholding
his own self in those he seeks to serve. Of such a one, Sri
Krishna says in the Gita: "He is the supreme *yogi* to whom
the pleasure or pain of others is his own pleasure and
pain." Such a one was Sadhu Vaswani. Thus he lived till
the last day of his earthly life. He was the very picture of
renunciation. Having renounced all, he announced the
Eternal. And he looked upon all, everyone, as his own self.
He regarded nothing in this world as being separate from
himself, and he endeavoured to bring joy into the lives of
those that came to him for help and healing and
wholeness. Their happiness was his happiness: their
sorrows were his sorrows. Every creature was, to him, an

image of the king of beauty.

One morning, he spoke to us of the teaching of the *Gita* concerning the *Atman*, the spirit. The true man is the *Atman*, he said, not the body. And the *Atman* cannot be destroyed. Death is an experience, not of the *Atman*, but of the body. The *Atman* is deathless, indestructible, eternal. It is the body that dies; it is the form that perishes. The *Atman* ever lives. So be not afraid of death, he told us; nor grieve over the passing away of your dear ones.

This teaching Sadhu Vaswani gave us in the morning. In the course of the day, he was called to the side of a mother who was disconsolate with grief. Her only son had died in an air-crash. She wept unending tears of sorrow. As Sadhu Vaswani met her, we were surprised to see that he too, shed tears!

Later on, we asked him, "This morning you taught us that we must not grieve over the passing away of our dear ones for there can be no death of the *Atman*. How is it then, that you shed tears as you sat in the presence of the bereaved mother?" Sadhu Vaswani answered: "As I sat by the side of the mother, I felt *I* was the mother!" Such was the secret of Sadhu Vaswani's life – identification with others. The others were not apart from him: they were a part of him. The pleasure or pain of others was his own pleasure or pain. He was, indeed, the *supreme yogi* of the *Gita*!

"You must not simply see the *Gita* reflected in the mirror of wisdom: you must *live* the *Gita*, *be* the *Gita*!" Such was his clarion-call to us.

'Krishna! Krishna!' we cry again and again. Certainly, His *name* is constantly upon our lips: but does our *life* bear witness to His message?

Sadhu Vaswani aspired to *live* the *Gita*, to assimilate the message of the *Gita* into his heart and mind through meditation, to reflect the spirit of the *Gita* in his daily actions, daily sacrifices. "May my study of the *Gita* be not in words," he said, "but in daily *yagna* to the *yagneshwara*, the Eternal!"

Referring to the three ways outlined by the *Gita* — the way of wisdom or knowledge *(gnana marga)*, the way of devotion *(bhakti marga)*,and the way of action *(karma marga)*, he raised the question:

"Why are the *margas* three? Why not less? Why not more?" To answer this question, he related them to the cycle of human evolution: we start with *karma* or activity; we grow into *gnana* or knowledge; and we flower into *bhakti* or loving devotion.

Let us not separate *karma, gnana,* and *bhakti,* he exhorted us, for we need all of the three. "And these three," he said, "are but three steps in the One Way, which may well be called *mukti marga,* the Way of Liberation."

What wonderful insight, what profound wisdom, that can perceive such a synthesis in the various "schools of thought" that have sprung up around the *Gita*! "The path, the *marga,* is neither *eastern* nor *western,*" he emphasized. "The path belongs to no one race, to no one religion. The triple path is known to mystics of East and West. It is... the triple path of purification, illumination, and union."

Karma (work) purifies. Right action, *punya karma*, prepares the seeker for truth, *gnana*, wisdom: step by step, the heart, purified through the discipline of work, and prepared to learn to be still, attains to the knowledge that God dwells within.

Knowledge is not possible without *sadhana* or self-discipline; and wisdom leads us on to true philosophy – communion with the Infinite "Not without reason," says Sadhu Vaswani, "has the *Gita* been called *Ananta Gita*, the Song of the Infinite."

Sri Krishna tells us in the *Gita*, "On whatever roads men approach Me, on that road I move to meet them, for all the roads are Mine!" Interpreting this great universal note in the *Gita*, Sadhu Vaswani said: "All religions are roads: all disciplines are roads: all lead to the one Lord. This is more than tolerance; it is reverence. The Lord has reverence for men: He goeth forth to meet men on whatever way they walk. All roads lead to Him – science, philosophy, literature, daily life!"

He told Indians not to think of the *Gita* as their monopoly; it was sung in India, it is true, but it was meant for humanity. 'It is foolish to say, "We are proud of the *rishis*". I ask you, "Are the *rishis* proud of you?"'

It is not enough to say that Krishna sang the Song Divine five thousand years ago in Kurukshetra: instead, he urged us, breathe out this aspiration: 'Master! Re-sing the Song in our daily life!'

Typically, Sadhu Vaswani identified with the 'little way', the hidden way, the way of simplicity, service, and sacrifice pointed out by the Lord. He said, "The little way is the *Gita*'s way to perfect life."

Patram, pushpam, phalam, toyam – a leaf, a flower, a fruit, a little water – no matter how poor or humble the offering, it is acceptable to Sri Krishna, provided it comes from an earnest heart with a sincere longing.

"He asks not for great things," said Sadhu Vaswani, "little things are ye asked to give Him. If you give the little ones, the broken ones, the thirsty ones, the world's disinherited ones, the poor ones in broken cottages, little cups of cold water, kind words, little gifts of love, the Lord will bless you!"

Dear to his heart was the ideal of *lokasangraha* (welfare of the world). He taught us that the life of fellowship with God is the life of true service, through which we may grow in reverence for the poor. "Look around you!" he called. "The world is in suffering; the world needs helpers. Serve and be ready to suffer in the service of suffering humanity." Beginning with the word "fight", he pointed out, the *Gita* ends with the word "surrender".

'Mamekam saranam vraja!'

In this surrender, this *saranam*, he taught us, is the secret of true freedom. Of this great scripture, on which he meditated constantly, he says: "What wisdom is in the *Gita*! It enchants the heart! It enthrals the soul! Methinks, these *slokas* sing in my body and my heart, my *buddhi* and my soul, and I hear in them the very voice of God!"

The wisdom of the *Gita* is not dry intellectualism or the

rationalism of a philosopher: the wisdom of the *Gita* is a music which lingers in the heart: and the melody of this wisdom must be heard, in actions of daily life!

8

The Gita:
A Universal Scripture

Sadhu Vaswani spoke of the *Gita* as "the Bible of Humanity." He was of the firm opinion that there was 'a unity of ethical intuitions and aspirations' among the various religions of the world. "There may be differences," he asserted, "but not discord."

Sri Krishna, the ancient *rishis* who gave us the *Vedas*, and the saints and the sages of India who built up the great Hindu civilization, believed in something far greater than the 'humanism' which the twentieth century glorified. They asserted the truth of the 'One Life in All' — all creatures, all races, all countries, all communities, all modes of worship, all approaches to the Ideal. This is why Sri Krishna tells us in the *Gita*: "By whatever path men approach Me, on that I meet them."

The paths to Him are many — infinite as the stars in the sky. 'The light of all lights is seated in the hearts of all,' the *Gita* tells us. Hence, the unity of all religions, of all nations, which my beloved Master asserted in the unforgettable lines:

'In all religions the light is Thine,
In all the Scriptures the inspiration is Thine.

"I went into solitude and heard them weeping," he wrote, of the great prophets. "They quarrel in our names, they who call themselves our disciples. They follow us not in the way we walk!"

Sadhu Vaswani emphasized that religion, in its highest form, was *ananda* – bliss, the joy of fellowship and service. Another name for religion is unity, harmony, love!

"It cannot be only in one temple that the great God is worshipped," he said. "It cannot be that only in one church shines His Glory. But how many have remembered this simple truth? Prophets and saints do not quarrel with one another. The quarrel is among the disciples when they deny Krishna's light – the light of all lights."

Truer words were never spoken!

We are told in the New Testament, that a man once approached Jesus, asking Him for the greatest law among the Ten Commandments (Matthew, Chapter 22, 35-40.) To him, Jesus said: *"Thou shalt love the Lord thy God with all thy heart and all thy soul, and with all thy mind.'* This is the first and the greatest commandment. And the second is like unto it: *'Thou shalt love thy neighbour as thyself.'* On these two commandments hang all the laws and the prophets."

Is this not what Sri Krishna tells us in the *Gita*:

'Fix thy mind on Me; be devoted to Me; worship Me; bow down to Me. Thus having controlled thyself, and making Me thy goal supreme, thou shalt come unto Me.'

IX: 34

Is this not the message of all religions? Love God with all your heart, mind, and soul; dedicate your every thought, word and action to Him, make Him your focus, your goal supreme, and you will surely attain Him!

This is much more than an emotional assertion. Much higher than an intellectual statement; it is a great spiritual truth. True religion, true belief, true faith requires that your total being must be involved in loving God.

Reading the Bible and reading the *Gita* are not enough; recitation of these divine scriptures is not enough; analysis of their chapters and verses cannot take us far. Love the Lord with your mind, heart, and soul! Love the Lord with thy whole being! Great scholars indeed have pointed out that Jesus's injunction combines *Bhakti Yoga, Gnana Yoga,* and *Raja Yoga,* the yoga of meditation. How is this to be understood?

Both the *Gita* and the Bible insist on wholehearted, indeed whole-souled love. All of us want to love and be loved, but perfect love is possible only when we realize that God loves us, and we offer Him our love. This is love's ultimate fulfillment, the path of devotion, or *Bhakti Yoga.*

This will kindle in us the awareness that God is the Supreme Reality in all creation. Therefore, loving our neighbours, loving humanity, loving every creature that breathes the breath of life, follows automatically, and in the pure love of God, we expand our activities to *lokasangraha,* the welfare of the world.

As we conquer the senses and the ego, we rise in the awareness that we are not the body, but the spirit within, and that this soul is identical with the Supreme Self. "Know ye not that ye are gods?" asked Jesus. He said, again, "The Kingdom of Heaven is within thee!"

What is this, if not the theme of *Gnana Yoga,* the path of wisdom? When one reaches this awareness, one beholds the light of all lights; one rises above the mind, the senses, and the ego, one reaches the supreme awareness: "I am that — the Supreme Self." This is the highest attainment that we can realise through *Raja Yoga,* the yoga of meditation.

The second important commandment of Jesus is: *Thou shalt love thy neighbour as thyself.* What is this but the ideal of Universal Brotherhood, Universal Self-hood? In the advanced stages of spiritual unfoldment, when you realise that Sri Krishna is the indweller in all that is, you begin to live and practise the ideal of *Vasudaiva kutumbakam* — all creation, you realise, is but one family. You feel a profound sense of unity with all creation. You become sensitive to the pain of others. You regard their sufferings as your own. You grow in the spirit of compassion, and this compassion is expressed in action. After all, when you perceive the Lord in all creation, your actions are devoted to the love of the Lord, and lead to universal welfare.

Is not this the ideal of *karma yoga,* desireless action? All of us can attain to the ideal of selfless action when we perform service of the Lord through the service of living beings. This is the best way of purifying your mind and heart. Therefore does the *Mahabharata* tell us: '*Doing good to others is the essence of righteousness, while doing ill to others is the essence of unrighteousness.*'

Thus Jesus' injunction and Sri Krishna's insistence on

right action assert but one truth: words are not enough; feelings and sentiments are not enough; right action is essential; good thoughts are no doubt valuable but they must be converted to action, action for the benefit of others.

Such selfless action purifies the *antahkarna*, (the inner instrument). It expands our consciousness and helps us advance on the three steps to *mukti-karma, bhakti,* and *gnana.*

A great saint of our times has described Jesus as 'the perfect proponent of integral *yoga*'. Through His teachings, His actions, and His life, He set a brilliant example before us all.

The same great truth is asserted by Sri Krishna in the *Gita:* 'The goal is the same; the paths are many. The truth may be taught in different languages by different religions.'

The Three-fold Path
of the Gita

Scholars divide the eighteen chapters of the *Gita* into three sections: the first six chapters deal with the path of action, and are described as the *karma kanda*. Chapters 7-12 deal with the path of devotion, and are called the *bhakti kanda*. The last six chapters deal with the path of knowledge, and are called the *gnana kanda*.

The *karma kanda* teaches us the ideal of right action, selfless action. We are taught that the performance of one's own duty — *swadharma* — is of paramount importance. We must serve not only our parents, our family, our near and dear ones, but also serve society, especially the sick and the needy, for this is our role in the larger family of creation. We must do our duty, but set aside all thought of reward and result. This attitude of selfless service will promote desirelessness and detachment in us. We then offer all our actions as a sacrifice to the Lord. This purifies heart, mind, and soul, filling our lives with peace and joy. We have now made ourselves His Instruments, and His Will works through us.

The *bhakti kanda* teaches us how we may transform *karma* or action into worship of the Lord. In the beautiful words of Kahlil Gibran, "Work is love made visible." When we do our duty in a spirit of joy and love, we grow in devotion, in pure love for Sri Krishna. All that we see around us, all that happens to us, all that we pass through, are just manifestations of His Will, His Divine Plan. Thus we learn to see Him everywhere, see everything as His visible expression. We love all humanity, all of creation, birds, animals, insects, plants, trees, rocks, rivers, seas, the earth, the sky, and space. *Karma yoga* becomes linked with *bhakti yoga*, and work becomes worship. We grow in the awareness of that glorious truth which is often cited as the *Gitasaram* or the essence of the *Gita*: All that has happened has happened for the best; all that is happening is happening for the best; all that is to happen, will happen for the best. This puts us firmly on the path of self-surrender that the Lord demands of Arjuna. Thus we have learnt to see the Lord everywhere; we have linked the heart and the hand, blended *karma* with *bhakti*.

In the third and final section called the *gnana kanda*, the Lord takes us further. This section includes the intellect in action and devotion so that total surrender to the will of the Lord is made possible. We are given the awareness that the self in us is not just the body, the mind, or the senses: it is the deathless *Atman* that is ever free from pain, misery and sorrow. We begin to understand the purpose of our life on earth and this is the beginning of our quest for God. We learn about the conquest of the *gunas*, so that the Lord's Will may work through us freely. We grow in detachment, we assimilate divine qualities that are necessary to tread the spiritual path. We learn the ultimate lesson of surrender and divine grace.

The concept of yoga in the *Gita*

Scholars tell us that the word yoga has been defined in three different ways, at three different places in the *Gita*. 'Equilibrium, at-one-ment, evenness of mind, is yoga,'we are told in Chapter II: verse 48. Yoga is seen here as inner peace, balance, serenity, equanimity; to be of balanced mind is to view with complete indifference success or failure, to work in a spirit of utter detachment.

Just two *slokas* later we are told, 'Yoga is skill in action', Chapter II: verse 50. Sri Krishna is talking of the right kind of action which casts away both good and evil; we do not need to renounce action, we only need to get rid of selfishness.

Finally, in Chapter VI: verse 23, we are told: 'Let that be known by the name of yoga, this breaking of contact with sorrow.' This yoga must be practised resolutely, and with an unwearied heart.

We can see that each of these definitions refers to different states of yoga. On the intellectual plane, yoga means looking at contradictions with an even mind, rising above the *dwandas* (pairs of opposites). In the field of *karma* (action), yoga refers to excellence and righteousness in the performance of duties and tasks. On the plane of emotions, yoga means the complete cessation of pain, a state of joy and perfect inner peace.

Finding Arjuna in utter despondency and misery, Sri Krishna first shows him the pathway to truth through knowledge. This has been called *Sankhya Yoga* or the yoga of knowledge in the *Gita*. We may summarize Sri Krishna's teachings on this aspect in the following manner:

- Life and death relate to the body; the *Atman* is eternal.

- The *Atman* is the Universal Reality, but it is linked with the individual soul and with nature.

- The individual soul is thus identical with the Universal Reality, and the external world of nature is just a manifestation of this Reality.

- The practice of meditation can help us to become aware of the unity of the entire universe.

In the yoga of knowledge, the Lord has told Arjuna who he really was; in the yoga of action, he tells Arjuna how he should act, in the knowledge of what he really is:

> 'Thus far have I spoken to thee of the *Sankhya*. Hearken now to the teachings of the yoga by following which thou shalt cast away the bondage of works.
>
> II: 39

Sankhyan knowledge must be galvanized by life, integrated with action. The Path of Knowledge is for men of contemplation, and the Path of Action is for men of action. However, the paths are not opposed to each other, or contradictory to each other; rather they complement each other. In fact, one follows the other logically. One must just try to obtain an apprehension or intellectual comprehension of reality.

After this, he should try to translate this knowledge into action. As Sri Krishna tells us later (V: 4), only the ignorant think that the Path of Knowledge and the Path of Action are different: he, who is established in one, gets the fruits of both.

In this part of the *Gita*, the Lord analyzes action:

- Even the wise cannot distinguish between action and inaction: therefore, it is necessary to understand the mysterious concepts of action, right action, and wrong action.

- One must always do one's duty.

- The laws of nature drive all of us to activity. We cannot survive without action. But the best type of action is action which is performed for the benefit of all living beings.

- The wise man acts without attachment and desire for results; success and failure do not influence his attitude.

- Such action (detached, desireless) contributes to our own inner purification.

- All such actions must be performed as offerings to the Lord.

To those of us who ask, 'Is it really possible for us to act without desiring any kind of results?' we can see that Sri Krishna has, in fact, given us not one, not two, but three strong motives which should guide all our actions:

- Duty for the sake of duty
- Work for the sake of inner purification
- Action as offering to the Lord

Arjuna enquires whether it is better to renounce all actions, or to act without selfish desire. The Lord's reply is categorical: both renunciation of action and unselfish performance of actions can lead to salvation. But of these two, unselfish, desireless action is better than renunciation of action (V: 2).

Renunciation therefore, is giving up our individual, selfish desires. By doing this we reach a stage where we realize our complete identification with the Universal Self. We not only know, but *act* in accordance with this truth.

Thus far, Arjuna has comprehended the Lord's teaching at the intellectual level and also been told to translate it into action at the ethical level; now the Lord accords him a vision of his Universal Form so that the teaching he has heard may now become a felt experience. In other words, the cognitive understanding of the yoga of Knowledge, which was sought to be put into action by the yoga of Action, is now *lived*, directly *felt* and experienced by the yoga of Devotion.

The concept of *bhakti* or devotion is nowhere defined directly in the *Gita*. However, it is described beautifully in several places:

- Neither a study of the scriptures, nor charity, nor rituals, rites or sacrifices can help us attain God. What is required is single-minded devotion.

- To those who worship Him with single-minded devotion, the Lord offers complete security and protection.

- The man of true devotion has the following qualities: he bears no ill will; he is friendly and compassionate; free from ego; balanced in pain and pleasure; forgiving; ever-content; ever in harmony, and master of himself; he is not disturbed by the world; he is ambitionless; he neither rejoices, nor hates, nor grieves; he is unmoved in pleasure and pain, in success and failure, by praise and blame; his mind and understanding are dedicated to the Lord, of whom he is dearly beloved.

The Path of Knowledge, the Path of Action, and finally, the Path of Devotion, have been revealed to Arjuna. He has been allowed to raise questions and clear his doubts. Repeatedly, he has asked the Lord: "Which path is the best?" Sri Krishna has assured him that all the paths can lead to the liberation of the soul. Yet again, Arjuna asks of the Lord: 'Who is a better *yogi* – the one who combines devotion with action, or the one who combines devotion with knowledge?' For Sri Krishna had earlier said that the yoga of Knowledge is difficult to accomplish, whereas the one who follows the Path of Action can realize the Supreme Reality successfully. Now, Arjuna wants to know which one of these would go hand in hand with the Path of Devotion.

Sri Krishna, in His considered reply, arranges the different disciplines both in the order of their intrinsic excellence, and also in the order of their ease of performance for the aspirant. What he emphasizes is that, though one of the paths may be intrinsically superior to the other, it is of no use if aspirants cannot practise them well. Thus the focus shifts to the receptivity, the response, the ability of the students. The preference and the aptitude of the aspirant thus become the criterion for the path that is to be selected. Sri Krishna relates the various techniques to achieve self-realisation:

- On Me alone fix your mind; let your understanding dwell in Me.

- If you are not able to fix your thoughts steadily on Me, try to reach Me through the practice of concentration and meditation.

- If you are unable to do this, even by performing actions for My sake, you shall attain perfection.

- If you are unable to do even this, then taking refuge in Me, renounce attachment to the fruits of all actions.

Thus, we may see that the different paths to attain the Supreme Reality are placed in order:

1. Comprehension of the Supreme Reality through rational understanding

2. Concentration on the Supreme Reality through meditation

3. Performing actions that are dedicated to God

4. Performing actions desirelessly and selflessly without expectation of results

5. Single-minded devotion to God

The first path is the most difficult, and the final one is perhaps, the simplest, the easiest, and the one that is accessible to us all! Those of us who are at a higher stage of spiritual evolution, may proceed from knowledge to devotion. But for the rest of us, devotion must be the starting point to attain divine knowledge.

The marvellous thing about the *Gita* is that it tells us to choose the path that appeals to us, the one that suits us best. This is in tune with the liberalism, pragmatism, and freedom from dogma that characterizes *sanatana dharma* at its best. What matters is the spiritual discipline that enables one to reach the goal – not its technique or methodology.

In fact, Sri Krishna assures us that none of us can go astray if we follow any one of the paths: '*In whatever way people approach me, on that way I meet them.*' In the final chapter of the *Gita*, the Lord integrates the paths to utter the final secret to Arjuna:

> 'Fix thy mind on Me; be devoted to Me; sacrifice to Me; prostrate thyself before Me. So shalt thou come to Me. I pledge thee My troth; thou art dear to Me!'
>
> XVIII: 65

And, even more emphatically:

> 'Abandoning all duties, come unto Me alone for shelter. Grieve not! I shall liberate thee from all sins.'
>
> XVIII: 66

This is the final and most inspiring message of the *Gita*. This is not escapism; this is not shifting our responsibility on to God; in fact the Lord has insisted that we should never shirk our duties; rather, we must free our mind from egoism and desire. Divine grace is obtained through unconditional surrender to the Lord. The Lord should be made the single goal of our life, the sole object of our worldly endeavours.

The essence of *gnana yoga* is beautifully summarized by Adi Shankara when he says: 'I express in half a verse what has been said in hundreds of books: God is real; the world is unreal; and the soul is one with God.'

Vedanta, the end of the *Vedas*, or the essence of the *Vedas*, is the philosophy that teaches us the unity of all life. Its teachings may be summarized thus:

- God dwells in every heart; He dwells in all aspects of the universe; He is without beginning, middle, and end. He is eternal, pure, perfect, and free. In Him the universe rests, and it is supported and sustained by Him.

- It is only knowledge of God that can bring us ultimate peace and happiness.

- The barrier that prevents us from knowing the reality of God is the mind. When the mind is at rest and in peace, we can realize the presence of God within us.

- Ego is the root cause of all human suffering. It creates in us the illusion of separateness, making us identify with the body. Conquest of the ego is essential to attain wisdom or *gnana*. Conquest of the ego subsumes the conquest of the senses.

- There is no lasting happiness to be found in the objects and pleasures of this material world. In God alone can we find true joy and peace.

Gnana Yoga is not abstract knowledge; nor is it a comfortable philosophy which one dissects and analyzes in the armchair. To the true seeker, it must become a living experience! It must teach you to love all living beings and live in harmony with them.

What are the qualities one must cultivate to tread the path of *Gnana Yoga?*

1. *Viveka* or discrimination. This helps us perceive the distinction between the real and the unreal, the good and the bad.

2. *Vairagya* or dispassion. You free yourself from slavery of sense-pleasures. You rise above pleasure and pain. You remember the words of the Lord in the Gita: 'The delights are born of sense-contacts and are verily wombs of pain.'

3. *Shad sampat* or the six-fold virtues which are:

   - *Shama* – calmness of mind, achieved through the conquest of desires

   - *Dama* – control of the senses

   - *Uparati* – contentment of mind, that is born out of disgust for worldly enjoyments.

   - *Titiksha* – power of endurance

   - *Shraddha* – intense faith in the scriptures and in the words of the guru

   - *Samadhana* – one-pointed concentration on the Lord, which is achieved by a combination of the above five qualities.

4. *Mumukshatwa* – or desire for liberation. The mind must be set unswervingly on the Lord. He must become the single goal, the sole focus of your life. The best way to develop this intense desire for liberation is to seek the company of saints and true devotees of the Lord. *Karma Yoga* has been described as the yoga of heroism.

It entails that we give up selfishness, which is very difficult to achieve! According to *Karma Yoga*, spiritual progress begins with selfless service.

What are the main teachings of *Karma Yoga?*

- Plunge yourself into selfless work. Do your duty, and a little more! Work for the welfare of others. Selfish work retards spiritual growth; selfless work elevates you to lofty heights of true joy and peace.

- Selflessness grows, but gradually! Work patiently and ceaselessly; bear in mind the splendid examples of the great *karma yogis.*

- Grow in the virtues of love and compassion. Put others before yourself.

- Dedicate your work to the Lord. Let your work become a form of worship.

- Develop the spirit of detachment, non-attachment to work and the results of work. Do not be swayed by success and failure, praise and blame. Do not expect rewards; offer your work to the Lord in the spirit of *yagna* or sacrifice.

- One important function of selfless work is that it makes possible the purification of the mind.

- Be calm and unattached. Act with wisdom and understanding, so that you may acquire 'skill in action'.

- The motive with which you act is the most important aspect of *Karma Yoga. Karma Yoga* is performed for the sake of God alone, with the sole aim of realizing God. Name, fame, philanthropy, social reform, power, release from sin — all these, when desired as results, detract from *Karma Yoga*. If the motive is pure and selfless, it is *Karma Yoga*. If the motive is impure, it is not.

What are the qualities of a *Karma Yogi?*

- He should be absolutely free from lust, greed, wrath, and selfishness.

- He should be detached and desireless.

- He should be humble, free from pride and vanity.

- He should be pure, simple and sweet in his expressions.

- He should have a loving and sociable nature.

- He should be flexible and adaptable by nature.

- He should rejoice in the welfare of others.

- He should exercise self-control over his emotions, actions, his palate, his speech, and his senses.

- He should lead a life of simplicity.

- He should work to maintain his body as a temple of the Lord: he should have a sound, strong, and healthy body, for in it dwells his eternal *Atman*.

- He should be dispassionate, not swayed by sensual attachments.

- He must possess equanimity, a balanced mind. Insult, injury, disrespect, and dishonour should not affect him. Respect, honour, praise, and power must not tempt him.

- He is a man of kindness, courtesy, and love. All that he does, he does with pure devotion and love of the Lord. For him *lokasangraha* is a form of worship.

- He must conquer the following weaknesses which will hinder his progress:

  ➤ Ego and irritability

  ➤ Self-assertive nature

  ➤ Fault-finding with others

  ➤ Idle gossip and vain arguments

  ➤ Half-hearted efforts, and

  ➤ Procrastination.

A true *karma yogi* should see the good in all people, while, at the same time, ignoring their weaknesses. Only then will he be worthy of calling himself a true devotee of the Lord. When it is properly understood and practised, *Karma Yoga* can give the aspirant rapid progress on the path of self-realisation.

Bhakti Yoga is the path of utter devotion, supreme love for God. It is pure and selfless love, which is far above worldly love. It does not involve bargaining with God over results; it is above and beyond all selfish motives. It is intense devotion and attachment to the Lord. It has to be felt, experienced – not talked about or discussed.

- *Bhakti* pervades the devotee's heart, mind, and soul.

- In its intensity, all impurities of the mind are destroyed, reduced to ashes.

- It makes the devotee simple and childlike in his absolute trust in God.

- It has none of the weaknesses and defects of human love, like selfishness, insincerity, attachment, and ego.

- It is the most pure and natural form of love, for we learn to love God even as He loves us.

What are the qualities of a true *bhakta?*

- He has a soft, loving, tender heart.

- He is free from pride, lust and anger, greed and egoism.

- In his great love for the Lord, he strives for perfection, and ceaselessly works to overcome his defects.

- He is free from all cares, fears, and worries. Like a child, he feels himself safe and secure in the Lord's divine protection.

- He treats everybody alike; he does not see people as 'enemies' or 'friends'; all people are his brothers and sisters. His love extends to all alike, for, in each and every human being, he perceives the form of the Lord.

- His faith in the Lord is firm, unwavering, and absolute. His strength and courage are derived from this faith. This faith roots out all anxiety and fear from his mind.

- He is firm in the conviction that all that happens to him, happens for the best, for it comes as God's Will. Happiness and sorrow are also forms of God's Grace.

Bhakti too, requires heroism. In its highest stages, the devotee even refrains from asking God to take away his pain, misery, and suffering. Thus it was that Kuntidevi prayed to Sri Krishna: 'O Lord, let me always have adversity, so that my mind may be ever fixed at Thy feet.'

Yes, pain and suffering are to be welcomed, accepted, for

they help us remember God constantly. They are blessings
in disguise, for they help to free us from the bondages of
this world. When we go through adversity, God also
bestows upon us the wisdom, courage, endurance, and
spiritual strength to overcome this adversity. In fact, the
Lord puts His devotees through severe tests and trials
only in order that they may be moulded, purified, evolved,
and made fit to receive His Divine Vision. Does He not
tell us in the Gita:

> 'Yet not by the *Vedas*, nor by austerities, nor by
> gifts, nor by sacrifices, can I be seen in the form
> in which thou (Arjuna) hast seen Me.
> But by devotion to Me alone, devotion
> undivided, may I thus be known and seen in
> essence, and entered into, O Arjuna!'
>
> XI: 53-54

What is the best way to develop such love for the Lord?
The answer is simple: we begin with guru *bhakti*. The guru
gives us a form, a visible outer form which we can take to
represent God. To serve and worship the guru is the best
way to cultivate devotion for the Lord.

The various attitudes to *bhakti*, the five *bhavas* – *santa*, *dasya*,
sakya, *vatsalya*, and *madurya* – will be discussed in detail in
the section on the Fourth Commandment '*Thou shalt not
forget thy daily appointment with God*'. We will also look at the
nine 'modes' of *bhakti* through which we may express our
devotion to the Lord. These are ways which will lead us on
the gradual, progressive path of *bhakti*, from the gross to
the subtle.

Sri Ramanuja also outlines certain fundamental disciplines

in *Bhakti Yoga.* These are:

1. *Abhyasa* – remembering God constantly. This helps us to attain steadiness of mind.

2. *Viveka* – abstention and discrimination, keeps the body and mind pure.

3. *Vimoka* – freeness of mind. By cultivating *vimoka* we reject all the gross desires that retard our progress and develop intense, single-minded love for the Lord.

4. *Satyam* – truthfulness, which is essential for a life of *bhakti.*

5. *Arjavam* – straightforwardness or honesty, which helps us overcome lies, deceit, hypocrisy, and insincerity.

6. *Kriya* – doing good to all. As compassion and mercy grow in our hearts, we learn to serve others.

7. *Kalyana* – virtuous conduct. This enables us to pray with a pure heart for the welfare of the world and the well-being of all people in it.

8. *Daya* – compassion, which is an aspect of God.

9. *Ahimsa* – the practice of non-violence in thought, word, and deed.

10. *Dana* – charity. This is born out of the generosity of a large heart. It destroys narrow-mindedness and meanness, and helps us evolve spiritually.

11. *Anavasada* – freedom from depression and pessimism. Cheerfulness and optimism are the characteristics of a true devotee.

Beginning with ordinary *bhakti,* which, for most of us, is

worship of a form or an idol, we are eventually led to
parabhakti – the highest form of devotion in which the
devotee feels completely one with the Lord. He sees the
Lord in all – he sees everything, everyone, as the Lord's
manifestation. *Parabhakti* eventually leads to *gnana*, the
highest wisdom. Both *gnana* and *parabhakti* enable us to
attain liberation, union with the Lord, which is the goal of
all *sadhana* and *abhaysa*.

Mahatma Gandhi: the True *Karma Yogi*

When Mahatma Gandhi fell to an assassin's bullet on
January 30, 1948, he died as he had lived – a private
citizen, an individual without power or position, a man
who did not possess great wealth or extensive powers. His
only 'possessions' were his change of clothes (the humble
loincloth and the *angavastra*), the shoes he wore, a pair of
spectacles, and his personal copy of the *Bhagavad Gita*. The
whole world mourned for this great man. The UN flag
flew at half-mast, and the Security Council cancelled all its
meetings to pay homage to this great man, who had used
the weapon of non-violence to achieve the most remarkable
victory over a great colonial power.

Prof. Gilbert Murray, a distinguished classical scholar at
Oxford University, said, "Be careful with a man who
altogether does not care about enjoyment, comfort,
prestige, or position, but who is simply confident in doing
what he considers right. He is a dangerous and unpleasant
opponent, because his body, which you may easily conquer,
will not give you any power over his soul."

Satya and *ahimsa* were the cardinal principles of his life.

Adhering to these principles was dearer to him than life itself. He had no personal needs or desires; he was equally at home sitting across the table from the British Viceroy, or seated on the mud floor of the humblest peasant's hut. He was indifferent to the pleasant and the unpleasant. *Ahimsa* did not make him a coward; rather it lent him the great virtue of *abhaya* (fearlessness). Fearlessness made him free. He was always open to debate and discussion. When he made mistakes, he admitted his faults openly, and changed his methods, but he remained steadfast in his adherence to his ideals.

For Gandhiji, there were no enemies — only opponents with a different point of view. He respected the people whom he had to confront in serious political situations. When he was jailed in South Africa, he made a pair of leather sandals which he gave to General Smuts, the white leader who had jailed him. General Smuts was proud of the unique gift he had received from his great 'adversary' and used the sandals for a long time. Much later, he returned them to Gandhi, saying, "I have been using these sandals during many summers, though I have to admit that I don't feel worthy of wearing the shoes of such a great man." This was Gandhiji's secret weapon, his great strength: he conquered hearts and minds! He disarmed his most rigid opponents with his humility. By renouncing violence he effectively made the moral disarmament of the enemy, his effective weapon.

Even as he was emerging as a leader of men in South Africa, he was deeply influenced by great writers like Thoreau and Tolstoy. Thoreau's essay 'Civil Disobedience' gave him the impetus to perfect his own concept of *satyagraha*. He also started the Tolstoy Farm, an agricultural commune that worked on the principles of collectivism, simplicity, unselfish work, celibacy, and a vegetarian diet. These ideals he carried with him to India, where he started *ashrams* at Sabarmati and Wardha.

Gandhiji's role in the Indian freedom is now recorded in history. But he did not seek high office or political power. What made him achieve such a tremendous moral, spiritual and political victory? Let us hear the reason in his own words:

'The reason why I let myself be totally absorbed in serving the community, was my wish for self-realisation.

'I had done it through serving my religion, since I felt God could only be reached through service. And service was for me to serve India, because I had the talent for it, and it came to me without taking the initiative. I travelled to South Africa to flee from an untenable situation and to earn my living. But instead, it became a search for God and a striving for self-realisation.'

'What I wanted to achieve, what I have striven for and sought after, these thirty years, is self-realisation, to see God face to face, to achieve *moksha* (liberation). I live and act for this goal. Everything I do, through what I say and write, and all my efforts in politics, is aimed at this same goal.'

Can there be a better manifesto for a *karma yogi?*

As the *Gita* teaches us, life demands action; most of us act to fulfill our narrow selfish needs and desires. But the true *karma yogis* of this world offer their actions to God, and serve Him in all they do. Thus they perform selfless work without expectation of personal gains and rewards. Action and effort become the means by which they transcend the lower self, and realize God through their efforts. So it was that Gandhi said of himself, "People say I am a saint who's lost himself in politics. But in reality, I am a politician who is doing his utmost to be a saint." He made the domain of politics sacred by dedicating his political efforts to public welfare and to God. To quote Thomas Merton, "His spiritual life was simply his participation in the life and *dharma* of his people."

He was a *karma yogi* beyond compare, engaging in desireless action, and practising integrity of thought, word, and deed. Nothing that I can say on Gandhiji as a *karma yogi* will be complete without this beautiful anecdote from his life.

A learned professor came to see Mahatma Gandhi at his ashram. He paid his respects to the Mahatma and said to him, "They say you have imbibed the doctrine of the *Gita* in your daily life. Can you please explain to me the very essence of the *Gita*?"

Gandhiji looked at the professor and said, "Professor, can you do something for me?"

'Yes, certainly,' said the professor.

Gandhiji pointed to a pile of bricks stacked in one corner of the courtyard. "Can you move these bricks across to the opposite side, please?"

"But... but Bapuji...' stammered the professor. 'I have asked you a serious question to which I believe you alone can give the answer!"

"Yes, yes, we will talk about it later. Now, if you will kindly start moving the bricks..."

The professor was puzzled, but eager to do the Mahatma's bidding. He carried the bricks across the courtyard and stacked them on the opposite side as he was told. Sweating profusely, he came to Gandhiji and invited him to come and see for himself if the work had been done as per his instructions.

"But this is not where I wanted them," Gandhiji exclaimed. "When I said *opposite*, I did not mean on the other side, but diagonally opposite ... there, in the northern corner."

"Right," sighed the professor. "I'll do it right away."

By now, he was huffing and puffing, as he carried piles of bricks across the yard. His hands were bruised, his shoulder was aching, and his back was stiff, when he returned to Gandhiji.

"The work is done," he panted. "Now Bapuji, if you would kindly answer my question..."

"Over here, in this corner, the bricks are blocking the entrance to the garden," said Gandhiji frowning.

"Do you think, Professor, we can have them stacked in the eastern corner?"

"But that's where they were stacked in the first place," said the professor, losing his temper. "I am a professor, Bapuji, and I came to you with a serious query, and you treat me like a labourer! Perhaps you imagine I cannot grasp your teaching – or perhaps you cannot express the essence of the *Gita* in a way that others can understand!"

"My dear friend," Mahatma Gandhi said, "I have given you a practical demonstration, put you through a working test of the *Gita*'s central teaching: it is just this – do your allotted task. Do not seek anything else!"

Sri Adi Shankara: the True *Gnana Yogi*

Sri Adi Shankara is today hailed as one of the world's greatest philosophers. Born in Kerala over 1500 years ago, he reaffirmed and re-established the principles of *sanatana dharma* (the eternal religion).

Born at a time when the practice of *dharma* was in decline, he propagated the ancient *Vedic* doctrines and the essence of the *Upanishads* in the form of his *Advaita* or the philosophy of non-duality.

He restructured all the extant forms of loose desultory religious practices into acceptable norms based on the *Vedas*. His commentaries on the *Brahma Sutras, Srimad Bhagavad Gita,* and the ten principal *Upanishads* remain invaluable source materials for our understanding of the Hindu religion.

Sri Adi Shankara taught that Oneness (*ekatvam*) is the essence of all knowledge. '*Ekameva advaiteeyam Brahma* – the Absolute is one alone, not two', he taught. There is the appearance of an enormous multiplicity, but there is no second to God. Beings may be many, but the breath is the same. Nations may be many, but the earth is one. In this manner, Shankara taught the principle of unity that underlies the apparent diversity of the universe. Shankara was well aware that *advaita* philosophy requires intense *sadhana* in order to remove all traces of ego and duality in the minds of men. The goal was *gnana* — the awareness of one's real unity with the self. But this, he felt, required the preparatory discipline of *bhakti* and *karma*, which would brighten the intellect and purify the heart. *Satsanga*, the company of the wise and holy ones, would also help the aspirants on the path, and promote the disappearance of *moha* (attachment). When this victory is achieved, one attains the wisdom and knowledge enshrined in the great teaching — '*Tat twam asi*, That art thou!' The attainment of this recognition is *mukti* (liberation).

Adi Shankara was brilliant in explicating the highly complex philosophy of *advaita*. It is, in its essence, a *bhava* — a conscious feeling or awareness, and cannot be applied to *kriya* (daily activity). Thus, you accept the divine presence in a human being, a lamb, and a snake; but for this reason, you cannot handle a snake or place it on your person. This is vindicated by the differential qualities of *asthi, bhathi,* and *priyam* in all beings, that is, existence, recognizability, and utility.

Once, when Shankara was giving spiritual lessons to his disciples, a young man demanded to know why all human beings in the world could not be regarded as absolute equals, since after all, the same kind of blood flowed in all of them. Shankara told him that one could adopt the idea of *advaita* (non-duality) in one's thoughts and attitudes, but it was not always possible to put everything into practice.

At this, the young man protested that such distinction and differentiation did not seem right. To explain the concept more clearly, Shankara asked the young man whether he had a mother, a wife, a sister, and a mother-in-law. "Are you treating all of them equally?" he demanded of the man. "Can you treat your wife as your mother and your mother as a wife?" The young man's doubts were cleared.

Once Shankara posed the question to his disciples: 'Who is the true conqueror in this world?' One disciple said that the true conqueror was the one who had subdued the world and brought it under his control. Another was of the opinion that he who had climbed up to the summit of the Himalayas was the real hero. A third disciple declared that he who crossed the seven oceans was the greatest hero.

Shankara told his disciples not to think of 'conquest' only in worldly terms. In such terms, anyone and everyone could be deemed a conqueror. Even animals and birds could fight each other, and establish 'victory'! A bird could fly over the Himalayas or cross the seven seas. Where was the victory in all this? "Only he who has subdued the mind is a real conqueror," Shankara asserted. No one can achieve victory without subduing his mind. '*Brahmam satyam jagath mithyam:* the Self is real, and the world is illusory,' Shankara declared. Equally, he asserted: '*Sarvam vishnumayam jagath* – the universe is permeated by God.'

When scholars pointed out the contradiction in his statements, Shankara explained the difference between permanence and impermanence. Worldly life is continually changing, moving – like moving scenes on a permanent screen. In this process, the world and the divine are one, but the world is impermanent, while the divine is permanent. 'Conquer *trishna* (desire)', Shankara taught. He equated desires with strong fetters that chained and bound man. While iron fetters would rust and so weaken, the chains of desire would only grow stronger.

Sri Shankara strove to re-establish in the heart of man, the faith that the divine Self was the indweller in him. In order to achieve this awareness, we have to drive out the vicious traits that have taken root in our minds. When we obtain even a glimpse of this sublime reality, that God dwells within us, we achieve equanimity, stability, egolessness, and we rest secure in the knowledge that we are of the Divine Essence.

Sri Adi Shankara went through an extensive, countrywide campaign of *tarka* (debates), trying to teach and persuade people to accept the truth. Having accomplished this *digvijaya yatra* successfully, he reached the holy city of Kashi, where he worshipped Lord Vishwanath, the presiding deity, saying: "O Lord, I come to Thee for the expiation of my sins."

How could this be? Within the short span of his life, he had studied all the sacred scriptures, written profound commentaries on them, and taught their truths to numerous followers. He had lived a pure, faultless life, and was even perceived as an incarnation of Lord Shiva Himself. How then could he have committed any sins?

In a beautiful prayer, he himself explained:

'O Lord! My first sin is that despite knowing and teaching that God is beyond mind and speech, I have still attempted to describe your divine attributes in my hymns and *slokas*. This shows lack of conformity between my thoughts and words.

'Next, even though I am convinced of the truth that God pervades and permeates all things, all creatures, all places in the manifested universe, and preaching this truth to all, I have come here to Kashi, to seek holy *darshan*. This is my second offence.

Thirdly, having firmly asserted that the One and the same Self is immanent in all beings, and that there is no difference between the *paramatma* (the over-soul) and the *jivatma* (the individual soul), I stand before you as if Thou and I are two separate and different entities. This is my third lapse.

'I beg you to absolve me of all three sins, of which I am guilty.'

Adi Shankara taught that *atma gnana* (knowledge of the Self) was essential for spiritual advancement. He preached and followed the *Vedic* dictum: '*Ekatma sarvabhoota antaratma*: the one *atma* is present in all beings.' He emphasized too, the concept: '*Ekam sath vipra bahuda vadanthi*: the one truth is described in many ways by the wise'. He firmly believed that *gnana* (wisdom) was nothing but *advaita darshana* – the vision of non-duality. I must add, however, that in his famous hymn *Bhaja Govindam*, Sri Adi Shankara emphasizes

that only the Path of Devotion can help man to get over
the cycle of birth and death:

'Bhaja Govindam bhaja Govindam
Govindam bhaja mudamathe
Samprapthe sannihite kale
Nahi nahi rakshati dukrung karane ...

Worship Govinda, worship Govinda, O foolish
one!
When death is near to you
Abstruse philosophy will be of no avail to you!'

Dhruva: the True *Bhakti Yogi*

Child Dhruva was the eldest son of his father, who was a
king. As the eldest, he should have been the closest to his
father's heart, he should have been the crown prince and
heir to the throne. But the child was meant for a greater
life!

Dhruva's father had two wives – Suniti, the older one, was
gentle, mild, and virtuous. She was Dhruva's mother.
Suruchi, the younger one, was beautiful and the king's
favourite. She had a son called Uttama.

One day, the two princes were playing together. Suddenly
Dhruva wanted to go and sit on the lap of his father, the
king. The little boy ran up to his father who was seated on
the throne, and climbed joyfully onto his knees. The king,
too, embraced his little son gladly, and lovingly stroked his
hair. Queen Suruchi happened to come there, at that time.
A proud and arrogant woman, she was incensed to see
Dhruva on the king's knee. Rudely, she pulled the little

boy by the ear and pushed him away.

"Get out from here!" she said to him in a rage. "You have
no right to be seated here on the lap of your father, or on
his throne! That is a position meant for my son alone!"

The king, who was infatuated with his younger wife, said
not a word in defence of his son.

Dhruva ran to his mother. "How is it that my father's lap
is not for me?" he questioned her in anguish. "Tell me how
I may obtain his love, so that no one can push me away
from my rightful place."

Suniti was a pious and devoted woman, and a loving
mother. She said to her son, "My dear child, look not to
your earthly father or earthly mother for comfort. Turn
instead, to your Divine Father. He has the power to grant
you your heart's desire." Dhruva's heart was touched with
his mother's words of wisdom. He went into the *tapovana*
(the forest of meditation) in order to find God, through
the practice of austerity and devotion. Maharishi Narad
came to meet him there. From the sage, Dhruva received
the *taraka mantra* that would enable him to have a *darshana*
of the Lord: '*Om namo bhagavate Vasudevaya*: "I offer
salutation to the Lord who is the all-pervading One!" For
days together, this five-year-old child sat in meditation
upon the Lord. Hunger, thirst, and all bodily demands
were put aside. As he uttered the *taraka mantra* repeatedly,
his consciousness was uplifted, and the Lord appeared to
give him *darshana*.

Dhruva had left the palace with the longing to regain his
rightful place on his father's throne and in his heart. But

the Lord's *darshana* wrought a tremendous transformation in his soul. The constant repetition of the *mantra* had kindled his highest aspirations. With folded hands and bowed head, Dhruva said to the Lord, "I want neither the reins of power, nor the pleasures of this earth. I want Thee and Thee alone!"

The Lord so blessed Dhruva that he was transformed into the most steadfast star on the horizon, the Pole Star. The boy, who had been pushed away from his father's knee, became the beloved of the Lord. As the Pole Star, the *Dhruva Nakshatra*, he shines on steadily, not moving from his place, come summer or winter!

Dhruva, is indeed, the shining example of *Bhakti Yoga!*

10

The Symbolism of the Gita

All the great religious scriptures of the world are deeply, profoundly, mystically symbolic. They speak to us at different levels: if we approach them simplistically, they have a simple but beautiful truth to teach us. As we evolve spiritually, we find that they have very many complex, powerful lessons to teach us.

Religion lends itself especially to the mode of symbolism. Narrow-minded bigots in the past dismissed Hinduism as a pagan religion, a religion restricted to idol worship. It was a wise Westerner who once remarked that a Hindu idol was "a window looking on to eternity"!

At a literal level, the *Mahabharata* is a story of spirited adventure and rousing warfare, even a text-book on politics, good governance, and ethics. But at a deeper level, it is concerned with the empire of the human mind: the myriad 'characters' in the epic are representations of the hundreds of psychological traits within many of us. Some of them are base, others are noble; some of them are virtuous, others vicious. Thus a Kurukshetra war is constantly being fought in our minds — a war between the forces of darkness and light, good and evil.

All that is good, all that is virtuous, all that is noble
within us, chooses God. All that is evil, wrong, and
ignoble, chooses the material world. Like the Pandavas, the
former seek righteousness; like the Kauravas, the latter
seek the gross world, kingdom, land, power. Both these
tendencies are part of us – aspects of our nature; they
belong to the same clan. However, the difference is inward,
spiritual. Scholars have studied the *Mahabharata* and the
Gita deeply, to draw out certain symbolic significances.

We are told that Pandu represents the soul, while
Dhritarashtra represents the mind. The latter, we know, is
born blind; for by itself, the mind cannot discriminate,
cannot perceive the truth clearly. The blind mind is likened
to a mirror: when the image of a dog or a cat or a flower
falls on the mirror, the mirror does not say, 'Aha, this is a
dog, a cat, a flower.' It only reflects what is before it; only
you, who looks at what is reflected in the mirror, can see
the reflection and conclude, with the help of your intellect
that the reflection is of this or that. The intellect is that
which defines what it sees reflected in the mind.

In our constant struggle with illusion and reality, the mind
is our enemy: it perceives only what it wants to perceive. It
is clogged with sense-impressions. And what the mind
puts out – its offspring – are also tied down to material
reality and the ego. Thus among the Kauravas,
Duryodhana, the offspring of the blind mind, represents
material desire. The Pandavas, the sons of the soul,
represent spiritual qualities.

The soul is the rightful ruler of the Self. Our birthright is
the divine consciousness that the soul alone can
experience. But Pandu dies, and his sons are not permitted

to succeed him. Duryodhana gambles with Yudhishtira, and the dice are loaded. The Pandavas lose, and are banished for thirteen years.

Yudhishtira, who represents soul-calmness, is utterly shattered. The soul-qualities are banished into the wilderness, deprived of the sovereignty which is their birthright.

When war becomes inevitable, Krishna gives Duryodhana (king of material desire) and Arjuna (fiery self-control, the main warrior of the Pandavas) a choice. One of them can have His entire army, with thousands of soldiers; the other can have Him, the Lord, but He will not fight. Arjuna has the wisdom to know that Krishna is God; and where God is, victory has to be! 'Yato dharma tato jaya', as the saying goes. He chooses Krishna for the Pandavas. Duryodhana is beside himself with joy, congratulating himself on acquiring the Narayan Sena.

Why does God tell Arjuna that He will not fight on their behalf? Is it not true that we often imagine God being deaf, dumb, and blind to our miserable cries for help? 'Comforter, where is thy comforting?' we call, in the words of the poet. Little do we realize that He is there with us, working through us, to perform His miracles. We may not see how He works, but He is sure to help us out of our sufferings. Is not this profound truth expressed in the words of the Lord in the Gita: 'Know this for certainty, Arjuna: My devotee is never lost.' All we have to do is cling to Him in faith and hope: He will not, indeed, He cannot let us down!

To recapitulate, Yudhishtira gambles, loses his birthright,

and is banished out of his own kingdom. The loaded dice (*maya*) lured him, and he fell of his own accord. He must pass through the required thirteen years that represent a cycle of spiritual growth. The exile is over, the Pandavas get back, but the Kauravas (material desires) are now so firmly entrenched that harmonious compromise is not possible. The Pandavas are ready to settle for less, for a fraction of their kingdom. Like so many of us, they would like to devote a *little* time to God and to spiritual practices, but material desires will not allow them to do even that little! They have to struggle, to fight, to gain the right to devote themselves to the Life of the Spirit.

There is a constant struggle between our sense-desires and our spiritual aspirations — between what we *want* to do, and what we *ought* to do. And this is what the battle of Kurukshetra is all about.

In the *Gita* you find the statement by Duryodhana: "Our army is difficult to count, but their army is so easy to count!" In other words, our weaknesses, our faults, our negative traits, are very many, but alas, our virtues are so few! The way of Divine Love is but one — the straight and narrow path. But the paths of passion are many — we can be infatuated with all kinds of things.

When we come to the actual beginning of the *Bhagavad Gita*, Dhritarashtra, who is blind, asks Sanjaya (who represents the introspective faculties) to tell him what is happening on the battlefield — the *karma kshetra*, the field of action — symbolic of the human body itself.

Duryodhana is proud of his army which, he says, is too numerous to count. And yet he adds, "Therefore, do everything you can to guard Bhishma." Bhishma is said to represent the ego. He fights on the side of the wrong, and he is subsequently killed. But he has the power of not dying until he himself chooses to yield to death. Here, he is the grand old man of the Kaurava clan whose very presence cheers Duryodhana. Dronacharya represents habit – the teacher of both the clans. But in the struggle between the senses and the spirit, habit supports the senses. As we say, habits die hard!

Arjuna asks Sri Krishna to drive his chariot to a place between the two armies. Seeing his kinsmen, relatives, and friends, he is deeply perplexed and saddened. His bow, Gandiva, drops from his hand. The point is, even those qualities that are his enemies, are yet his own relatives, members of his own psyche. How can he kill them? How can he destroy them? It would be like killing a part of his own nature.

"If I were to kill my own people, what a sin it would be!" he exclaims. He is discouraged. He rationalizes; he makes excuses, he proffers subtle arguments – all of them different reasons for choosing the wrong option: "I will not fight!" They all sound very good and righteous, but they are all false justifications for doing what he should not do! When we are involved in an internal struggle between our lower desires and our higher spiritual aspirations, the mind is weakened. "I cannot give up this!" we think. But actually, we are only expected to conquer our weaknesses. When we give up such a battle, then indeed, will everyone look on us in contempt, as Krishna tells Arjuna. You have lost a psychological battle, and you are defeated. The message of the Gita is thus to remind us

that life is a constant battle, until we are able to conquer
the forces of darkness, and win a resounding victory for
the forces of light.

As I have repeatedly stressed, the *Gita* is a dynamic
scripture, a gospel of action. It is not meant for
philosophers and renunciates alone; nor is it reserved
solely for the benefit of people who have turned their back
on worldly life. It is for you and me! And we can put its
principles into practice in deeds of daily life. Therefore, let
me share with you, a few simple practical suggestions
which I call 'The Seven Commandments of the *Gita*'.

The First Commandment:
'Thou Shalt Not Identify Thyself with the Body'

Lord Sri Krishna's teaching begins in the second *adhyaya* of the *Gita*. The very first thought in the teaching is the difference, the distinction between the soul and the body, between the *Atman* and the *deha*. The problem with many of us is that we have completely identified ourselves with the body – the physical, material aspects of our existence. If I were to ask, "Who are you?" you would immediately point to your physical form. If I were to ask you, "Who is J.P. Vaswani?" you would point to my form, my physical body. But we are not the bodies we wear! This is the first teaching that the Lord gives us in the *Gita*. The body is only a garment we have worn during this present earth incarnation.

> 'As the soul experienceth, in the body, childhood, youth' and age, so passeth he on to another body. The *dheera*, the sage, is not perplexed by this.'
>
> II: 13

When I urge you not to identify yourself with the body, I am asking you to move away from the allures of the materialistic world. The more we identify with the body, the more we want, the more we crave, the more we possess, the more we get entangled in *maya*.

Once upon a time, there lived a wise and holy sage who had attained spiritual illumination. Many were the people who knocked at his door, eager to see him, speak to him and be blessed by him. Whenever there was a knock at his door, he would ask, "Who are you?"

The visitor would invariably say, "I am so-and-so, son of so-and-so, from such-and-such-a-village."

"Why have you come?" the sage would ask next.

"O holy one, give me your blessings so that ..." and the visitors would place their desires before the holy one. 'So that I can have a rich harvest ...' "So that I may have a son..." and so on.

Receiving such answers, the sage would lapse into silence. He would not open the door. Thus many people came to him and went away disappointed.

One day, a seeker came to knock at the holy man's door.

"Who are you?" called out the sage.

"I wish I knew," came the answer. "Oh holy one, I beg you to enlighten me, for I don't know who I am, and why I came into this world. Please show me the way, so that I may attain the true goal of this, my human life."

The holy man was well pleased with this reply and opened his door to admit the seeker. He realised that the man was a genuine aspirant, thirsting for the Truth. He took him as his disciple, and initiated him on the path of self-realisation.

Ask yourself, 'Who am I?' Look for the answer in the heart within. 'Where do I come from? Why am I here? What is the purpose of this existence of mine?' You will be led to the truth that you are not the body you wear!

Identification with the body leads to the illusion that power, pleasures, and possessions of this world can make us happy. But this is not true; instead, these material possessions only keep us in bondage — the bondage of ignorance, *avidya*. Once you are freed from this illusion, you will realize the truth of the Self, and move towards God-realisation. This is the process by which we may all move from illusion to reality; from darkness to light; from death to immortality.

The soul, the *Atman*, the indwelling one, passes from body to body. It is unaffected by outer things. The Self abides; the bodies are transient.

You may well ask: Why does the soul pass from body to body? My answer is: To gather experiences, and to evolve towards its abode in the Eternal. Just as the diverse bodies of our childhood, youth, and age do not cause a doubt in our minds about the continuity of the Self, so too, the diverse bodies of different incarnations, especially the new body after death, should not cause us to doubt the continuity of the *Atman*.

Of course at this point, many of you will want to question me about reincarnation. If it is true that we pass through several incarnations, how is it that we do not remember about our so-called 'previous' lives? Let me ask you: how many of you remember clearly and vividly all the details of your early childhood? If we can't remember these, how then may we be expected to remember the details of our past lives?

The Lord tells Arjuna: 'You have always been; you will always be. This is the awareness that we must try to attain — that we are immortal, that we abide in Eternity.'

You are not the body! You are the immortal soul within! Therefore, do not become a slave of the body. Do not keep running after the shadow shapes that come and go!

St. Francis of Assisi once observed that the root of all evil, the root of all sin, is this sense of identification with the body. You are not this body that you wear; this body is only your present, temporary address. You inhabit the body now. In your earlier incarnation, you lived elsewhere, you were in a different body. Now you live in another, but not for long. Sooner or later, your address will change. You will move on. The body is the dress you have worn. It is a boat which you are rowing, to cross the *sansar sagar* — the ocean of transmigration. It is meant to take you to the other shore.

There are some people who go one step further. They identify themselves with the body-mind complex.

> 'Contacts with their objects, O Arjuna, give rise
> to cold and heat, pleasure and pain. They come
> and go, are impermanent. Endure them, Arjuna!'
>> II: 14

It is the body-mind complex that is affected by the

impressions of sense-life. These impressions are impermanent, transient. Therefore, the Roman thinker Marcus Aurelius said, "Things themselves do not touch the soul. Let *that* part of thy soul which leads and governs, be untouched by the movements of the flesh, whether of pleasure or of pain."

The mind receives its impressions from the outside world, conveyed to it through the five senses. And the mind swings between joy and sorrow, happiness and dejection, excitement and inertia, elation and defeat. Have I won the lottery? I am excited. Have I won an award? I am delighted. Have I received a substantial increment in my salary? I am pleased. Has someone praised me? Are good things happening to me? I'm content. I think life is just fine.

But life is not always so pleasant. Sometimes I lose money in business. I am depressed. Someone criticizes me. I am downcast. My work is not recognized or appreciated. I lose all interest in work. I withdraw. I cut myself off from others. I grow in despondency and despair ...

We are not the body, or the mind. What *are* we then? '*Tat twam asi,* That art Thou!' What *That* is, we have yet to discover. We have to enter upon a voyage of discovery – not like the voyages taken up by Drake and Magellan who circumnavigated the world – but the voyage of self-discovery.

My friends, I urge you to become aware of the value of this human birth. It is priceless! It has been bestowed upon each one of us for a specific purpose, that we may realize what we are, whence we came, and whither we are to return. We are not the bodies that we wear. We are immortal spirits. We are not this; we are *That*! Every day, as you wake up in the morning, I request you to repeat this *mahavakya* given to us by the *rishis* of our ancient land: '*Tat twam asi* ! *That* Thou art!' Thou art not this, the body, that thou take thyself to be. Thou art the immortal soul! This is the very first commandment of the *Bhagavad Gita*: Thou shalt never, never identify thyself with the body!

Scholars have linked the *Atman* to the lamp shining within; it is surrounded by three separate covers; three separate layers. The mind is the first cover from the inside; the senses come next; the world, the flesh outside is the third. When the mind is unaware of the reality of the *Atman* within, when it thinks egoistically that *it* thinks and does everything, it wallows in error. The mind must turn within, it must acknowledge the supremacy of the *Atman*.

The difficulty with Arjuna is that he has allowed his *mind* to dominate his action. "I will not fight," he asserts, even as he begs Sri Krishna to guide him: "I am Thy disciple. I seek refuge in Thee. Teach me." The Lord does not dictate terms to His disciple. He does not order; He does not command; He does not impose a decision on him. Instead, He offers Arjuna the supreme knowledge which will help him to become conscious of his true Self, which will lead him from ignorance to knowledge, from mere physical awareness to the highest spiritual awareness.

One of the results of our identification with the body is the intense fear of death, from which many of us suffer. The psychiatrist, Carl Jung, tells us that even people who say they *want* to die, are deeply afraid of death. Arjuna too, is afraid — afraid to cause the death of his near and dear ones.

> 'Never was there a time when I was not, nor
> thou, nor these lords of men, nor verily shall we
> ever cease to be.'
>
> II: 12

The Lord tells Arjuna that the outer man, the body, may die. But the *Atman* lives on. Arjuna has identified the 'man' with the 'body'. He confounds the real with the unreal. The body is *asat*: it is material; it is destructible. But the *Atman* is imperishable; of this imperishable soul, the Lord says:

> 'He never is born, nor does he, at any time, die.
> Nor, having once come to be, does he cease to
> be. He is unborn, perpetual, eternal, ancient. He
> is not slain when the body is slain.'
>
> II: 20

Does not this assert the truth – *Tat twam asi!*

'Ye are gods,' said Jesus to the Jews.

'Your substance is that of God Himself,' said a great Sufi saint.

'Whoso knows himself has light,' said LaoTse, the Chinese seer.

> 'Weapons cleave him not, nor fire burneth him.
> Waters wet him not, nor wind drieth him away.'
>
> II: 23

Alas, we are unaware of this great Truth. We are obsessed with the physical and the material. We look at the mirror, and we are dismayed by the wrinkles on our foreheads, and the grey hair on our heads. I am told that the film stars suffer from severe stress and insecurity with each passing year, and that they are prepared to spend hundreds of thousands of dollars on cosmetic surgery, just to remove wrinkles and lines and creases.

Is it not a paradox that, when we cling to the body, it tends to wither and lose its shine? When we disregard the body and use it merely as an instrument of service, it begins to glow with health and radiance! When I urge you not to identify yourself with the body, I am asking you to move away from the allures of the materialistic world. The more we identify with the body, the more we want, the more we crave, the more we possess, the more we get entangled in *maya*.

There was a king who received great comfort and solace from the wise words of a holy man. Grateful beyond words, he wanted to express his appreciation, and offered him an expensive gift – a pair of golden slippers.

The holy man smiled. He wanted to make the king understand that worldly gifts were unsuitable to a man of God.

"O king," he said, "if I accept this gift, you must also give me fine clothes to match these golden slippers."

"And so I will," promised the king readily. "You will have royal robes studded with gems and precious stones."

"But, Your Highness," said the holy man "would it not appear ridiculous if I wore royal robes and golden slippers, and moved on my own feet from place to place?"

"That's easily settled," said the king. "I will give the best Arabian mare from my stable, for you to ride on."

"H'mm," said the holy man thoughtfully. "Would it not be strange for a man to have all this and lack a beautiful abode, a lovely wife, and servants?"

"All this, I shall arrange for you to have," the king assured him.

"But then, Sire," said the holy man, "if I should have a son, and if he should chance to die, will you bear my grief and weep instead of me?"

"How could I do that for you?" said the king, startled out of his fit of generosity. "You must bear your own grief, you must weep for yourself."

"Then, O King," said the *sanyasi*, "I will not take the golden slippers, the royal robes, the Arabian mare, the beautiful house and servants, or the lovely wife! I do not wish to be led into pain and misery."

The king understood the message. He realized that material things, identification with the physical, can never lead to true joy.

What we need, more than material wealth, is the wealth of the spirit, for it offers us the freedom of liberation from *maya* !

The stories of Paramartha guru and his five followers are well known in South India. The poor deluded *sishyas* of this guru were constantly struggling to achieve awareness and wisdom; and their misguided efforts are told in comic stories that are meant to teach us, through laughter, that we have a long way to go before we attain realisation.

Once, the five *sishyas* had to cross a river in spate. Having reached the other shore safely, they set about counting themselves to make sure that everyone was safe. The eldest *sishya* began to count. He left himself out and counted everyone else.

"Oh no!" he exclaimed. "We are just four! Who is missing?"

The second offered to do the counting again. He made the same mistake of leaving himself out of the count. "But this is terrible", he wailed, "one of us is gone, lost, drowned to death!"

All the *sishyas* took turns to count, and all of them fell into the same error. Soon there was terrible weeping and wailing. Seeing them in this miserable condition, lamenting the loss of their imaginary friend, a passer-by enquired, "Why are you weeping so bitterly?"

They related the story of the 'death' in their group.

"How many of you crossed the river?" asked the man.

"Five of us," wailed the senior *sishya* "And, alas, we are only four now."

"Four?" said the man. "Four? Are you sure?"

"Sure, we are sure," said the *sishya*. "Here, see for yourself," he counted his companions. "One, two, three, four ..."

The man understood. He sat them down in a circle and

made each one call out, 'one', 'two', 'three', 'four', and 'five, until it dawned on them that all of them were alive and well.

We may laugh at the hapless *sishyas,* but even as each one of them left himself out, we leave our *soul* out of the reckoning. We fail to realise that our true selves are the immortal souls — the *Atman* within, and not the body without.

When Prophet Muhammad was talking to a group of his disciples, he asked each one of them to tell him what they possessed.

The first one, Hazrat Uman, replied, "I have a wife and children, some wealth, and quite a few worldly possessions, as is natural for a man in my position."

The others too, answered on similar lines until it was the turn of Hazrat Ali. Ali declared, "Master, my only possessions are God and the Prophet. Except these, I have nothing!"

Muhammad said to the others, "Ali knows the truth. For worldly possessions matter very little. We cannot take them with us to the world beyond. Attachment to them leads only to pain and suffering."

"This is the lot of those who love the world. But the true devotees of God have withdrawn their attachment completely from the world. They are always engaged in contemplation of the Beloved. They have transcended the region of births and deaths."

Sant Kabir sings:

'Some are in suffering because of their body,
Some the mind sickens;
Others are plagued by wealth.
Sayeth Kabir, all are aggrieved.
Happy are the Lord's servants alone.'

Let me share with you a beautiful story I read some years ago. There lived a wealthy merchant in the kingdom of Arabia. He had three daughters whom he loved dearly. He also had a clever parrot which he kept in a golden cage in his room. The parrot was his prized possession, for it could speak wisely and well. Once, the merchant had to travel to India to buy silks, spices, and precious gems for his trade. He asked each of his daughters what they would like from India. Like all young girls, they demanded gold, jewels, silken robes, and other valuable gifts.

"You shall have all that your heart desires," he assured them heartily. Then he turned to his pet parrot "And what about you, dear creature?" he said. "You are no less dear to me than my daughters. Tell me, what can I bring for you from the famed and historical land of *Bharata*?"

"There is something I particularly want from there," said the parrot. "I would like you to find a flock of parrots in India, and ask them to answer just one question of mine: How can I attain freedom? Bring back to me their answer, for I have heard that even birds are wise in that ancient land."

The merchant laughed loudly, as he fed delicious berries to the parrot. "I can give you the answer to your question, precious pet," he said, not in anger, but in love. 'I will *never* ever let you go — so much for your freedom! Have I not given you a golden cage? Do I not feed you with the choicest tidbits that you enjoy? Do I not love you even as I love my own children? Why can't you enjoy the comfort and security of my palatial home. and be happy with your life here? Why do you want freedom? What will you do with freedom?'

"Whatever it may be, I would like you to find the answer to my question," insisted the parrot. "Let us say, it is of academic interest to me."

"Very well, I promise," the merchant assured him. "I will definitely talk to your brothers and sisters in India, and bring you back the answer you seek — mind you, for academic interest only! For I will never let you go."

The merchant kept his word. Having finished his business in India, having bought gifts for his family, he visited the holy city of Varanasi about which he had heard a lot. Here, on the banks of the holy river Ganga, he found a flock of parrots seated on a parapet wall. He decided to address his pet's question to these birds.

"Tell me, parrots, for one of your kin who lives with me, wants to know this from you: how can he attain his freedom?"

At the mention of the word *freedom*, the parrots flew away, as if to prove their love for that very idea. Only one parrot, the leader of the flock, remained before the merchant. He looked deep into the eyes of the merchant, almost mesmerizing him.

"How may he attain his freedom?" the merchant repeated, his eyes locked with the eyes of the bird.

Without uttering a word, the parrot dropped down lifeless before the stunned gaze of the merchant. He lay on the ground, inert, dead, a heap of green feathers.

The merchant was shocked and grieved. "I should not have asked that question," he thought to himself. "It was a terrible blunder on my part."

When he returned home, he was received with great joy by his family. When everyone had received their gifts, he sent them all away, and came to talk to his pet, all alone.

"Well?" said the bird. "Did you get the answer to my question?"

"I really should not have done it," said the merchant, with a heavy heart. "I found a lovely group of your kin on the banks of the holy river Ganga. I put your question before them, and they all flew away except one – the leader of the flock."

"What did he say?" asked the bird eagerly.

"That's just it," said the merchant. "He did not say a word! He just dropped down, dead! Oh, it was unbearable, I wish I had not asked him!"

"Never mind what you felt," said the parrot. "Tell me exactly what happened."

Patiently, the merchant narrated the incident, exactly as it had happened: how the parrot had stared silently at him, how he had repeated the question, and how the bird had fallen before his very eyes, lifeless!

"Why are you so obsessed about your freedom?" he asked his pet. "What does it mean to you?"

The parrot stared at him wordlessly. Then, it fell from its perch in the golden cage, and lay in a lifeless heap on the floor of the cage.

"Oh, no!" cried the merchant. "You, too! I've lost you now forever!"

Grieving, he opened the cage door and lifted the inert form of his beloved pet. He was determined that he would perform its final rites like a father, and have a beautiful memorial built for it in his garden. To his utter amazement, when he took the lifeless parrot out of the cage, it fluttered out of his hand onto the nearest window. Perched on the windowsill, it addressed the merchant.

"My kinsman in India was truly wise," it said. "He taught me that the answer to my question was within me! He showed me that the way to attain freedom was through death. I followed his instruction, and now I am free! Please do not try to retain me here. I belong to the wide open spaces, the green trees, the clear air, and to the blue skies! And I am going to find my true home!"

So saying, the bird fluttered away.

The way to *mukti* (liberation) is through death. Dying to the body, we gain immortal life. We are released from the golden cage of earthly life which only restricts and binds us with the chains of *maya*. Released from the cage, we attain to our true state. Thus, Sri Krishna tells His dear, devoted disciple, Arjuna:

> 'The man, who is serene in pleasure and pain, undisturbed by either, he lives in the Life undying, O chief amongst the sons of men Arjuna.'
>
> II: 15

And again:

> 'He never is born, nor does he, at any time, die. Nor, having once come to be, does he cease to be. He is unborn, perpetual, eternal, ancient. He is not slain when the body is slain.'
>
> II: 20

Perhaps the greatest thing we gain when we cease to identify with the body, is freedom from the fear of death. It has been said that the only certainty of human life is death – the unalterable fact that all that is born must, one day, die. The fact also remains that in any given life, each of us can only die once. Yet, how the fear of death haunts us!

There was a brave soldier who had fought in many glorious wars and vanquished several deadly foes. One morning, as he took a dip in the river for his bath, he saw a strange, mournful figure, sitting on the riverbank and staring at him solemnly. The form and face of the sober figure unnerved him.

"Who are you?" he demanded. "Why do you stare at me thus?"

The figure sighed deeply. "I am the spirit of death," it said. "Today, I have an appointment with you ..."

The soldier was taken aback. In an instant, he collected his wits and fled from there. Harnessing his trusted steed, he rode fast to a garrison town that was a hundred miles away. Riding into the high-walled fortress, he ordered the guards to close the huge gates after him and rode into the stable, where he tethered his horse.

Stroking the panting beast, he said, "Thank you, my faithful friend! You have indeed, saved me from death!"

Just then, he heard a chuckle. Turning, he saw the spirit of death standing at the stable door. "I was given an appointment to meet you in a stable," said the spirit. "Therefore, I was puzzled when I saw you on the riverbank this morning. This is the right place and the right time. I can keep my appointment with you now."

If a brave soldier who lives with death on the battlefield can be so afraid of mortality, what about us ordinary mortals?

In the *Mahabharata*, Yudhishtira is confronted by a spirit which poses several difficult questions which he has to answer. At one point, the spirit asks him, "What is the greatest *aascharya* (wonder) on this earth?"

Yudhishtira replies, "Everyone hears of people dying around them, all the time. But yet, no one believes that one day, they themselves will have to die. This, to me, is the greatest wonder of all!"

The fact is, as the *Gita* tells us, there is no death for the soul, for it was never born, and it will never die. Perhaps this is the reason why, in our subconscious mind, we refuse to accept the fact of death! When you realise that you are not the body, fear of death is dismissed, as a fear born of ignorance.

The *Yoga Vasishta* tells us the story of two brothers. When their parents die, the younger one is inconsolable, but the older and wiser brother says to him, "Grieve not, brother. You have had many parents, many relatives and friends, through several births, and several embodiments. You are not grieving for any of them now. So why do you lament the loss of just one set of parents?"

There was a poor man who was weary with lifting his heavy burden on the road of life. One day, he decided he had had enough. He dropped his heavy load with a thud and cried out, "Oh Death! Come to me now, for I am ready to go with you!"

In a trice, Death appeared before him. "Did someone call upon me?" he enquired puzzled.

"Er ... umm ..." mumbled the man, taken quite aback. "It was only me. I wanted someone to lift this load on to my back ... just a helping hand ... so that I could get on with my work."

"Sure", said the polite spirit of Death. He helped the man lift the load and placed it on his back. The man went off from the place, as fast as his legs could carry him. The burden of life seemed light to him, compared to the awesome 'freedom' offered by death!

Fear of death arises from the illusory notion that life on earth is pleasant, profitable, desirable, and therefore worth clinging on to at all costs. Caught up in the toils of life, in the allurements and entanglements of the body, it is difficult, indeed, for the mind to concentrate on Self-realisation and God-realisation. We are caught up in the disappointments of yesterday, the problems of today, and the anxieties of tomorrow. We are bounded, constricted by this world of multiplicity. But as we shake off the material bondage and the identification with the body, we awaken into the life of eternity. We shake off the ego, we shake off the false sense of individuality, we take the first step towards liberation.

Freeing the self from identification with the body, we become aware of the truth that nothing belongs to us, no one belongs to us. Therefore, the multiplicity of conditions, the manifold problems that we confront in life will not overwhelm us any more. We will remember Sri Krishna's words to Arjuna:

> 'Nimitra matram savya sachin:
>
> O, Arjuna, be thou a mere instrument only.'

Arjuna realised that Kurukshetra was his *karma kshetra*. He was not there to kill or be killed — he was there as an instrument of God's Will.

Ignorance of this great truth brings misery and affliction upon us. Like the Arab merchant's parrot, we remain imprisoned by the cage of mind and senses. Freedom can be attained by dying to the egotistic Self, and asserting the immortality of the soul within.

Swami Vivekananda tells us, 'The essence of *Vedanta* is: *Aham Brhmasmi*. I am *Brahman*. *Tat twam asi*, That art thou!'

You are essentially divine. *Vedanta* recognises no sin; it recognises only error. And the greatest error, it says, is to think that you are weak, that you are a sinner, a miserable creature ... There is no room in the Hindu way of life for such defeatism or negative thinking! *Tat twam asi,* That art thou! In the *Mundaka Upanishad*, we are told of two birds perched on the branches of the self-same tree. One of them is always looking up at the sky; it is ecstatic, energetic, and sings a song of divine beauty. The other bird, perched on a lower branch, glances downwards, and is overwhelmed by anguish and misery.

The two birds symbolize the self: the first, which looks upward, has discovered the essential glory of the Divine Self within. The second is attached to the body, to the earth, and is weighed down by attachment and grief.

Raja Janaka, whom most of you know as the father of Sita in the *Ramayana*, was also renowned as a great philosopher-king. He often gathered together sages and philosophers at his court, so that he could listen to their wise discourses. At one such gathering, eminent *rishis* and scholars were seated in conclave in the king's *darbar*, when sage Ashtavakra entered. This wise seer was called Ashtavakra because his body was bent, twisted in eight different places due to a birth defect. As he hobbled into the hall, moving his crooked figure towards the conclave, the sages who were already seated burst out in derisive laughter.

Ashtavakra paused, and then addressed the king. "I thought I was going to attend a meeting of philosophers," he said to Janaka. "But it appears that I have walked into a gathering of cobblers!"

"How dare you ..." protested one of the sages, rising to his feet in anger.

Raja Janaka said to the sage in humility, "Please explain yourself, wise one."

"The men whom you have gathered here are looking at my flesh, my skin. What can they be but cobblers? This physical body that I wear is but a shoe. These men are judging me by the shoes I wear. They do not realise that I am not this body. How can these men be philosophers?"

Alas, the world judges people by outward appearances. Go anywhere, and you are judged by the clothes you wear, the car you drive, even your hairstyle. Your exterior is what counts! If you would progress on the path of self-realisation, you must stop identifying yourself with the body. You must move away from the 'shoes' you wear. This is, indeed, the significance of the custom practised by Hindu — removing one's shoes before one enters a temple or a holy place. This is symbolic of the idea that we move away from body-consciousness to walk upon sanctified ground, which will help us move towards God-realisation. We cannot cast off the body, literally. But we can change our perspective by dwelling on the idea that we are not the bodies we wear — we are the immortal spirits within. This makes a tremendous change in our outlook!

In the *Gita*, Lord Krishna singles out King Janaka as the perfect example of desireless action. Let me tell you a beautiful story that illustrates King Janaka's superior sense of awareness.

Once, Lord Vishnu took the form of a Brahmin, and allowed Himself to be brought to Janaka's court as someone who had committed a heinous offence. The appropriate sentence for the offence was exile from the kingdom, and the king pronounced the judgement of exile on the Brahmin.

The Brahmin bowed his head in acceptance of the sentence, and asked the king, "Will you kindly let me know, Your Majesty, how far your kingdom extends?"

Janaka was taken aback. A wise man, he realised that the kingdom which had been ruled by his forefathers, did not really belong to him. Even his body was not his, for it was but an instrument of God! On the other hand, from the point of view of the soul, the vast universe was his! When this realisation dawned on him, the king said, "Oh Brahmin! Endless is the kingdom of my soul! Live happily, anywhere you choose!"

Janaka was truly wise. He realised the immortality, the limitlessness of the true Self! The great poet-saint Kabir tells us that we are like the grains of wheat caught between the grinding-stones of life. The grains that cling to the central axle of the grinding-stones are uncrushed, while those that move away from the centre are crushed into powder.

So too, when the soul moves away from God, we are crushed by the powerful wheels of *maya*. We can never be at peace, when we have identified with our lower self, the body. But when we move away from body-consciousness, we transcend the limitations of the physical self and move closer to God.

This transcendence is not easy! '*Kastarati, kastarati, kastarati mayam* ...', says sage Narada in his *Bhakti Sutra* : "He who crosses over, crosses over, crosses over *maya* ..." The thrice-repeated term stresses the fact that this cross-over is not easy! Tied down by *maya*, led by *maya*, how we have whirled in the cycle of birth and death! But the moment we cut ourselves off from identification with the body, the moment we cross over *maya*, we realise our oneness with the Self, and we move towards emancipation, *jivan mukti*.

The Bible tells us of the young man who approached Jesus and asked to be his follower. When Jesus spoke to him of the Ten Commandments, he assured the Master that he had been observing them for several years.

Then Jesus said to him, "If you wish to enter the kingdom of Heaven, then sell everything you have, and come and follow me."

The young man was not prepared to do this. He backed away, not without regret.

Selling everything one has is not to be interpreted literally. It means moving away from the ego, from identification with the body. Sanskrit scriptures talk of *maya, mamata,* and *moha,* that is, illusion, possession, and attachment. These must be transcended if we are to attain God-realisation. I am a little saddened, even a little amused, when I hear people berating us Hindus for worshipping 'monkey-gods'.

Hanuman is represented as a monkey because he

represented the power of the mind. The minds of most of
us are distracted, jumping about from one idea to another,
literally monkey-like. However, when we have discovered
the Hanuman — the spiritual *shakti* within us — we
overcome body-consciousness, and tap the *atmabal* that
Hanuman truly symbolizes: the power that enables us to
transcend the physical and the material. Have you read
that beautiful part of the *Ramayana*, where Jambhavan
awakens Hanuman's spiritual power and reminds him that
he is not what he seems, a mere *vanara*? Hanuman is
diffident and doubtful at first; he feels that he will never
be able to cross the sea and travel to Lanka. But the wise
Jambhavan helps him unleash his divine potential.

Each one of us has a Hanuman asleep inside us — a
tremendous soul-force that will help us cross the ocean of
maya. This hidden *shakti* can be awakened by a guru's grace.
The guru will unfold to our consciousness the truth that,
inside each one of us, is '*Sat chit ananda*, true, eternal,
blissful knowledge'. Alas, so busy are we in living the life
of the body, that we have forgotten this, our essential
nature. The guru can awaken us anew to this realisation.

There is a story told to us, according to which Sri Rama
once asked Hanuman to explain to him how the two of
them were related to each other.

Hanuman is said to have replied, "O Lord, from a physical
point of view, when I regard myself as the body, I am your
slave. From the mental perspective, I am a ray, an
emanation, while you are the sun, the Light everlasting.
But from the perspective of the spirit, I am none other
than your Self!"

What a wonderful story this is! Insofar as we do have a body, let this body be an instrument, a slave of the Lord. Let us seek union with the Lord through all that we are — in body, in mind, and spirit. Let us use the body to perform God's Will. Let us use the mind to radiate God's love and wisdom. In the spirit within, let us seek identity with God.

The question that every spiritual aspirant has to ask himself again and again is this: 'Who am I? Who am I?'

There were a husband and a wife who quarrelled so violently with each other that they stopped talking to each other. They even began to occupy different rooms in the house so that they did not have to see each other. One day, a stranger knocked at the door. The father and the mother did not budge, and their little son opened the door.

"Why, look at you!" exclaimed the stranger. "Why are you sent to open the door? Where are mama and papa?"

"Mama and papa are in different parts of the house because they are not talking to each other. But tell me who you are, uncle, and I will tell them separately that you have arrived."

The stranger saw his chance: here was a house divided, where he could get a comfortable stay and several meals, if he played his cards right. Aloud, he said to the child, "Tell your mama and papa that *mamaji* (maternal uncle) is here to visit them."

The child did as he was told, informing his parents that *mamaji* was there to visit them. The husband thought that it was the wife's *mamaji*. He hastened to greet him and welcome him; he had no quarrels with his in-laws, and he wished to observe the laws of hospitality.

The wife peeped out and saw the visitor being received. She assumed that it was the husband's uncle who had arrived. So she set about preparing an elaborate meal to place before the visitor. When the husband left the room, she hastened to touch the visitor's feet and offer her respects to him.

For the next few days, the stranger revelled in the hospitality of the house, receiving the courteous attention of husband and wife — separately, of course. It was like a free vacation at a home-like resort for him. Soon, however, the husband and the wife settled their differences and began to communicate with each other as before. They talked about 'mamaji' and found out that he was neither *her* uncle, nor *his* uncle! When the stranger realised that his game was up, he quietly slipped away!

When the soul refuses to communicate with God, when the soul refuses to acknowledge His Divinity, ego steps in, asserting its importance. Alas, the human mind is easily duped, and starts pampering the ego.

The spiritual aspirant must never, ever cut off his link with God. He must not allow his ego to take advantage of him. When the true Self has established its link with God, the ego vanishes. For many of us, our life on earth is nothing more than a parade of ego-desires. As the ego changes, our desires too change. The little child craves toys; the young boy wants computer games and gadgets; the young man chases after fast cars and girls; the grown-

up man chases wealth and power. And so we hanker after
shadow shapes, fondly imagining that fulfilling the ego-
desires will make us happy. From birth to birth, from one
life to another, the ego changes its shape and form like a
cloud – the cloud that hides the sun, the source of light,
the sense of our real identity.

Identification with the body, egoism, and ignorance of the
true nature of the Self – these three are identified by sages
as the cause of all human suffering. Egoism can only be
removed by the purification of the mind and the senses,
and this is best achieved through selfless, desireless action
(*nishkama karma*), about which I will tell you more, when we
discuss the Second Commandment of the *Gita*.

However, it is not true to say that one *cannot* perform any
action without the ego. When a true artist becomes
absorbed in his work, when a great singer is pouring his
soul forth through song, when a powerful orator is
uttering profound words of wisdom, when a gifted writer
is penning his immortal poem, none of them is aware of
the ego – and they excel in what they do, because they have
left the ego behind them!

Ego leads to arrogance and pride. Every little worldly
achievement flatters the ego. Perishable, transient wealth,
vain acquisitions of this world, haunt us. All human misery
is created by egoism. It leads to greed, pride, lust, and
hypocrisy. It is only the true Light of the Self that can
finally destroy the terrible ignorance bred by ego. When we
learn to love, serve, meditate, be good and do good, we
grow in the awareness that we are divine!

A holy teacher narrated this parable of life to illustrate

this point. In each human embodiment, a man finds himself perched on a high wall, overcome by thirst. He is confronted by darkness, in which he hears the roar of wild animals, the hissing of snakes, and the hooting of vultures. But when he turns his consciousness away from this darkness, he sees a sparkling, beautiful river flowing beneath the wall, filling him with hope and joy, just with the knowledge that it is there, that he can quench his thirst if he gets to it!

How can he get down to the clean, sparkling, sweet waters of the river? By removing the bricks from the wall, one by one. As he continues to do this, he gets closer to the river, and the splashing of its lovely waters is like music to his ears.

The river represents the waters of Eternity. The darkness represents the dangerous world of the senses. The wall the man is sitting on symbolises the ego. The moral of the story: turn your face and thoughts away from the material world. Focus on your divinity, destroy the ego, and your thirst will be quenched by true realisation of the Self! Let me add, friends, destroying the ego is achieved only through sadhana (discipline). Each time you utter the Name Divine, you throw a brick; each time you perform an act of selfless service, you throw a brick, sometimes a very large one; occasionally, it may be a whole mass of bricks! But you're getting there, eventually, if you keep on trying!

There is a parable narrated in the Mahabharata which captures the predicament of the ignorant being in bondage to the senses.

A powerful king was defeated by his enemies. Driven out

of his kingdom, he escaped from the palace carrying as much gold with him as possible. He ran to find cover in a forest, but was beaten and robbed by bandits who took away everything he had. Soon thereafter, he was chased by a herd of wild elephants. Running blindly to save himself, he stumbled and fell into a disused well, clinging desperately to the aerial roots of a banyan tree which had penetrated into the walls of the well.

The king's life hung by a thread, literally. Above him, the herd of wild elephants stood around the well; beneath him, on the dry floor of the disused well, a python lay with its mouth wide open, ready to swallow him when he fell; close to his hands, two rats were busy gnawing away at the root to which he held on. What does the king do? He notices a beehive, close to his face. Honey is dripping from the hive. Forgetting his desperate predicament, he begins to lick the delicious honey oozing from the hive, little realising that his action will set off a hundred poisonous bees to attack him and sting him. What will become of the king, we all wonder. Better it is if we ask, what will become of *us*? For we are in the king's predicament when we identify with the body. The coils of the senses bind us, and we are unable to escape.

Bondage is caused by the concepts of 'I', 'me' and 'mine'. When we discard *rajas* and *tamas* (the robbers), when we move far from the wild elephants (anger, greed, hate, and pride), when we cease to cling to the creepers (attachments due to *karma*), when we overcome the fear of death (the python with its open jaws waiting to eat us), and we are aware that the rats (time) are eating away our fragile hold on life, we must then seek the truly sweet honey of Divine Knowledge, and not be distracted by poisonous sense-pleasures that will only aggravate our situation!

Therefore, have the *rishis* of ancient India taught us: Assert your essential nature and be free! Realise the divine within you and be free! Expand your consciousness, purify the mind, discover the true Self, and you will recollect your essential nature: '*Soham* – I am That!'

Do not be a miser, do not cling to the body, unable to spend your infinite spiritual wealth. Let go of ignorance, let go of the ego, and the humiliating notion that you are limited, restricted by the body and the mind. Realize that you belong to infinity, that your soul is immortal, that God's power and grace sustain you, and that you are essentially divine!

The prospect of death unnerves all of us – not only our death, but the death of our near and dear ones, too. Thus was Arjuna unnerved, to contemplate the death of Bhishma and Drona, whom he loved and revered.

"You grieve for those for whom you should not grieve," Lord Krishna said to him. "The wise man never grieves for the dead or the living."

There is a moving incident from the life of Lokmanya Tilak which bears witness to Sri Krishna's teaching. In 1902, the city of Pune was ravaged by a plague epidemic. Hundreds upon hundreds of hapless victims lost their lives, and every family was afflicted with bereavement. Tilak's family was no exception. He lost his young son Vishwanath, and two of his dear nephews, all within one week.

A close friend came to offer his condolences to Tilak. "This is indeed too much," he said to the great philosopher and thinker. "To lose three young men at one go is too much for anyone to bear!"

"But it is the Will of God and we must accept it," said the *brahmagnani*, Lokmanya Tilak. "It seems that the Lord of Death is lighting a Holi fire, to which every family has to contribute its share of *chharu* (cowdung cakes). How could we fail to give our share?"

I do not need to remind you that Tilak has written one of the most illuminating commentaries on the *Gita*.

"Know thyself!" This is what Eastern and Western philosophers considered the ultimate form of knowledge. Sages and saints from East and West gave their disciples the same message. This is the essence of that bold *Vedic* assertion, '*Tat twam asi, That* art Thou!' It proclaims to us that we are not the bodies we wear – we are the spirit Everlasting; the spirit Universal; the spirit Undecaying; the spirit Supreme. We are the *Atman*, which is beyond birth and death.

Why then do so many of us get caught in the chains of human bondage? Why do we allow ourselves to be entangled in the web of *maya*? Why do we wallow in misery and suffering, unmindful of the fact that we are of the Divine Essence? It is due to the limitations of the human mind that we are unable to grasp and retain our essential identity as spirits.

Existentialist philosophers too, encourage you to ask yourself, 'Who am I?'

Who are you? You might begin by answering, "I am Ram, or Rahim or Robert." But if the question persists, you might add, "I'm a teacher, or a doctor, or a scientist, or a businessman."

You might take it further: "I'm so and so's father, or husband, or son, or neighbour." You may add, with a trace of pride, "I'm a rich man, a millionaire, an industrialist, a minister." Mothers may add, with motherly affection, 'I'm Chintu's or Bunty's or Nikki's mom.' Some of you may say, "I'm the President or Secretary of the Chamber of Commerce."

But beyond all this – who *are* you?

"I'm a good human being," some of you may be able to assert, quite truthfully.

Which is all very well, but the truth is that all these answers are incomplete. They reveal that you really do not know yourself. This might irritate you. You may protest, "Of course I know myself. How can you or any one else tell me something that I don't know about myself?"

The truth is, we are all ignorant of our true nature. We identify ourselves with the body, with a physical form, which is smaller than a speck of dust in the infinite vastness of the cosmos. We identify with our profession and social status, which is about as insignificant as a fly on the windowpane. Farmers smile indulgently as a lone sparrow pecks at a grain of wheat in their granary. Children smile at the ants which diligently carry a tiny speck of sugar to their holes. Let me tell you, human beings, their achievements, accomplishments, and successes are just as insignificant in the cosmic scheme of things! We all are like little sparrows pecking away at grains of wheat! And we preen our feathers when we have two more grains than the others!

The great Spanish philosopher, Diego Y Garcia, once described a 'specialist' in any academic discipline as a person with a 'painfully vast amount of knowledge in a pathetically small area of study.'

So much for the vanity of knowledge!

Have you heard of a man who was suffering from a painful boil on the side of his nose? It was hurting him so badly that he decided to see a doctor about it. "I'm only a general physician," said his family doctor. "I suggest you see an ENT specialist."

The specialist took one look at him and showed him the door. "Sorry," he said, "I'm a left nostril specialist. Your boil is on the right nostril."

Men and women who are young and beautiful are proud of their looks. Alas, their beauty and youth are transient, and will not withstand the onslaught of time! Politicians are proud when they acquire power. They hold themselves to be above the law; they forget their accountability to the people who elected them. They are brought to earth with a thud when the people teach them a lesson in the next election.

Vanity of vanities, all is vanity!

How much greater, how significant you will feel when you

consider yourself part of the Universal Spirit that sustains and moves through earth, sky, water, air, and fire! What will be your feeling when you realise that you are deathless – and that you belong to the Infinite?

When you grow in this awareness, you identify yourself with the Everlasting. You begin to say to yourself, "I am not this body. I am the *Atman*, the deathless spirit. My spirit is the universe. My essence is of God."

This realisation releases a tremendous energy of the spirit within you, so that it can transform your life and your personality completely! Aware of the divine within you, you begin to recognize and respect the divinity in others, and your consciousness expands; you become more understanding, more tolerant, more loving and forgiving, more magnanimous – in short, more divine than human!

When such a state lies within your grasp, what is it that deters you from attaining this awareness? The answer is: it's all in the mind – both the possibility and (for some of us) the impossibility of reaching this state of divine conciousness.

The *Upanishads* tell us that the mind is the cause of both bondage and release. By educating the mind, by consciously changing our thought-patterns, we can train our mind to grow in the awareness of the spirit. The mind expands, and is no longer tied down by its identification with the body. It is released from the terrible burden of negative emotions like anger, greed, envy, and jealousy. It is no longer haunted by the fear of death, nor tainted by selfishness.

When the mind has been controlled, purify your conscious and subconscious by *sadhana*, meditation, *nama japa*, prayer, *kirtan*, and *satsang*. These are spiritual disciplines that can bring about a transformation in your attitude to life.

Finally, conquer yourself by dismissing negative thought patterns, and move towards concentration and positive focus.

It is not really difficult, when you set out to achieve it with determination. And the reward is great — you discover the hidden treasure of divinity within you!

Identification with the *Atman* is not merely of abstract value. In practical terms, it can make life joyous, peaceful, and secure. I often narrate to my friends, the story of the Persian king who had his ring inscribed with the words: '*This too, shall pass away*'. When he read these words, he gained equanimity and wisdom. He was no longer unduly elated by good news, nor did defeat and bad news depress his spirits. He had learnt the secret that the world is transient, changing, and therefore, it is futile to cling to changing objects and changing events. This is what Sri Krishna tells us in the *Gita*:

> 'Having come to this fleeting, joyless world, do thou worship Me.'
>
> IX: 33

There was a villager who was invited to visit his rich cousin, who lived in a city. The villager was amazed by the gadgets and electronic marvels that filled his cousin's house. He touched the height of amazement when he was whisked off to the fifteenth floor office of his cousin, in an elevator. "You are indeed great," said the villager. "Why, you can even make us rise up at the touch of the button!"

Just then, there was a power-failure. The elevator came to a standstill, and the lights faded out.

"Can't you do something?" the villager asked in panic.

His rich cousin had to admit that it was actually the electricity which made all the 'marvels' possible. On his own, he could do nothing without its power! Even so, it is the Divine in us that is responsible for our achievements. When this realisation comes to you, you conquer the ego, and you attain to the basis of the life spiritual: that God is in all. God is in everything. God is in you!

Let me add, when I talk about attaining God-realisation and self-realisation, I am not referring to a journey in space or time. I am talking about a state-of-awareness, a state of mind which awakens within you — and awakens you from the dream of *maya* (illusion).

There was a great painter who had a beautiful wife. She was struck by a mysterious illness and the doctors declared that, unless she were nursed carefully, she would not have very long to live. Now it suddenly dawned on the painter that he had not painted a single portrait of his wife. What a fool he had been, failing to capture her beauty on canvas! He decided that the lapse should be set right at once.

He had his wife sit up in the bed for hours together. He insisted that she should smile. He made her gaze fixedly in one direction, while he painted desperately, to capture her fragile beauty. Alas, the inevitable came to pass. Unable to stand the strain, the poor woman passed away, even before the 'immortal' painting could be completed. The doctors accused the painter of gross negligence and folly. He was tortured by guilt and shame. Eager to preserve her image for posterity, he had failed to protect her from death!

We too, are foolish like the painter. We devote our energy to worldly pursuits – building bigger houses, buying faster cars, acquiring more wealth and power, while we ignore the Divine Self that abides in us!

In the *Virata Parva* of the *Mahabharata*, we are told how the Pandavas and Draupadi spent a whole year living *incognito*, unrecognised, unknown. We know the story, but we must see its spiritual symbolism. Nakula becomes Granthika, a steward who handles horses. Sahadeva takes on the name of Arishtanemi, a cowherd. Now, horses and cows symbolize human senses and sentiments. These must be controlled, before one advances on the path of self-realisation.

Bhima becomes the cook, Ballabha. This represents *pranic* energy which is devoted to the task of spiritual sustenance and nourishment. Arjuna dons a woman's clothes and becomes a sexless eunuch, Brihannala. This symbolizes the soul's evolution beyond sex-identity and sex-consciousness.

Draupadi becomes Sairandari, a maidservant. Conquering the ego, she represents the intellect which devotes itself to the pursuit of the four *dharmas*. Yudhishtira becomes Kanka, a skilled dice-player. This symbolizes the process by which he exchanges material values for spiritual values. Thus each of the 'roles' adopted by the Pandavas and

Draupadi, actually symbolize stages and aspects of inner purification through which one attains self-realisation.

Think of Jesus Who says to us, 'He that findeth his life shall lose it: and he that loseth his life for My sake, shall find it.'

When we are tied down by the 'I-me-mine' syndrome, we cut ourselves off from God-realisation. Only self-denial and self-discipline can lead us on the path of self-discovery.

There was a Persian king who was fast asleep in his palace, when he was awakened by the noise of footsteps on his roof.

"Who goes there?" he called angrily.

A very sweet, loving, and gentle voice replied. "It's me! I've lost my camel and I'm looking for it!"

The king was startled by the absurdity of the answer, and the temerity of the man who could climb on to the roof of the palace and get away with such an excuse. He sent his guards up on the roof to find the intruder but the man had, of course, disappeared by then.

The next morning, the king was in his *darbar*, presiding over an important gathering of sages, wise men, and philosophers. The topic of discussion that morning was God-realisation, and the priests and scholars were forcefully putting across their views on the topic. The king was listening to them with great interest as he sat in royal splendour on his jewel-encrusted throne. Every now and then, he too contributed to the discussion, with his views or by disagreeing with the views expressed by others. Suddenly, the learned conclave was interrupted by a commotion at the entrance to the *darbar*. The king's guards were physically restraining a *fakir* (holy man) from entering the court. They hesitated to use their weapons on him, because he appeared to be saintly and venerable.

"Let me in," he demanded loudly. "I wish to rest in this *musafirkhana* (travellers' inn) for a few days!"

The king recognised the voice: it was the voice of the man who claimed to be looking for the camel on the roof.

"Who are you?" he demanded. "How dare you misbehave in the king's court? What on earth makes you think this is a *musafirkhana* where every passerby can rest for the night? Don't you know that this is a royal palace, and that my ancestors have lived here and ruled this kingdom for hundreds of years?"

The *fakir* replied, "I don't know all that! I only know I came here fifty years ago, and I saw an old man seated on this throne. I came here again, twenty years ago, and I saw a middle-aged man on the same throne. Now here I am today, and I see you, a much younger man, seated on the self-same throne. What is this place, if not an inn, where people come and go, and different occupants are found every time?"

The king was startled at the *fakir's* question. He invited him to come into the court and acknowledged the wisdom of his words. "True it is, my grandfather ruled this kingdom, then my father. I rule it now, and this too shall pass! But I have something to ask you. You, who are so wise, what were you doing up on my roof last night, looking for a lost camel? How can you explain that absurdity?"

"Oh king, if you can be so absurd as to sit here in the *darbar* and discuss God-realisation, why do you find it absurd that I should be looking for a camel on the roof?"

The king was an evolved soul, and he understood the spiritual significance of the *fakir's* question. He gave up his kingdom and became a renunciate, looking for God. The *fakir* had taught the king the vital truth that one had to rise above the material manifestations of this world, if one wishes to seek the truth.

A holy man lived just outside the capital of Indraprastha, under the shade of a banyan tree. Visitors and travellers arrived at the capital every day, and often sought instructions from him on how to get to the 'basti' or the colony as they called it in those days. They were very confused by the fact that there were seven different gateways to enter the city.

"How can we go to the *basti*?" they would demand of the holy man.

He would show them the way, and give them directions. But when they followed his instructions, they found themselves at the burning *ghats* (cremation grounds) on the river Yamuna. Some of them dismissed his directions as a prank. But a few came back to rebuke him for deliberately misleading and misdirecting them.

The holy man said to them, "You asked me to tell you the

way to the *basti*. Now, the *basti* means a place of permanent residence. The great capital Indraprastha is only a transit camp where people are queuing up to get to their ultimate destination – the *smasan* (burning *ghat*). Once they are taken there, they do not go elsewhere. They end up there permanently. This is why it is really a *basti*."

The people realized the truth of the holy man's words: that all that is born must surely die one day. It has been my privilege to be blessed by several saints and men of God, who have made the land of my birth, Sind, sacred by their presence. One of them was he, whom I in loving reverence, still think of simply as 'the unknown Baba'.

When I first met him, it seemed to me that I had known him in many bygone births. He passed on to me a five-fold teaching which firmly instilled in me the truth of the First Commandment of the Gita, '*Thou shalt not identify thyself with the body*'. May I share those beautiful teachings with you?

- Remember, that you are a pilgrim here, a wayfarer in quest of your lost homeland. Your home is in eternity.

- Be patient in the midst of the difficulties and dangers of life. Remind yourself again and again, 'This too shall pass away!'

- Each day, meditate on death, for death approaches us with each passing moment.

- Give the service of love to all.

- Seek fellowship with saints and holy men so that the tiny drop that you are may become a mighty ocean, wide enough to hold within it a thousand oceans.

The Second Commandment:
'Thou Shalt Not Fail To Do Thy Duty'

Thou shalt not fail in doing thy duty! Duty first!

Does not the English poet say:

> 'I slept and dreamt that life was beauty,
> I woke and found that life was duty.'

We must do our duty. Duty is religion, even as work is worship.

> 'Do thou thy allotted work, for action is better than inaction. Even the pilgrimage of thy body is not possible without activity.'
>
> III: 8

Work is a necessity of life! Even eating and talking are activities. It has truly been said that when God gave us each a mouth to feed ourselves, he also gave us two hands to put food into that mouth, that is, by working, and literally, by the activity of taking food to the mouth.

Action is better than inaction. In the Bible we are told that Adam was condemned 'to labour by the sweat of his brow.' It is not a bad thing at all, that we should all work, for work is a blessing; work is therapeutic; work is a tonic. An idle mind, we know, is the devil's workshop. Even on the physical plane, idleness breeds illness.

But what kind of work?

'Lokoyam karmabandanah,

> The world is in bondage to work', except when
> the work is done as sacrifice.
> 'Therefore, O Arjuna, do thy work for the sake
> of that, free from all attachment.'

III: 9

The world is in bondage to work, the Lord tells Arjuna, the world is imprisoned in selfish action. This is what most of us devote ourselves to: we work hard for the sake of power, pleasure, and profit. This can hardly contribute to the welfare of society, or indeed our own true welfare. Therefore, the Lord recommends that Arjuna should act selflessly, without any thought of profit, without any sense of attachment, offering work as a sacrifice to the Lord.

> 'Therefore, without attachment, perform always
> the action which is thy duty, for by doing work
> without attachment, man verily reacheth the
> parama, the Supreme.

III: 19

Most of us enjoy doing work that we like. I know a man who loves driving his car. He is in the best of moods when he is driving; he loves being at the wheel of his car. But when the drive is over, he loses his good humour. Similarly, there are students who love to work on the computer. When they are doing their assignments on the computer, or surfing the Net for information, they are very happy. Ask them to go to the library and read something; or ask them to write something down — then it is a different matter altogether. Maidservants are hired to do much of the housework in India. Even they have their 'preferred' activities. Some of them love to work in the kitchen, but do not like to clean the house or wash the clothes. Even children, doing homework, have their 'likes' and 'dislikes'. They will do their drawing and painting happily, but when it comes to sums, they begin to complain.

Most of us are excellent at doing the work we enjoy, but we cannot pick and choose. As the saying goes, it is good to do what you like, but it is better to *like* whatever you do. In other words, we must also be able to do the things we do *not* like.

There was a young woman who was highly dissatisfied with her job. It seemed to her that she was called upon all the time to do what she liked least. In a huff she quit her job. She got a new job soon enough; only, it turned out to be worse than the previous one!

It is a great law of life that when you do not actively dislike any work, you will find that you will actually enjoy doing everything. To take it one step further, you will find that only the kind of work which you like comes your way! Even the Lord works constantly for our benefit, though no work is incumbent on Him.

> 'There is nothing in the three worlds, O Arjuna, that should not be done by Me, nor anything to be obtained which has not been obtained; yet I mingle in action.'
>
> III: 22

The Lord, Who is omnipotent, omnipresent, omniscient, works ceaselessly for our benefit. As Brahma, the Creator, He is constantly at work; as Vishnu, the Protector, we are permanently calling upon Him; as Shiva, the Destroyer, His work goes on. And in immortal incarnations like *Sri Rama avtar*, the Lord personified the very sense of duty – as disciple, as son, as brother, as husband, as friend, as king, Sri Rama set the noblest example of doing one's duty. We must never fail in doing our duty. For this is true religion. Sri Krishna adds, significantly:

> 'Better is one's own duty (or path or law, *swadharma*) though imperfectly done, than the duty (or law) of another, well discharged. Better death in the discharge of one's own duty. To follow another's duty is full of danger.'
>
> III: 35

Perform your duty first; abandoning your duty to pursue another's duty is both foolish and dangerous! There is a very interesting fable which draws our attention to the distinction between *paradharma* (others' duties) and *swadharma* (one's own duties).

A poor villager had two household animals, a donkey and a dog. The donkey carried the man's burdens on his back every day. He was not stroked or petted by his master. The dog, on the other hand, stayed at his post at the doorstep, barking at all strangers. He wagged his tail at his master, who stroked him, and lavished love and attention on him.

Enviously, the donkey said to the dog, "How I wish I could be you, even if for a short while!"

"Why not?" said the dog. "Let's exchange duties tonight. I shall lie down and snore, as you do every night. You can stay in my place and watch out for thieves."

"Sure," agreed the donkey. "But don't forget, you will have to carry the master's burdens tomorrow!"

The exchange of duties agreed, the animals took up their posts. As luck would have it, a thief approached the cottage. Instinctively, the dog awakened, and urged the donkey, "Come on, do it now! Alert the master!"

The donkey started braying loudly. The master, who was in deep sleep, was so irritated by the harsh braying that he came out of the house and beat the donkey up severely. The thief of course, ran away with the commotion raised, and that the master did not even realise what the donkey had done for him!

The donkey, badly beaten up, groaned to his friend the dog, "Enough is enough! You do your duty, and I shall do mine!"

The spirit of detachment and selflessness are impossible when you take on *paradharma*. Nor can it bring you real joy and satisfaction. On the other hand, doing your own duty will lead to a sense of satisfaction and fulfillment.

There are many politicians and leaders who exhort the people to make sacrifices for the sake of the country. 'Tighten your belts,' they tell the people. 'Give up luxuries,' or 'Do not waste oil'. However, none of this is applicable to themselves! It would appear that the duty of these 'leaders' consists merely in verbalizing appeals to the people. But nowadays, voices are beginning to be raised against such hypocrisy and lack of accountability. In India, every Member of Parliament is allotted several crores during his tenure as an MP, to be spent on welfare, or development activities and projects in his own constituency. I am told that many Members of Parliament put this fund to good use – some of them build bus shelters; some of them construct school buildings, or provide facilities to existing schools; some contribute to better medical facilities and so on.

Recently, when the Parliament secretariat went into these accounts, it was discovered that several MPs had simply *not* utilized the funds allotted to them. Not only was this a dereliction of duty, but they had failed to benefit the people for whom these funds were meant!

Nowadays, people are ever ready to blame *others* for failing to do their duty. Students blame teachers; teachers blame the authorities. Wives accuse husbands of indifference and neglect; husbands feel that their wives lack sympathy and understanding. No one seems to look into their own hearts and assess whether *they* are doing their duty conscientiously.

There are some people, who, out of the 'kindness of their heart' as they call it, take up 'noble' duties, neglecting their own. Now, I am not suggesting that we should not undertake selfless actions. If you can spare the time, energy, and effort to do others' duties *after* performing your own duty to perfection – hats off to you! But this should not be an excuse or pretext to neglect your own duties!

There was a student, who was very concerned about his best friend, who was unable to concentrate on his studies. He spent a lot of time with his friend, cheering him up, encouraging him, even trying to teach him. Later, both of them failed in the examinations!

There was a lady, a housewife and mother of three children, who was elected as the secretary of her Ladies' Club. She devoted herself energetically to club activities and 'social service' programmes, neglecting her family. She told them to make their own breakfast, and order pizzas for dinner. This was surely a gross neglect of her duty!

Many people in India exclaim that the officials and policemen are corrupt; but if they are stopped by a policeman in a traffic offence, they are happy to offer him a bribe and get away with it! By doing so, not only are they failing in their own duty as good citizens, but they also prevent the policeman from doing his duty as an honest defender of the law! The trouble with human nature is that many of us are dissatisfied with our own duties, and are apt to imagine that we can perform wonders and miracles everywhere else! Many people in India, for example, begin their comments on cricket by saying, "If I were the captain of the Indian team ..." But what about the homes, families, shops, and offices where they are actually players or members?

Our students like to say, "If I were the Principal, or the Vice-Chancellor of the University, or the Education Minister, I would declare more holidays and abolish all exams." What they need to do is attend to their duties as students, so that they can qualify themselves to become principals, vice-chancellors and ministers in the future!

The performance of one's *swadharma* or allotted duty is not always pleasant or easy. But, as wise men say, the hardest duty can be smoothened, softened, 'oiled' with love.

Take a mother. Who says her job is easy! She is the most unselfish person in the family, and also the most patient, the most understanding, and the least demanding. She always puts her family before herself. She does not look for rewards or recognition. And, as western nations are beginning to realise, she is like the Chief Executive Officer (CEO) or the Managing Director (MD) of the organization which we simply call H-O-M-E. Her duties include Marketing, Purchase, Human Resource Management, Administration, Finance, and Budgeting. She is also the cook, chauffeur, housekeeper, nurse, laundry maid, cleaner, nutritionist, counsellor and hostess – all rolled in one. Some proud husbands even refer to their 'better half' as the 'Home Minister'. And yet, no mother has ever complained (seriously!) about her duties and responsibilities. Most of them accept these duties happily and willingly, and do their best for their families and homes. A mother is truly an inspiring example to us all!

There is a story in the *Mahabharata* which emphasizes the sanctity attached to one's duty. A young seeker took to the life of renunciation (*sanyas*). He lived a life of austerity and penance in the forest, and thus acquired tremendous *taposhakti* (power of *tapasya*). One day, as he was sitting in deep meditation under a tree, a few leaves fell on him, disturbing his concentration. He glanced up at the tree in anger, and saw two birds, a crow and a crane, fighting with each other over their perch on a branch. The moment his angry glance fell on them, they were burnt away by the sheer power of his annoyance, reduced to cinders and ashes before his astonished eyes!

The *sanyasi* was delighted and impressed by this display of his own power. "I am well on my way towards becoming a great *yogi*," he thought proudly. A few days later, he went to a neighbouring village to beg for food, as was his daily custom. He stood at the door of a house and called out, 'Mother, give me *bhiksha!*'

A young woman's voice called from inside the house, "Please wait for a while. I am attending to my duty. I will be with you soon."

The *sanyasi* grew angry at what he considered to be the temerity of this insignificant person, a mere housewife.

"You wretched woman," he thought to himself. "How dare you keep me waiting! Do you know what kind of *shakti* I possess?"

As if she could *read* his thoughts, the voice from inside called out, "And, my dear brother, be patient. Don't think too much of yourself. I'm *not* a crow or a crane!"

The *sanyasi* was taken aback. Abashed, he waited silently till the woman of the house came out with food. When he saw her, he simply fell at her feet for, to his limited mind, she seemed to possess a far greater *shakti* than he did: the power of mind-reading, no less!

"Mother," he said to her with great reverence, "tell me how you acquired such a great gift. What are the *yogic* techniques you practised? What are the austerities you performed? Do enlighten me!"

"My dear brother, I do not know what you are talking about," said the young woman. "I made you wait because I was attending to the needs of my husband who is ill. That is my prime duty now as a housewife. All my life, I have tried my best to do my duty well. At first, I did my duty towards my parents. Now that I am a married woman, I do my duty as a wife. This is all the yoga that I practise! But doing my duty has helped me to grow in wisdom and understanding. This is why I was able to read your thoughts, and came to know the fate of the crow and the crane."

"Doing your duty – is that all? Can it make you so powerful? I beg you to tell me more!" pleaded the *sanyasi*.

"There is nothing more that I can say to you," said the housewife. "But if you wish to know more, I suggest you go to the market, where you will find a *vyadha*. He can teach you something valuable."

The *sanyasi's* ego raised its ugly head again. "A *vyadha*?" he said to himself. "What can a *vyadha* have to teach me?"

A *vyadha* in those days was regarded as being very low in social status. He was a man who eked out a living as a hunter or a butcher.

Arrogant as he was, the *sanyasi* was determined to acquire greater *shakti*, and decided to seek out the *vyadha* in question. He found him easily in the market place, a big, fat man, bare-chested, cutting up animal carcasses and bargaining with people over the price of the meat.

Disgusted at this sight, the *sanyasi* thought to himself, 'God forbid that I should seek out such a low creature. What can he possibly teach me?' Just then the *vyadha* looked up, and saw the *sanyasi* standing at a distance and staring at him.

"Oh, so you are the *sanyasi* whom the housewife has sent to me!" he exclaimed "Please sit here until I have finished with my business."

The *sanyasi* did as he was told, while the *vyadha* attended to his work. After some time, he shut his shop and said to the *sanyasi*, "Let us go to my house now."

The man's home was a humble thatched hut. Here too, the *sanyasi* was made to wait outside while the man disappeared. The *sanyasi* peeped inside the hut and found that the man was attending to his old parents. He washed them, he fed them, and made them comfortable. Then he came out and said to his visitor, "Tell me what I can do for you."

"What is the nature of the Self?" asked the *sanyasi*. "What is the relationship of God and the individual Self? How may one attain liberation?"

Calmly, the *vyadha* delivered a discourse on *Vedanta*, which, in the *Mahabharata* is called the *Vyadha Gita*. The *sanyasi* was amazed by the depth and insight of his wisdom.

"Why are you trapped in this lowly form and this filthy occupation?" he exclaimed. "Why are you doing such filthy and degrading work?"

"My dear friend," said the *vyadha*, "no work is degrading.

No duty is filthy. My birth and circumstances have placed me in this position, and I do my job to the best of my ability. I have no attachment to this job — I do it well because it is my duty. I also attend to my duty as a son, and try to keep my parents happy. All that I have told you came to me through doing my duty with detachment. Apart from this, I practise no yoga; I have never been to a forest to meditate either. I only do my duty."

Both the *vyadha* and the housewife in the story had a great sense of devotion to duty. They did their duty joyously, cheerfully, and wholeheartedly. This was the secret of their illumination.

To the unattached worker, all duties are equally important, equally good. He regards his duty as an action which will kill selfishness and indulgence, and lead him to salvation.

Detachment is not for *sanyasis* alone! All of us must practise it, in the spirit of the *karma yogi*. For people who grumble, complain and moan all the time, all work is distasteful and unsatisfactory. Nothing will ever make them content, and their efforts are doomed to bring them nothing but disappointment.

How may we avoid such disappointment, frustration and dissatisfaction? Sri Krishna has the answer:

> 'Surrendering all actions unto Me, with thy thoughts resting on the Self Supreme, from desire and egoism freed, and of mental fever cured, fight thou, O Arjuna!'

                                        III: 30

Let us surrender the fruits of action to the Lord! Let us stop chasing after personal satisfaction; or individual happiness. The Lord urges us to perform all actions as dedications to Him. When you dedicate your duty to the Lord, you will indeed feel the difference:

- When you surrender to His Will, and act to do His Work, you will not do anything that is bad or evil.

- When you allow yourself to become an instrument of God, your work will be better, more useful, more effective, for you are freed from your own limitations.

- This will also enable you to cultivate the virtues of perseverance and persistence, self-confidence and strength.

- When you rid yourself of the desire for the fruits of action, when you are free from the anxiety about the result, you are content to leave it to the Lord. You also feel happy, that you are acquiescing in His Will, and being a part of His Divine Plan.

- You escape the great dangers of pride, arrogance on the one hand, and depression and dejection on the other. If your efforts meet with great success, it is His doing; if you should face failure, it is His Will.

- You really put into practice the maxim: Work is Worship. Doing your duty thus becomes a beautiful prayer.

- Performed in this spirit, work will always be a pleasant experience for you.

- You will find that the greatest good accrues to you, through utter surrender to God's Will.

Lokmanya Tilak writes:

> The comprehensive doctrine of the *Gita* is that a human being comes into existence to perform, as a duty, whatever duties come to his share. His action should be motivated by the maintenance of society, and according to the arrangement of society which may then be in vogue. He should act desirelessly, courageously, and enthusiastically, for the public good and not merely for the enjoyment of pleasure.

It was in this spirit that Tilak and Mahatma Gandhi undertook to fight for India's freedom — a task which they regarded as their sacred duty. It was in this spirit too, that Sadhu Vaswani turned his back on personal profit and personal power, to dedicate his life to the service of suffering humanity. The concepts of 'right action' and 'duty', as we see, overlap. Also, the idea of duty varies with different people. For example, in conservative Indian families, it is the 'duty' of the parents to arrange a suitable match for their daughter; while in western countries, this would be rejected by the daughter as undue interference! Thus, it is hard to generalize on personal duties.

However, we can deduce the following aspects from the *Gita*:

- Renunciation must be of the ego, not of work.
- In doing our duty, we must bear in mind the welfare of society, *lokasangraha*. We must always be conscious of

our social responsibilities.

- We should not yield to weakness of heart or mind in the performance of our duty.

- We must do our duty with cheerfulness and enthusiasm.

- Whatever is our condition in life, we must do the duty that is specific to us.

- Duty must be dedicated to God as a selfless offering.

- We must not shirk our duty out of fear or disappointment.

- We must not desire the fruits of our actions. 'Do your duty, the fruit is not your concern,' the *Gita* teaches us.

- We must act without attachment. We must act without anxiety.

- We must be steadfast, single-minded in success or failure. We must hold our mind in equilibrium.

As Sri Krishna unfolds his doctrine of *Karma Yoga*, the doctrine of action, the doctrine of work, the very first thing he emphasizes is devotion to duty. Devotion to one's duty is what the *Gita* calls *swadharma*. Each one of us has his duties, his obligations to fulfill. My duties may be 'high' or 'low'. It may be someone's duty to govern the nation; it may be another's duty to manage billions of dollars worth of finances and investments; it may be your duty to teach a nursery class; it may be your friend's duty to tend a garden; it may be my duty to run an office efficiently; it may be my duty to sweep the roads clean.

The Master is careful to point out to us that it is *not what we do* that matters; it is the *way we do it* that matters.

I may be a humble office assistant in a government department; but if I do my duty sincerely and honestly, faithfully and conscientiously, the portals of perfection would be readily open, as easily open to me, as they are to the highest in the land! For the Lord makes no discrimination on the basis of caste or creed or social status; I may be the lowest of the low; but if I perform my duty to the best of my ability, the Lord will accept my work with loving grace.

There was a great leader who was fighting the presidential election. He was addressing a huge public rally, when a heckler arose from the crowd and shouted at him: "Today you want to be the President of this country. But own up to the truth about your past to this crowd: is it not true that a few years ago, you were just a cobbler?"

The great leader was unmoved by this outburst. He smiled and said, "It is true I was just a cobbler; but I'm proud to say I cobbled well!"

The crowd heard his answer and broke into thunderous applause. They saw a man before them, who embodied the true sense of duty – whatever he did, he did well. Whatever he was given to do, he would do well!

There is a great cosmic drama of life which is being unfolded before us day after day. Each one of us has a part to play in this drama of life. Your role may be a major one, my role may be a minor one: but both of us need to perform well; both of us need to play our roles to perfection, otherwise, the drama will be a failure.

If each one of us attended to our duties in the right spirit, this world will surely be a kingdom of God! If there is chaos, confusion, anarchy, and indiscipline rampant in the world today, it is because the emphasis has changed from duties to rights.

Today, everyone is claiming rights — workers, teachers, farmers, builders, investors, women, government servants, doctors, and others. Everyone is clamouring for their rights, but nobody talks of the duties that they have to attend to. I feel that if each one of us gave first priority to our duties, if each one of us fulfilled our obligations conscientiously, everybody's rights would be automatically protected. If the employer fulfilled his duties well, the employees would have no reason to go on strike; if the men fulfilled their duties conscientiously, rights would automatically accrue to women. There would be no fight against injustice, there would be no need to struggle for equality! Let me add too, there are a hundred ways of doing the same thing. Some of these ways are right, some of these ways are wrong, but only one is the very best. We must do our duty in the best way possible, because it is our offering at the lotus-feet of the Lord. How can we offer Him the second-best or worse? How can we offer Him anything but the best?

When Pandit Jawaharlal Nehru was the prime minister of India, he was travelling by car to attend an urgent meeting. His car was made to stop at a railway crossing. The driver, an officious individual, went to the gatekeeper at the railway crossing and said to him, "Do you know who is in that car which you have stopped at this gate? It is none other than the prime minister of the country! Now, get cracking and open the gates at once. You cannot keep the PM waiting!"

The gatekeeper said to him politely, "My duty is to close the gates when I receive a signal to that effect. I have no authority to open it until the train has passed through."

The driver's mood turned ugly. "I warn you," he threatened, "I will have you dismissed from your post. You will lose your job if you do not open the gates right away."

When Pandit Nehru heard of this incident, he was delighted with the gatekeeper's strong sense of duty and responsibility. He saw to it that the man was recognized, appreciated, and promoted for his devotion to duty.

We need more and more people like this gatekeeper in India today. We have so much indiscipline, confusion, and corruption today, because people have forgotten what it is to do their duty!

When Pandit Nehru died, they found the words of a beautiful poem by Robert Frost on his bedside table:

'The woods are lovely, dark and deep,
But I have promises to keep,
And miles to go before I sleep
And miles to go before I sleep ...'

There may be a thousand temptations to distract us; there may be a hundred other things that we would rather be doing; but it is our duty that has the first call upon us.

Two teachers met each other after an exam session. The

first one said, "Let me tell you, examination work wears me out! I am tense and stressed all the time during invigilation, and being upon my feet for three long hours is very very painful!"

The other teacher laughed. "I find examination work relaxing," she said. "I distribute the papers, come back to my table and write letters to my family, or read a novel."

This is how people fall from their sense of duty and responsibility. Supervising examinations, invigilation as it is called, is an onerous responsibility. Not only is the invigilator guarding against malpractices, she is also ensuring that the examination is fair and just, and that honest students do not suffer because of dishonest practices by others. If the invigilator treats the exam as an opportunity to relax, read a novel, or write a letter, she is guilty of gross neglect!

I am saddened when young married couples, in the guise of asserting their rights, actually impose their will on each other, and erect barriers between them! If a marriage is to be successful and happy, the partners must forget about their rights and concentrate on their duties.

Sri Krishna points out to us that man finds God-realisation by being devoted to his own duty. Duty is *swakarma*; duty is *swadharma*. Therefore cling to your duty; do not shirk your duty. Toil on, and you will attain to the Supreme! Toil on, and offer your work to the Lord, in the spirit of *tyaga*, without thought of reward. Through worship wrought by work, you reach the Supreme.

'Man reacheth perfection, by each being devoted
to his own duty. Listen thou, how perfection is
won by him who is devoted to his own duty.'

XVIII: 45

Do thy duty, for it is the best way Godward. Many people
complain that they find the concept of duty complicated
and unclear. If you should ever feel this, my advice to you
is, choose that which you ought to do, not what you *wish*
to do or *like* to do!

Even as a young man, Sadhu Vaswani had set his heart on
a life of renunciation. But his mother would not hear of it.
It was her dream to see her beloved son well-placed in life,
earning a handsome salary and living a comfortable life.
She wept bitter tears even to hear him utter the word *fakir.*

This saintly son set aside his own aspirations and
submitted himself to his mother's will. To please her, he
became a professor. To make her happy, he took up the
post of a principal. And when he took her to stay with him
in the palatial bungalow provided to him by the Raja of
Patiala, her joy knew no bounds! He did his duty towards
his mother, fulfilling her expectations as best as he could,
paying off the debts incurred by the family, providing a
comfortable living for them. It was only after his mother
passed away, that he followed the road less travelled, as his
spirit dictated.

Not what you want – but what you ought to do! This is
the *mantra* of duty.

Sadhu Navalrai, a pillar of the Sindhi community, rose to
become the deputy collector of a district – the highest

civil service post to which an Indian could be elevated under the British regime. As a deputy collector, he had magisterial duties too, adjudicating civil cases brought before him.

Imagine his shock when his own father was brought before him one fine day! The old man had transported opium without paying octroi duty. He was confident that he could get away with it, as his son was deputy collector. He secretly smiled to himself, as his case was presented before his son, quite sure that he would be let off lightly.

To his shock and horror, the deputy collector levied the maximum possible fine on him for the offence.

When the proceedings were over, he invited his father into his chamber and said to him, "Father, I am a public servant, and I had to do my duty as a magistrate. Forgive me if this action of mine offended you. As your dear son, allow *me* to pay the large fine that I had to impose on you. I hope this will make amends for your hurt feelings."

I have also been profoundly moved by the story of the judge whose son was brought to his court on murder charges. It became clear at the end of the trial that the young man had indeed committed the crime. With a heavy heart, the learned justice went home to write the sentence. His wife pleaded with him to spare the life of their only son, but he knew his duty as upholder of the law. On the following day, he pronounced the death sentence on his only son; on the same evening, he died of a massive cardiac arrest. He had steeled himself to do his duty at the price of his dear son's life and he paid for his grief with his own life!

Who in India has not heard of Raja Harishchandra, the king who was committed to truth and duty! Having lost his kingdom, and forced to work as a menial in the cremation ground, what must he have gone through when his own dear son was brought for cremation! And yet, he would not allow the boy's last rites to be performed until the dues were paid by his wife.

A distinguished Spanish general who was fighting against insurgents, faced a terrible predicament when his only son was captured by the enemies. They forced the son to talk to his father on the phone.

"Father, my life is in danger," the boy pleaded. "My kidnappers say that they will spare my life and set me free, if only you will withdraw the Spanish forces from their post."

"My dear son, you know I love you, and will do anything for you," said the general. "But I have brought you up to be a true Spaniard, a patriot. And you know we owe a great debt to the land of our birth. Be brave and do your duty as a brave son of Spain, even as your father does his duty as a general."

The son was killed ruthlessly by the enemies but the general had refused to compromise Spain's security!

Think of Sri Rama who, after fourteen years of *vanvas* and the ordeal of separation from his beloved Sita, at long last returned to his native Ayodhya to be crowned king. Alas, his happiness could not last long. Due to questions raised over Sita's imprisonment in Lanka, he was forced to banish her, whom he loved more dearly than his life! As the king

of Ayodhya, his duty as a ruler – *raja dharma* – was of
paramount importance. He sacrificed his every happiness
for the sake of his people to whom he owed his
responsibility as a ruler!

This was indeed the ultimate example of duty, set before
us by the Lord Himself in His *avatar* as the *maryada
purushottam*, the ideal man! When we learn to do our duty
selflessly, dispassionately, without desire, without expectation of a reward, we grow in the wonderful awareness, "I
am not the doer; I do not expect, deserve, depend on the
fruit of action." This is selfless action at its best!

Swadharma performed without desire is truly fulfilling. For
example, if you are a teacher by choice, by natural
inclination, you will find that you are teaching because you
love it! On the other hand if you are teaching because you
want the money, then expectations and desires will cloud
your joy. As I stressed in the stories narrated above, doing
your duty may not always be pleasing to your ego!

When there is no domestic help available, the mother has
to wash, cook, clean, and clear up, all by herself. Under
such circumstances, a loving mother will surely not shout
at her family, "I am *not* your cook or your servant!" She
cannot say, "Washing and sweeping are *paradharma* for me, I
will not do it!"

Swadharma does not always imply ease and pleasure. As Sri
Rama's example shows, it can even involve intense struggle
within. In the case of Mahatma Gandhi, it even led him to
risk his life many times, and ultimately, he paid for his
beliefs with his life! But nothing could stop him from his
swadharma.

When you do your duty selflessly, without expectation of reward, you achieve inner fulfillment. But I am also bound to add – external results will also accrue to your benefit. For when you perform the right action in the right way, you will attain the results. Do your duty in the spirit of an offering to the Lord. This helps you grow in the awareness that you are an instrument of God, and that He is working through you! When people perform their duties with delight, when their deeds are dedicated to the Lord, action is fused with *yoga*, and the world will become a garden of peace and harmony!

How may we grow in the spirit of *Karma Yoga*, as advocated in the *Gita*? Let me pass on to you a few practical suggestions:

- Realise that selfishness is a curse of human life. Selfishness makes us narrowminded, petty, and greedy. We confine ourselves to material goals and work only for money and reward. Such a narrow vision shuts out the Divine Light of God from our lives. We are restricted into a groove. Our hearts and minds are contracted.

- Cultivate the quality of selflessness. This is not easy at first. But as we grow in awareness, we will also grow in unselfishness. Feel your oneness with the Divine Spirit. Feel your oneness with all creation. Be aware of your kinship with all the creatures that breathe the breath of life. Above all, draw inspiration from the great *karma yogis* who devoted their lives for the benefit of humanity.

It has been said that you only require 'a little capital' to cultivate selflessness: a little love, a little mercy, and a little sympathy. If you start with just a little, they will multiply in good time, and you will prosper in your chosen path of selfless action. Remember too, that expecting fruits for our actions will only bind us to the wheel of *karma*. We will have to take birth again to enjoy the fruits that we seek. This retards our spiritual progress.

On the other hand, selfless work promotes inner joy and peace. Motivation need not be lacking either, for we are seeking the ultimate goal of freedom and liberation.

- Conquer the lower passions; conquer the ego self within you. Negative emotions like lust, greed, egoism, envy, and anger stay in the heart and mind. Even a trace of these emotions sullies the purity of your character. A *karma yogi* should have perfect self-control over his thoughts, words, deeds, appetite, and senses. He should not give in to excess or self-indulgence. He should lead a simple life.

- Learn to be amiable and adaptable. Accommodate yourself to others. Do not develop rigidity about what you can do and what you want to do. The spirit of give-and-take is vital in our social relationships. A true *karma yogi* fits in happily into any kind of situation or environment. Trials, difficulties, obstacles, and challenges do not deter him. He is always calm and cool and collected.

- Keep a healthy mind in a healthy body. Without a strong and healthy body, and a pure and vital mind, no one can do his duty well. Take good care of your body for it must be put to the best possible use as an instrument of God. Take good care of your body, but do not be attached to your body! Do not give in to vanity and pride. If you so desire, practise yoga. Exercise regularly. Take long walks. Enjoy the fresh air and sunshine. Eat good, nourishing, simple food. Maintain personal hygiene.

- Cultivate the *yogic* quality of equanimity. The *Gita* tells us: *'Samattwam yoga uchyate.'* Equanimity is called yoga. You must have a balanced mind, whatever the conditions around you. You must develop a balanced approach to life.

- Always be loving and courteous in your dealings with others. Do not complain; do not curse; always speak lovingly and gently. Be polite and courteous to everyone you come across. Let not your best behaviour be reserved for the rich and powerful.

What are the weaknesses, obstacles, personal defects that a *karma yogi* must overcome? For it is not enough to nurture the intellect while neglecting those qualities that management experts now call 'soft skills'. Unfortunately our *karmic* residues have left several negative qualities in us, which we must work to overcome:

- Accept criticism in the right spirit. Let it be the means to make you better in every way. So avoid being irritated by trifles. Accept your own weaknesses and work to eliminate them gradually.

- Avoid aggression and over-assertion of your own will upon others. Do not seek to dominate others. Do not impose your will, your opinions on others. Appreciate others' concerns, look at problems and issues from their point of view. The tendency towards aggression and self-assertion are controlled when we develop respect and love for others.

- Do not find fault with others. Learn to see the good in every one. Appreciate others and learn from them.

- Avoid arguments, vain gossip, and futile discussions. What are we trying to prove by getting the better of others by verbal gymnastics? This only agitates the mind and disrupts our spiritual progress.

- Do not be half-hearted in your efforts. Put in your best, give your 100% to the action you are doing. Careless and half-hearted efforts do no good to anyone, least of all to you. How can you offer your actions to the Lord in the spirit of a *karma yogi*, when your heart and soul are not in them? Whether you are folding pamphlets, washing dishes, sticking postage stamps, or dusting the furniture – do it as best as you can!

Bipin was an upcoming, bright, successful doctor. Knowing that a bright future lay ahead for him, a wealthy man had arranged to offer his daughter's hand in marriage to Bipin. Her name was Smita, and she was proud to have 'caught' an eligible bachelor like Bipin. She was beautiful and vain. She was also egotistic and demanding. She had already told her father that a state-of-the-art hospital with the best facilities must be presented to her future husband, and that she would be its chief administrator.

But that was in the future. One morning, Smita dropped in at Bipin's clinic to discuss their marriage arrangements. She walked into his consulting room, and was not at all pleased when Bipin told her to wait in his office, while he dealt with the remaining patients.

When Bipin had finished his consultations and came in to join her, Smita said sulkily, "Do I always have to be second to your patients?"

"Don't take it so badly," laughed Bipin, who was essentially a good-natured person. "Remember, you are going to marry a doctor. Shouldn't you be happy that he is sought after?"

Smita thought of all the money that the patients would bring, and she cheered up instantly. She and Bipin began to discuss the guest list, the music, and the menu for the lavish reception that her father would be hosting at a five-star hotel.

Suddenly, they heard desperate knocks on the door, and Bipin opened it to see a poor, emaciated woman with tears streaming down her eyes.

"Doctor *sahib*, please come with me at once," she begged. "My little daughter is having convulsions, and I need your help to save her life!"

"Where is the child?" asked Bipin.

"I work at the construction site opposite your clinic," said the woman. "That's where the child is, with my fellow-workers. You only have to cross the road, and you can attend to her in a matter of minutes! Oh please save my baby!"

"Don't worry, sister," said Bipin reassuringly, reaching for his bag. "Let us go across at once, and attend to your child."

"Excuse me," said Smita loudly. "Do you remember who I am? Do you remember what we were discussing before this woman barged in?"

"Come on, Smita," said Bipin. "I cannot ignore the call of a patient in need of my attention! It is, after all, my duty as a doctor!"

"What about your duty towards me, the girl who is going to marry you?"

"To save a patient's life is my first duty. Everything else comes next," Bipin answered, getting ready to leave.

"I must warn you Bipin, I don't like to be second on anyone's list. If you walk out on me now, I shall break off our engagement."

"As you wish," said Bipin. "But I am going to attend to the child now. For me, every patient is a picture of God, and I cannot keep God waiting because of my marriage arrangements."

Duty demands that we set aside pleasures and our personal preferences. Duty is an obligation we owe to man and God, and it is a price which should be paid in time, when it is required.

The great musician Brahms was invited to perform in Hungary. He was excited and delighted, for he looked forward to visiting the country. And as an added bonus, his friend and fellow musician, the violinist Joachim, was to accompany him. The pair travelled to Budapest in eager anticipation, looking forward to interested audiences and a rewarding concert-tour. Imagine their disappointment when they learnt that there was only *one* man who had purchased a ticket to attend their first concert!

"This is ridiculous," said Joachim disgustedly. "Let us cancel the concert and return the man's money."

"I don't think we should do that," Brahms observed. "He has come here especially to hear us. How can we disappoint him because others have failed to come? As musicians it is our duty to entertain this gentleman to the best of our ability."

And so, the one-man audience had the pleasure of attending a full-fledged concert by two distinguished musicians. Brahms and Joachim played for him throughout the scheduled three hours of the concert, delighting him with the items he requested. He shook their hands warmly at the end of the concert, and said that he would cherish the experience all his life.

"You see, Jo", Brahms said with a happy smile, "we owe our duty to our profession and above all else to ourselves, as committed artists!"

The distinguished Indian classical musician, Vishnu Digambar Pandit, also had to face the same predicament. Pandit had done yeoman service to Hindustani classical music by popularizing it among the masses. Once, he was to perform in a small town, where he too, was confronted by a single listener. Vishnu Digambar and his whole entourage of musicians performed for the man who had paid just four *annas* (twenty-five paise) to attend a three-hour programme.

When Marcus Aurelius, the great Roman statesman and philosopher, appointed a prefect as his personal guard, he gave the young man a sword and said to him, "You will use this sword to defend my life as long as I am faithful to my duty. But if I should fail in my duty, you will use the same sword to punish me. And remember, my duty is to make the Roman people happy."

An Athenian, who was lame in one foot, was laughed at by other soldiers because he had volunteered to defend Athens.

"I am here to do my duty as a citizen of Athens," he told them. "I am not here to run a race. Why do you laugh at me?"

In western countries, even minor officials and other functionaries fulfill their obligations to their duty, without fear or favour. Once, three famous British actors were riding together in a car, which was stopped by a policeman for a minor traffic offence.

"Officer," said Ralph Richardson, who was seated in front. "Do you recognize me?"

"Yes, sir," said the constable. "You are Sir Ralph Richardson. I have seen you on television."

"This is Sir Cedric Hardwicke, seated next to me," continued Sir Ralph. "And behind me is Sir Laurence Olivier. Surely you are not going to give us a ticket."

And the policeman replied, "Sir, I have a duty to perform. Even if you were the knights of King Arthur's Round

Table, I would have to give you a ticket."

Lord Lawrence, the Governor-General of India, was on board a ship bound for India. Also travelling on the ship was a lady with a baby. She neglected her child to such an extent that it was practically crying day and night. This became a source of great annoyance to the passengers and some of them even threatened to throw the child overboard. The mother was obviously neglecting her duty. But Lord Lawrence decided to do something which no one thought of doing. He took the baby from the mother and began to laugh and play with it. The happy and contented baby soon stopped crying. The mother was ashamed of herself, for a great man had taught her how to do her duty well!

To perform a duty well is to give it your all – your 100% effort and attention. Time set aside for a particular goal is precious, and it must not be squandered away on any account.

This was the spirit in which Mahatma Gandhi and his comrades devoted themselves to the cause of Indian freedom. To Gandhiji, every moment was precious. It could not be wasted under any pretext or circumstances. Every moment had to be spent in the cause of the nation – all else could wait. Once, Gandhiji came to know that his dear, trusted secretary, Mahadev Desai, was spending nearly an hour every day to study French. He was being taught French by Mirabehn, a European lady who had come to live in the ashram as the Mahatma's disciple.

"Mahadev, is it true that you are studying French nowadays?" he asked his secretary.

"Yes, Bapu," said Mahadevbhai.

"When do you study? And how much time do you spend on your French lessons?"

"About an hour, Bapu."

"And how long will it continue?"

"About six months, Bapu."

"Let me see. That means an hour a day for 180 days!"

"I can manage it very well, Bapu. I'm learning fast ..."

"That would mean you are taking that much time *away* from national work!. said the Mahatma, pained. 'Have we not pledged every moment of our life to the nation? All other tasks, however good and desirable, are luxuries, and we cannot waste our time on luxuries now!"

Mahadevbhai respected Gandhiji's admonition. He dropped his French studies immediately.

"Do your duties!" Sri Krishna urges us in the *Bhagavad Gita*. "Don't cut yourself off from humanity! Thus may you be free by doing work, and thus, when you are free, you may continue to work."

Sri Krishna also tells us how we should work:

> Work, freed from selfish desire! Work, asking
> nothing for yourself! Thus may you find action
> in inaction and inaction in action. Thus may you
> be a free man.

Thus is revealed to us the secret of *Karma Yoga*. When we step on the path of *Karma Yoga*, we gain awareness of the distinction between *swadharma* and *paradharma*. It is ignorance that causes us to prefer *paradharma* — ignorance caused by *raga* (attachment) and *dwesha* (hatred). When these are set aside, and we adopt the right attitude, *swadharma* turns into *Karma Yoga*. This is even better than creating good *karma*, for it enables you to break the bonds of *karma* altogether and step on to the highway of *mukti* (liberation).

Inaction in itself is *not* the desired goal; for even when we are inactive — doing nothing — we are creating neutral *karma*. Further, inaction and inertia are *tamasic*, and can lead to lethargy of the body and dullness of mind. Even at a basic physical level, we know that laziness leads to boredom, while an active body in an active mind promotes energy and enthusiasm. When we act in ignorance of the doctrine of *Karma Yoga*, we become involved in worldly bonds. But when we act with awareness, we develop awareness and grow in purity of spirit.

A beautiful story is told to us concerning Samartha Ramdas, which illustrates the power of doing one's *swadharma*.

A young disciple of Samartha Ramdas had just been initiated into the path of an ascetic. As was the routine, he was sent out to beg for alms one morning. He went from door to door, begging the householders: '*Bhavati biksham dehi*, give me alms!'

Later, he would have to cook the grains with his own hand to feed the guru and himself, for this was the only kind of food ascetics ate in those days. And so the disciple begged for a few grains, moving from door to door. The householders, who were not very wealthy, gave him what little they could.

'*Bhavati biksham dehi* !' he called at a house with a closed door.

The door opened and an irate Brahmin came out. "*Murkha!*" he said to the young man. "You are not aware of what is to come upon you and so you beg for food in ignorance. Let me tell you — I who can anticipate how each planet moves — let me tell you that your appointment with death is at 12 o'clock (midday) today!"

So saying, he banged the door in the young ascetic's face. The young man became a nervous wreck. He ran back to the guru as fast as his legs could carry him and fell at his feet, clutching them with both hands.

"Oh guruji! Save me, for I'm about to die!" he wailed.

"Explain yourself," said Samartha Ramdas.

The young man narrated the Brahmin's prophecy to him.

"Well, he said 12 o'clock, didn't he?" said Samartha Ramdas calmly. "It's only nine in the morning now. So please go and beg for food. You must complete your morning routine, come what may."

Guru bhakti gave the young man the impetus to fulfill his task, but Oh! the state he was in! He was like one bemused, with a sore, distracted aspect, and a fear-filled mind.

When he returned with the food grains, the guru said to him, "Kindly cook the food at once. For I am very hungry today."

The disciple wept in the heart within: "How could my guru be so hard-hearted that he bids me cook his food, when he knows I have only minutes left to live?" But such was his devotion that he managed to cook the food and serve the guru.

"Now eat with me," the guru bade him. The pathetic young man forced himself to swallow a little food, but he was ready to choke with the strain.

"I wish to rest," the guru said to him. "Kindly spread the *ghongdi* (blanket) on the floor."

When this was done, Samartha Ramdas lay down and said to the disciple, "Now seat yourself on the *ghongdi* and kindly press my feet, for they are aching. Please continue to do this till I tell you to stop. I order you, on no account to leave your seat on the blanket, no matter who calls."

In utter misery, the disciple did as he was told. As Samartha Ramdas fell asleep, he continued to press the guru's feet with great devotion and fortitude, despite the fear and sorrow that gripped his heart. People came to the door to call him; someone wanted to see the guru; someone called to offer fruits — the disciple did not budge. He continued to press the guru's feet.

At 12 sharp, *Yama*, the Lord of Death arrived. "Come," he said to the disciple. "You must go with me now; for your time is up."

The disciple did not even look up to see who was calling, so intent was he on his allotted task. "I'm sorry I cannot go anywhere now," he said, as he bent down to press the guru's feet gently. "My guru has ordered me to stay here, and I cannot leave without his permission." Having waited a few minutes, Lord *Yama* went on his way, for the man's time was now past!

Not long after, the guru opened his eyes. He asked the disciple what time it was. He was told that it was well past midday, by the disciple who was still intent on his task.

"Get up now," the guru told him lovingly, "and be at peace, for your appointment with death is now past."

The disciple realised with a start that it was indeed long past midday, and death had come to him, but gone back empty-handed, as he was engaged in his *swadharma* as a disciple — devoted to the task of *guru seva*. Even death could not touch him when he was performing his allotted duty!

There is an incident from my boyhood days, which is still fresh in my memory. Looking back on it, I realize now that it was an early lesson in being dedicated to one's duty, doing one's allotted task! A few of us boys, belonging to the Sadhu Hiranand Boy Scouts Troupe were putting up a few skits, as part of our annual theatrical programme. In one of these skits, your humble servant was given the role of Napoleon. As I was short-statured, our scout master had decided that the role fitted me like a glove. There I stood, acting the role of Napoleon, my chest puffed up with dignified pride.

"Forward, men!" I ordered energetically, as my "army" rushed across the stage. I was thrilled with myself!

Soon the skit came to an end, and the curtain fell. We rushed to change our clothes and get ready for the next skit. In the next play, I was given the role of a boy servant to a rich *zamindar.*

"Hey Teoo, bring me a cup of tea!" ordered the *zamindar* arrogantly.

Stripped of my grand Napoleon costume, standing with folded arms before my 'boss', I was, tempted just for a minute, to exclaim, "How dare you order me about like this? Only a little while ago I was Napoleon, and you were one of my common soldiers!"

However, wisdom prevailed. I was well aware that I was now playing the role of a humble servant. Had I given vent to my emotions, the whole play would have been a flop, a disaster! This incident taught me a valuable lesson that, in this vast panorama of life, each one of us is assigned a specific role. Let us play our parts well, and all will be well with our life!

Sadhu Vaswani himself gave me an unforgettable lesson on this noble commandment, *'Do thy duty'.* At that time, I was in Sri Lanka with Sadhu Vaswani, but it felt like I was in seventh heaven! My alma mater, the D.J. Sindh College, Karachi, had offered me the post of a lecturer. But my heart prompted me to reject the worldly career, and be with my Gurudev. Fortunately for me, my brother Ram spoke to my mother in Karachi, and obtained her consent for me to stay on with Sadhu Vaswani in Sri Lanka.

Happy with the thought that my mother understood my aspirations, I rejoiced in every second I was able to spend with my Master. However, I had to face a tough test soon. A visitor from home arrived to see Sadhu Vaswani. He mentioned that he had met my mother, who had expressed regret over the fact that the son whom she had brought up with love and care, the son over whom she had taken great pains to ensure that he grew up to be a brilliant scholar, namely myself, had been taken away from her!

When my Master heard this, he summoned me and said "Jashan, I want you to go back home. Your duty is to be with your beloved mother."

I was broken-hearted, but I obeyed his order implicitly. He was, of course, right. I could not neglect my duty to my mother. I travelled back to Karachi, and I did not utter a word about the pain and anguish I felt in my heart.

Friends and well-wishers of the family told my mother that a high post in the Customs Department would aptly suit my qualifications. My mother expressed the desire that I should apply for the post. Wordlessly, I consented, although, deep within my heart, I longed to return to where I felt I truly belonged, at the feet of my Gurudev. Is it not true that a mother understands her child even when he does not speak to her of his aspirations? My mother, a sensitive, caring, and devout lady, looked into my heart and realized where my future lay. On the morning of the third day after my return to Karachi, she called me to her side and told me, "You may return to your revered uncle with my blessings."

My joy knew no bounds. But I knew that my Master would

not accept me if I returned forthwith; therefore, I entreated my mother to put her consent in writing, to write a letter to Sadhu Vaswani expressing her whole-hearted approval of my choice to be with him.

My mother, a wonderfully kind and understanding soul, obliged readily. She wrote a letter to her brother-in-law, that she was handing over her son to his care, wholly and completely. My future was in his hands, to shape as he desired, she added.

Thus did my Master teach me to put duty above all else. It was only with my mother's blessings that he accepted me, and allowed me to travel forward with him on the path I had chosen!

13

The Third Commandment:
'Thou Shalt Do Thy Duty and a Little More'

Sri Krishna talks about *lokasangraha* in the *Gita*:

> 'Janaka and others, indeed, attained to perfection by action. And thou, too, Arjuna, shouldst perform action with a view to the welfare of the world.'

III: 20

Welfare of the world is *lokasangraha*. It is the good of mankind. Action prompted by the good of mankind is right action. Altruistic action does not create bondage — instead it liberates.

I said that the Second Commandment of the *Gita* was: '*Do your duty*'. Indeed that is primary; it is vital. But do not stop with just doing your duty. Do your duty and a little more — contribute your mite to the welfare of the world!

When we start living and working for others, our lives become richer, more rewarding, more meaningful. We are able to tap our inner *shakti* to its highest potential; we become more energetic; we become more creative; we solve problems easily.

Above all, we grow in the consciousness that all life is One, all life is reverent, all men are brothers, and that birds and animals too, are our brothers and sisters in the one family of creation. Is not this the highest form of consciousness – this awareness of the unity of all life?

Lokasangraha is what we, in simple terms, call *seva* (service). We start off by doing our duty towards our family, our profession, our near and dear ones. This purifies our inner instrument. Then, we grow in the awareness that we do not belong merely to our immediate family, we belong to a larger family: to the community, to society, to the nation, to humanity at large, to creation in all its variety and splendour!

Today, when I visit huge metros like Mumbai, London, New York, and Chicago, I am saddened by the fact that people are so indifferent to the needs of those around them. When they are confronted by human pain, suffering and misery, their attitude seems to be, "This is none of my doing; and so it's none of my business."

Surely friends, it *is* your business! I spoke of the family of humanity: here, every man is my brother, every woman is my sister! How can I be indifferent to their pain and suffering? It is my duty, to the best of my ability, to help as many as I can, to lift their load on the rough road of life!

This incident was narrated to me by one of my NRI friends. She was travelling on a city bus in West Midlands, UK. At a crowded bus stop, an old, shabbily dressed Sardarji got on to the bus. Now this bus was run as a one-man operation: this means there is no conductor to take money from you, issue your ticket, and give you change. There is only a driver, and each passenger drops the exact money for his fare into a glass-topped counter before the driver, where he can actually see the amount is right, and then he presses the button so that a ticket of that denomination is issued automatically.

Thus each passenger enters the bus, deposits the exact amount of cash and says, 'Thirty pence,' or 'Fifty pence,' or 'One pound'. The driver presses the button to issue the ticket, and the passengers move in quickly and take their seats. Now, the old Sardarji was unaware of this practice. He entered the bus and held out a five-pound note and mumbled the name of his destination.

"No, no, not that way!" exclaimed the driver. "Exact change, please!" But even as he talked, he realized that the old man could not understand what he was saying. The passengers who were behind him in the queue began to murmur angrily. One or two roughly brushed passed him, got their tickets and sat down. The other passengers looked on, curiously. It was 'none of their business'! My NRI friend told me that she turned her face away in embarrassment. She did not want to be associated with the shabby old man in any way.

When the other passengers had all got in, and the old man was still standing there helplessly, the driver said to him impatiently, "Come on! Say something! Do something! Don't just stand there!"

Just then, a lady from the top deck of the bus who heard what was going on, came down to see what was happening. In a trice she realized the problem, and walked briskly to the old man. With a friendly smile and several patient questions, she elicited from him the information needed: where he was going, and whether he had change. When he told her he had no coins, she readily put her own money before the driver, obtained the ticket for the old man, and then invited him to come and sit next to her, so that she could show him where to get off.

"That's really nice of you Ma'am," said the driver. "I couldn't have left this place, if you hadn't come to the old man's help. I say, you are really public-spirited!"

"Not really," smiled the woman. "This gentleman is new to our country. He does not speak our language. Isn't it my duty as an English citizen, to help him out?"

My friend heard this, and felt ashamed; she had not thought it *her* duty as an Indian, to go to the help of her own countryman. She had turned her face away, unwilling to help him as a fellow Indian. As for the other passengers, they had all done their duty; they had got their tickets and found their seats. Why should they bother about an old and ignorant stranger who did not know their language and their ways?

I always say, the opposite of love is not hatred; the opposite of love is apathy, indifference to the needs of those around you. While everyone on the bus was indifferent to the plight of the old man, one lone Englishwoman had cared enough to come to his aid. Her idea of duty was not so narrow that she could ignore him – it extended to his care. She was ready to do her duty, and a little more!

This 'little more' is *lokasangraha*. Alas, we have forgotten this concept today. Why, there are people today who do not even do their own duty properly! It was Andrew Carnegie, a great American, who spoke of three types of men: the first type does not want to do his duty. He will shun his duty, neglect his duty, if he is not supervised, if someone is not watching over him constantly. The second type of man will do his duty and nothing more, not a jot more.

I know some people who leave their seats at 5 p.m. sharp, no matter if crucial work is pending before them; no matter if desperate people are waiting to see them. I am told that there are doctors who refuse to see patients in distress, when their 'duty time' is past. Their idea of duty is indeed, narrow!

Andrew Carnegie spoke of a third type of men: men who will do their duty, and a little more. It is these people, he said, who will truly succeed in life! Success belongs to those who do their duty, and a little more. This 'little more' is going out of your way and serving someone in need.

One day, a man came to meet Sadhu Vaswani. There was a gleam in his eye, a smile on his lips, a vigour in his step, as he eagerly greeted the Master and said, "Bless me, Master, for today has been a lucky day, a happy day, a wonderful day for me!"

Sadhu Vaswani asked him, "What has happened today?"

The man replied, "Today, I have signed a contract worth Rs.Ten lakhs, and in a single day, I have earned a profit of

Rs.Three lakhs!"

Let me tell you that in those days, Rs.Three lakhs would
have been the equivalent of Rs.Three crores today! In
those days people hardly spoke of crores or millions. A
lakh was a lot of money!

The Master looked at this man lovingly, and asked him in
a very soft and gentle voice, "Did you feed a poor man
today? Did you offer water to a thirsty one? Did you offer
a piece of cloth to a naked one? Did you utter a word of
comfort to someone in distress?"

The man was taken aback. "No, Dada," he confessed
honestly. "I haven't done any of these things." He added
after a little thought, "It didn't even occur to me to do any
of those things."

Then Sadhu Vaswani said to him, "How can this be your
lucky day, a wonderful, happy day? Your day has been
wasted if you have not helped someone in need!"

Alas, we keep on wasting day after day if we neglect the
opportunity to save others, to bring comfort to the
depressed, to help the poor and the underprivileged, to
bring joy into the lives of joyless ones.

This should be the mark of our daily schedule — to do our
duty and a little more! Let service be a part of our larger
duty. Unless we go *out* of ourselves, we can never be truly
happy. Look around you, and you will find the world is
sad, torn by tragedy and smitten with suffering. Living in
such a world we must share with others, whatever God has
given to us in His infinite mercy. It has rightly been said

that service is a debt, it is the rent that we have to pay for inhabiting the human body.

It is a debt we have to pay for the many favours that we have received from God and the surrounding universe. We can pay off this debt only by serving those less fortunate than ourselves: the poor, the needy, the disabled, the old, and the orphaned ones.

The ancient legends tell us of a great and noble king who devoted his life to the service of his people. His every moment, every breath, every effort, was spent towards working for *lokasangraha*, the welfare of his people. When the call of death came to this king, whom the people loved and revered as a saint, an angel of God came to escort him to Heaven, which he had earned as his right, with his good deeds.

To the angel, the king, made an unusual request: "May I be permitted to visit hell before I enter the Kingdom of Heaven?"

Perhaps the angel was a little surprised by this request! However he consented graciously, promising to take the king to hell, as well as to be with him as an escort during the visit.

The king went to hell, accompanied by the angel. But he was amazed by the sight that met his eyes. Happy faces surrounded him. People were delighted to see him; they greeted him with great joy. There was rejoicing and contentment wherever he turned.

"Surely, this is not hell!" He whispered to the angel. "You

have brought me to Heaven directly."

"No, Your Majesty," said the angel. "This is indeed the other place."

"But..." protested the king, "I had always imagined hell to be a place of terrible pain and suffering! This place radiates joy and contentment."

"Alas, this place is full of pain and suffering, though you may not see it before you. Everywhere else, where you cannot see, people groan in misery. But being in your holy presence has brought peace and joy to these people."

"If that is so, I have found my Heaven right here," said the king. "This is where I shall stay. For what is greater than bringing joy to the joyless ones?"

There are terrible problems confronting the world today — starvation, poverty, war, violence, religious fanaticism, environmental degradation, and more! It is enough to depress the most optimistic among us. And so, even good people exclaim in despair: "What can we do? How much can we do? Whatever we do, it's not going to be enough!"

True, it may not be enough. But that should be no reason for us to desist from *all* action. Rather, we must do what we can, in the firm faith and belief that, 'I *can* make a difference! I *will* make a difference.' If all of us worked in this spirit, the world will surely be a better place!

Many people in India, when they are urged to be selfless, honest, loving, and forgiving, retort angrily, 'I am not Mahatma Gandhi!' Too true, we are not Mahatmas. But then Gandhiji was not transformed into a Mahatma overnight. He had to struggle; he had to confront failure and hardship; he was even kicked and beaten in South Africa, before he decided to devote his life to the service of the downtrodden, the deprived, and the oppressed of the world.

Many were the people who had to face the same failure and ill treatment before Gandhi. Why, thousands of Indians must have been victims of the inhuman apartheid regime in South Africa before he even set foot in that country. But these bitter, harsh experiences transformed a young, struggling lawyer into a 'great soul' determined to fight against all forms of oppressions and injustice. He went to South Africa to earn a living. He learnt the most valuable lesson of his life — that one had to live and fight for others, not just for oneself.

Gandhiji was angry, upset, and hurt, when a white South African hurled him out of the first-class railway compartment onto the platform at Maritzburg station, and threw his luggage after him. But anger and wrath, those negative emotions, were transformed into positive, selfless forces, making him determined to promote the welfare of all people.

Sri Ramakrishna makes a similar point when he talks about greed. "You say you are greedy?" he said to his disciples once. "Why not be more greedy, *really* greedy? Don't just want things for yourself; want them for everybody. Don't ask for less, ask for more, so every one can benefit."

"Patience is bitter, but its fruit is sweet," said Rousseau.

Anger is the killer of patience, it can destroy, demolish patience, utterly.

The story is told us of the weaver-saint Thiruvalluvar of South India, that a cheeky young man once came to buy a saree from him. In truth, he had come to provoke the saint beyond the point of endurance, to prove that the saint was only human!

"How much does this saree cost?" he asked, picking up a valuable saree.

The saint named the price.

"And this?" said the young man, tearing the saree into two. The saint halved his price.

"And now?" the youth continued, tearing up the half-saree into two.

Thus it went on, the youth tearing the saree into pieces until it was reduced to the width of a small rag, and the saint remaining calm and quiet in the face of such deliberate provocation. The young man was overcome with repentance as he saw the beautiful saree reduced to useless bits.

"I beg your pardon, Sir," he said to the saint, "let me pay you the price of the whole saree."

"No, you need not," said the saint. "The pieces are useless to you. In any case the hard work and the effort that went to make that saree are invaluable. You cannot pay for *that!*"

"But it was my arrogance and stupidity which destroyed

the saree," pleaded the young man.

"I can weave another saree like that easily," said the saint. "But if your life is torn apart by such actions, it cannot be mended!"

The saint did not mind his personal loss and the insults he had to bear. His concern was for the young man's spiritual welfare. Sure enough, his blessings transformed the life of the young man. The weaver-saint was not merely doing his duty as an honest weaver, refusing to accept money for a torn saree which could be of no use to anyone. He also went one step further, for he was able to see into the mind of the rude young man, and realize that he needed motivation to change. The saint did not mind the loss he had incurred, or the insult meted out to him. He had dealt with a recalcitrant youth so effectively as to cure him of his negative traits.

This is the great spiritual advantage of *lokasangraha* — it purifies our *antakarna*, the inner instrument. When we do our duty, and a little more, when we act selflessly, we grow in interior purification.

The greatest challenge before the spiritual aspirant is just this: how may I grow in interior purity? Let me tell you, dear friends, if only you could look inside your mind and heart, the vision you see therein would shock you beyond words! Within us, there is a clash of conflicting desires; within us are ugly blots of egoism and arrogance. Alas, we are unaware of the ugly horrors within; we go about in this world with puff and powder and lipstick, or with made-up outer appearances, which give no indication of the ugliness within.

A holy man and his disciples were passing by a cemetery on a moonlit night. The sky was cloudless and the moon was shining in all its silvery splendour. Its rays fell upon the graves which shone, glowed, as if they were made of marble and silver. Pointing to the graves, radiant in the moonlight, the holy man said to his disciples, "Look at these sepulchres, how they glow and shine in the moonlight! But within them, lie worms and snakes and scorpions crawling over decaying flesh and rotting bones! This is also our condition. We appear clean and presentable externally. But within us are worms and snakes and scorpions of greed, envy, jealousy, and pride!"

The English use the phrase 'whited sepulchre' to refer to a person who is beautiful and impressive on the outside, but evil and ugly inside. Alas, we all need inner purification! As we do our duty, and a little more, we grow in inner purification!

Lokasangraha is not just welfare of the *people*, for, to the enlightened soul comes a realisation that all creation is one family. And in this one family of creation, birds and animals are our younger brothers and sisters. It is our duty too, to give the love of our hearts to our younger brothers and sisters. It is our sacred responsibility to save our younger brothers and sisters from the cruel knife of the butcher.

I recall the powerful words of Sadhu Vaswani. "The day is coming," he said with the foresight of a seer, a sage, and a visionary, "the day is coming, when meat-eating will be condemned as murder!"

Think of the highly evolved human beings of the 24th and

the 25th centuries: what will they think of us and our eating habits? They would probably say, "How could those people kill birds and animals and live off their flesh? How is it possible that human beings could be so cruel and violent?"

Today, we think of cannibals in the same way, don't we? We are told that a few centuries ago they used to snatch away babies, kill them and eat their flesh. Today, aren't we doing the same to animals? The generations of the future will say that we are also like cannibals, whom we now regard as *junglee*, uncivilised, barbarian.

The year 1789 is a landmark in the history of human civilisation. It was in that year that the French National Assembly passed the Bill of Human Rights. In the 18th century, the world recognized the rights of human beings to live with dignity. The 19th century, thanks to the indefatigable labour of saintly souls like Abraham Lincoln, gave rights to the blacks and slaves, who were treated as personal possessions of the plantation owners. The 20th century recognized women's rights, and accorded them equal status in the eye of the law. What about the 21st century?

It is my dearest hope and wish that the 21st century will give animals their rights – and that would indeed be a great and glorious moment in the history of human civilization.

When you grow in the awareness that you belong to the larger family of creation, you live up to the ancient Indian ideal of *'Vasudaiva kutumbakam'*. This whole world, this vast universe, this unexplored cosmos with its magnificent creation is ONE family. Then you realize, in the memorable words of my Master: these hands are not given to us to hurt, but to heal! These hands are given to us to bless, not to butcher! These hands are given to us to save, not to slaughter! These hearts are given to us to love, not to hate!

There are certain words which I read years ago which capture the essence of *lokasangraha*: 'I shall pass this way but once. Therefore, any good that I can do, any kindness that I can show to a fellow being, let me do it *now*. Let me not defer it, for I may not pass this way again!'

Is not this the ideal of *lokasangraha*?

The Chinese have a wonderful saying: 'If you want to be happy for an hour, go and take a nap. If you want to be happy for a day, go out for a picnic. If you want to be happy for a month, go and get married. If you want to be happy for a year, inherit a fortune. But if you want to be happy all your life, then go and help others!'

This then is the secret of being happy all your life – devote your efforts to *lokasangraha*. Do your duty, and a little more!

Sri Krishna's precept of desireless action is easy to achieve when you do your duty and a little more! You learn to do your duty without a thought of personal reward. 'Not expecting fruit' does not mean that you do not care about the outcome of your actions. In practical terms, we know that every action will have its result. But the point is that, when your action is selfless, you are not affected by the result, attached to the fruit. But rewarded you will be!

When you are purified, internally harmonized by selfless service, you will begin to radiate love and peace and joy. Your relationships will improve, and you will grow in maturity, wisdom and love.

Rudyard Kipling, the famous writer, had purchased a farmhouse on a hilly estate. He and his wife spent a vacation in their new getaway retreat, and were delighted with the green hills and the rolling pastures — a welcome change from their town residence.

On their morning walk one day, they met an old and feeble woman, bent low with age, hobbling with a stick, but happy to enjoy the sunshine and the fresh air. She took one look at the fashionably dressed couple, and asked, shrewdly, "Are you the people who have bought the farmhouse on the hilltop?"

"Yes ma'am," said Kipling politely, taking off his hat.

'Are you staying up there now, in the farmhouse on the hilltop?' the woman asked again, her voice quivering.

"Yes, grandma, we are," Mrs. Kipling replied, holding out a friendly hand.

"Then it must be your window that is so brightly lit up at night!" said the woman.

"Oh yes!"

"Thank you! Oh thank you!" exclaimed the old lady. "You do not know — you cannot imagine — what a comfort those lighted windows are to me! You know I am old and often lonely," she continued, "the lighted windows make me feel happy and cheerful!"

"I'm so glad," said Mr. Kipling warmly, "you make us feel wanted and welcome in the neighbourhood."

"I do hope you will stay here long," said the woman anxiously. "And I do hope you will come here often."

"We do hope to, Ma'am," said Kipling.

"Oh good," said the woman happily. "Do keep those lights burning — they matter a lot to me!"

"We promise we will," said the distinguished writer. A couple of days later, when they left the farm after their brief vacation, they instructed the caretaker to remove the curtains of the windows, and to keep the lights burning late into the night. Little deeds of kindness, little acts of love can make life on earth heavenly!

Bhagavat-saptah was being celebrated in the temple of a small town. Several devotees came to attend the daily functions and discourses, some even travelling from outlying villages. On the last day of the *saptah*, a devotee hastened to the local cobbler during a break in the programme.

"Can you mend my *chappals*, please?" he asked the cobbler. "I want them back as soon as possible!"

"They are completely worn out," said the cobbler. "They have to be resoled."

"I am not surprised," said the stranger with a sigh. "I have been walking for miles up and down every day to attend the *saptah* at the temple."

"So you are new here," remarked the cobbler, as he set to work on the *chappals*, quickly and efficiently. "I thought I had not seen you earlier."

'You're right,' agreed the stranger. 'It is the *saptah* which brings me here daily. Do you attend it, too?'

"I am tied down by my duty," smiled the cobbler. "But I'm happy to see so many like you, who take the trouble to spend time and effort on God and devotion."

Very soon, the *chappals* were resoled, and placed before the visitor.

"They are so comfortable," he exclaimed with delight. "Tell me how much I owe you."

"Nothing!" smiled the cobbler. "Let me have the opportunity to serve a *bhakta* — for that is the best offering I can make to *bhagwan*."

The cobbler may not have attended the *Bhagavat* discourses, but he lived the *Bhagavat* in deeds of daily life!

"Mingle, mingle, mingle!" said Sadhu Vaswani. "Don't be single!" To talk of 'renunciation' and 'worship of God' while ignoring human suffering is futile, for God loves those who love the poor and the helpless ones!

A *sanyasi* sat on the banks of the holy Ganga river, meditating quietly. He had chosen a lonely and quiet spot so that he would not be disturbed. However, his concentration was broken by the sound of sobbing.

Distressed, he opened his eyes to see a woman climbing down the steps to the river, carrying a small bundle in her arms. She was obviously a destitute, for her clothes were ragged and torn. She sobbed even louder, as she waded into the river as far as she could, and then let go of the object wrapped in the bundle.

It was her dead child, as the *sanyasi* saw with shock and grief. Removing the white piece of cloth in which the baby had been wrapped, the woman waded back to the steps, and collapsed on the bank, now weeping uncontrollably. The *sanyasi* saw it all, and understood at once the poverty of the woman, the tragedy that had struck her, the helplessness, and the terrible grief. He saw and understood the misery and the suffering of the downtrodden and the deprived. He decided there and then, that he would take religion to the masses, and serve them through religion.

He was none other than Maharishi Dayanand Saraswati, the founder of the Arya Samaj.

Noble blood and inherited wealth are merely accidents of birth; it is nobility of actions that characterize the truly great ones of humanity. The famous Italian soprano Mabribon, a celebrated superstar in her profession, was receiving visitors one evening.

"Now I'm tired," she said to her maid as the last one of her guests left. "Do not allow any more visitors to come in."

As a famous singer, she had always regarded it as a duty she owed to her fans and admirers to receive their visits and accept their wishes in person. She spared time for this whenever she could. But today had been hectic, and she wished to retire to bed early.

"There's only one visitor left, Ma'am,' said the maid hesitantly. 'He's just a little boy in unkempt clothes."

"All right," sighed the soprano, "send him in!"

A little urchin appeared at the door of the room. "Come on in, my son," she called encouragingly. "Tell me your name!"

"Pierre," the boy murmured, entering the room slowly, afraid to move closer to her.

"Come here," she called. "And tell me, what I can do for you."

The boy swallowed hard and big tears rolled down his pale cheeks. "It's my mother," he mumbled. "She's very ill, and we don't have money to pay for her medicine."

"I don't wish to beg," he stammered. "I have brought a poem that I have written. I thought that if you use it in your programme, I mean, if you could sing it ... You could pay me, I mean, give me whatever you wish ... And I will never ever forget your kindness ..."

"How clever of you, dear!" said the great singer kindly. "Give me your poem... And don't forget to give me your address, too!"

She read the poem, and she liked it very much. On the very next day, she sang it at the Opera, and her rendering won a tremendous applause. Directly after the programme she went to Pierre's house and met his mother lovingly. With her she had brought the entire day's collection at the Opera House, which she handed over to young Pierre.

"Your song was just beautiful, son!" she said, "I loved it, and everybody loved it. Please accept this small payment from me, and give your mother the treatment that she needs!"

No outward show, no grand gestures, no display of 'magnanimity' or 'generosity' – such is *lokasangraha*, performed in the spirit of the *Gita*!

Arbino was a sincere and devoted worker, who had served the great artist Michelangelo faithfully, for over twenty years. Arbino became old and weak. He knew he did not have long to live. The master-artist told Arbino that he would have to rest and conserve his energies, so that he could live longer.

'But, Master,' Arbino protested, 'I do not want to be a burden to you!'

'It would be no burden', Michelangelo assured him. 'I will care for you, and look after you day and night.'

The great artist was true to his word. Despite his hectic work schedule, he devoted time to attend to Arbino, nursing him through sickness. He also produced a great masterpiece, painting Arbino's last days on his sickbed.

A grand coach drove up to the gates of the Chittaranjan Loco Works. A gentleman alighted from the coach and entered the huge mansion which housed the offices.

As he entered the building, his eye fell on an old man who
was waiting anxiously in the corridor. The old man met his
glance and came over quickly to talk to him.

"Can you help me please, Sir?" he said urgently. "I have
come to see the owner of the Loco Works. I have heard
that he is a great philanthropist, and I need his help. My
daughter's wedding has been arranged, but I need some
money to help with the expenses."

"Come with me,' said the gentleman. 'I am going to his
office, and I will tell him about you."

The old man followed him gratefully. When they reached
the proprietor's office, the gentleman told him to wait and
went inside. A short while later, a company clerk came out
and handed an envelope over to the old man. "Sahib has
sent you Rs.500 for your daughter's wedding," he said to
the old man.

"Oh, but I wanted to meet Chittaranjan Das and invite
him to the wedding. Now, I must thank him for his
kindness and generosity!"

"But you just met him," said the clerk, surprised. "The
gentleman who brought you here was none other than
Deshbandhu Das himself! And it is he who has sent this
money to you."

To help people is in itself very good – but not to reveal
your identity to your beneficiary is great! It was the great
French physician Boerhave, who said, "The poor are my
best patients. God pays for them."

A famous surgeon was offering his free consultancy at a charitable dispensary, when he came across a poor patient, a primary school teacher, who was diagnosed to be suffering from cancer.

"You must be operated on without delay," said the doctor. "You must go to the city and get yourself admitted to the hospital today itself."

"But ... but, doctor ..." stammered the young man. "It would all cost too much! I have old parents and two sisters who depend on me, and as it is, we find it difficult to make ends meet!"

"That can be discussed later, young man," said the doctor. "Please take this note from me and report to the _____ Hospital. You will be admitted in a free ward."

"Doctor, you are so kind!" said the young man. "I will pay your fees as soon as I get back to work. Can I ask you how much ..."

"Five thousand rupees!" said the surgeon, with a twinkle in his eyes. "And don't worry, you can pay me in instalments! Fifty rupees a month. OK. Now, off you go... I want to see you in my hospital tomorrow!"

Thanks to the surgeon, the young man's surgery was performed the very next day, and his life was saved. After his recovery, he regularly paid the instalments to the doctor. More than eight years later, when his last instalment had been sent, he received a letter from the surgeon, which read as follows:

"I deeply appreciate your hard work and honesty. I am sending you herewith a cheque of Rs. 10,000, adding my own share to your amount. Please use this money to help other deserving patients you know, and this will truly turn into a service movement."

Truly has it been said that goodness is self-propagating. The joy and satisfaction we derive from *lokasangraha* is truly indescribable — and it can only be termed as God's warmest blessing upon us! When people attain to levels of true greatness, they view the world from a different perspective altogether. They are unaffected by petty ego clashes; questions of 'big' and 'small' tasks do not affect them.

When America was fighting for its independence under the overall military command of General George Washington, he came across a platoon of soldiers who were trying to shift a huge fallen tree-trunk from one place to another. The tree-trunk was blocking the road and had to be cleared urgently, to allow the free movement of troops.

The corporal was ordering the soldiers rudely.

"Heave, heave!" he shouted. "Get going! Push with all your might!" And again, "Is that your best? Well, it's pathetic!"

Washington was in civilian clothes and no one recognized the distinguished general. Gently, he said to the shouting officer, "Don't you think you should give them a helping hand so that they can do their job better, instead of simply ordering them about?"

"Give them a helping hand?" sneered the man. "You don't know what you're talking about! For your information, I'm a corporal. These soldiers work *under* me, and it's beneath my dignity to do their job!"

"All right, *Sir*," said the chief commander to the lowest-ranking official in his army. "I will offer my help to your men."

He took off his overcoat and joined the soldiers. Not only did he encourage them with appreciative words, he also pushed and heaved with them until the tree-trunk was pushed aside and the road was cleared. When the job was done, he turned to the arrogant corporal: 'Whenever you find your men unable to do a job, please send for the Chief Commander of the Army! He will be glad to come and help his men any time!'

The corporal who had a narrow, egotistical notion of his own dignity and duty, stood gaping at the impressive gentleman who stood before him. Only then did it dawn on him that the 'gentleman' was none other than General Washington himself! It was to the great general that he had held forth on his superior position as a corporal!

US President Cleveland was travelling by train once. His biographer, Richard Gilder, also boarded the same train. On being told that the president was travelling in the train, Gilder went in search of him, for he had something important to communicate to the president. But a long and thorough search up and down the train failed to reveal the presence of the president in any one of the crowded coaches. Puzzled, Gilder went into the baggage-car to question the conductor. There, to his great surprise, he

found the nation's Chief Executive seated on a wooden
crate! A woman with a baby had boarded the train, and
Cleveland had offered his seat to her. He was a man who
did his duty – and more!

Charles Andrews was a young man who had dedicated his
life to God very early in life. He decided to go among the
people of a notorious locality in London, for he wished to
serve them in all sincerity and devotion. Criminals, cheats,
rogues, and drunkards thronged the locality, day and night.
Charles Andrews saw a man staggering out of a tavern,
dead drunk.

'Look here, friend. You must stop drinking,' Andrews said
to him, as he helped him get on to the pavement.

'Mind your business,'snapped the drunkard, pushing him
roughly.

'Oh Lord Christ, forgive this man and bless him,' prayed
Andrews.

This became a daily occurrence. One day, the drunkard
said to Andrews, 'You are an absolute fool if you think
God will ever forgive me!' He added morosely, 'And
besides, I have no trust in Him.'

'My friend, my brother!'said Andrews with infinite
compassion 'Whether you have faith in the Lord or not,
He has full faith in you! A day will come when you will
surely give up drinking!'

"You think so?" asked the drunkard. "Are you sure God has
faith in me?"

"I assure you, He does!" Andrews told him.

The man turned over a new leaf. He left drinking from that day.

Charles Andrews, when he went to India later, became known as *Dinabandhu,* for he served poor people as if he were their own brother.

It was Kahlil Gibran who said, "You give but little when you give of your possessions. It is when you give of yourself that you truly give."

Is it not true that genuine selflessness consists in caring for others, sharing the interests of others? On the tomb of the British philanthropist, John Howard, in St. Paul's Cathedral, you will find engraved the following inscription:

> 'He who lives for others treads an open, but unfrequented, path to immortality.'

When Pompeii was excavated after the eruption of Mt. Vesuvius, they found the body of a crippled boy, whose foot was lame. Around his body was a woman's arm, bejewelled with valuable trinkets and rings. Obviously, a rich lady had taken pity on the crippled boy and tried to save him. Only her outstretched arm was saved, she was probably lost in the eruption. But she must have died in the satisfaction that her final effort in life had been spent trying to save the life of a fellow human being!

A little Japanese boy went to the house of a retired gentleman and offered a few picture postcards for sale. The postcards cost very little, about ten cents.

"What are you going to do with the money?" the gentleman asked him indulgently.

"I am going to raise one million dollars for earthquake relief," said the little boy in all solemnity. He was so tiny, and the sum he named was so huge that the gentleman could not help smiling.

"One million dollars!" he exclaimed. "Do you expect to raise it all by yourself?"

"No, Sir," the little boy replied gravely. "My younger sister is also helping me!"

When St. Vincent de Paul was a small boy, he used to work with the shepherds. When he was twelve years old, he was sent to work for a neighbouring farmer, who paid him thirty sous. Little Vincent had never ever had so much money in life! He was happily speculating on what he would do with the money, when he saw a poor man, whose rags and misery moved him to pity. Without a moment's hesitation he took out his thirty sous and gave him the lot. Such was his spirit of service.

In the good old days when Portuguese merchants sailed across the seas to seek their fortune, a young adventurer returned from India, having made a fortune, which was laden on to several ships. However, he did not at first reveal his good fortune to his family and friends. Instead, he put on some worn-out clothes and went out to see his near and dear ones. In turn, he told each of them that he was in dire straits and badly in need of their help.

"Could you put me up in your house for a few days?" he

begged them.

But everywhere, people made excuses. "Alas, there is no room in my house," said one. "I wish I could help you, but my hands are tied," said another. No door would open to receive a poor relation!

The young man returned to his ships. He put on his rich attire and rode into the city with a great retinue of servants. He purchased a huge mansion in the best locality and let it be known everywhere that he had returned from India with a huge fortune. In a day or two his fabulous wealth was the talk of the town! The friends and the relatives who had turned him away, were ashamed of themselves. "If only we had known how rich he was..." they sighed, "we would have acted very differently! But it's no good now – we have spoilt our chance with him forever!"

How many of us can act selflessly – *without* any ulterior motives?

Have you seen a stagnant pond that has no outlet and does not flow into a canal or stream? Its water becomes stale, dirty, and gets covered with thick moss; it begins to smell bad; it becomes the habitation of frogs. So it happens with a life that does not flow out through good deeds performed for others' benefit; it too, becomes stale and stagnant with vanity, ego, selfishness, and desire. But a life that is spent in the service of others, flows clean and free like a sparkling river, and ultimately reaches the ocean of the Supreme Self. Thus, doing good to others, serving others, always turns out to be the best that one can do for oneself!

It is good that those who seek to serve others bear this in mind: that service is meant to purify the mind, the heart, and the intellect, and to move us on the path of God-realisation. We are also blessed with the unique, selfless joy that comes from serving those in affliction, and bringing the light of love into dark, unhappy lives. These are the genuine feelings to be nourished by those who serve others — and not vanity, ego, and self-seeking pride. Do not seek to serve others to prove your superiority. This brings disgrace to you, and it degrades those whom you 'serve' in this spirit. It destroys the very spirit and concept of service. Prepare yourself mentally and spiritually to serve others.

Get into the habit of prayer, meditation, and reading the scriptures, so that you gain insight into the truth about life and the Self. Draw inspiration from your guru and his *satsang*, so that you may assimilate the true spirit of service. Next, assess the needs of people around you, and see how best you may serve them, with your unique God-given endowments. Thus, a doctor can offer free medical care to poor patients; a lawyer can offer legal services to the poor and defenceless. Whatever you are — teacher, artist, scientist, or musician — you are endowed with a unique gift or capacity that can be spent in the service of those in need.

There is also a practical, down-to-earth aspect of serving others. When you come across hunger, your first impulse should be to feed the hungry, and not offer them profound spiritual discourses on philosophy and God-realisation. When you come across those in pain and suffering, you must mitigate their misery before you begin to talk to them on self-improvement.

Therefore, I tell my friends that when they set out to do good to others, they must practise what I call 'the Five Fingers of Service' :

1. Serve silently! Do not serve for show or publicity. Let the right hand not know what your left hand gives away. Do not seek to serve for name, fame, popularity, or publicity.

2. Serve humbly! Be grateful to those who give you the opportunity to serve them. You are not doing *meherbani* on them — they are offering *you* the chance to show your gratitude to the Lord, for the numerous blessings we have received from Him.

3. Serve lovingly! Do not speak harsh words to the people you serve. A sense of identification is very essential to the spirit of true service. Do not criticize or condemn others. Give and serve in the spirit of love and sympathy to all.

4. Serve unconditionally! Therefore, seek no reward for your service, nor 'recognition' from the world. Don't let your service become an interference; don't serve others with an ulterior motive — to convert them to your ideology; to force them to follow your beliefs; or to support your political party. This is not true service.

5. Cultivate the soul through service! In other words, become aware that you are only an instrument of God. He is the One Worker — you are but His tool, His agent. Therefore, renounce all idea of egoism, of the narrow Self, and become an instrument of the eternal *shakti* that shapes the lives of individuals and nations. I

repeat, service, *lokasangraha,* is a God-given opportunity for the upliftment of mind and soul. Therefore, let us serve others in the spirit of serving God.

The essence of Vedanta may be summed up in one concept: All life is one. If such oneness is accepted, where is the question of ego or superiority in service? Service thus becomes a spiritual discipline for the enlightened mind. It helps us to expand our vision beyond our own narrow, restricted life. Service makes us sensitive to the needs of others, who are not apart from us, but *a part* of our essential self. Service makes us evolve spiritually, and helps us realize in deeds of daily life, the great truth of the brotherhood of all creation. Such service helps us on the path of spiritual advancement; it leads us towards God-realisation; it awakens the divine within us!

Give in humility! Serve with love and devotion! Share all that you have with others. For, in the beautiful words of Sadhu Vaswani, "I know of no religion higher than the religion of unity and love, of service and sacrifice!"

He taught us that all that we have, all that we are, all that we possess, is but a loan given to us, to be passed on to those whose need is greater than ours. Nothing belongs to us. Nothing has been given to us absolutely; everything has been given to us as a loan – our time and talents, our knowledge, our experience, our wisdom, our influence in society, our bank accounts, our property and possessions, our life itself, is a loan given to us to be passed on to those whose need is greater than ours. This is the true spirit of *lokasangraha.*

The Fourth Commandment:
'Thou Shalt Not Miss Thy Daily Appointment with God'

Thou shalt not miss thy daily appointment with God! Howsoever strong be the pressure of work on you, howsoever demanding be your other commitments, set aside time for your daily practice of silence, prayer, meditation, and communication with God.

I come across so many brothers and sisters in my travels, who tell me they have no time for daily prayer, no time for the practice of daily silence. I think to myself, they may as well say they have no time to breathe!

> 'Let the *yogi*, seated in solitude and alone, try constantly to concentrate his mind on the Supreme Self, with his self subdued, free from desires and from all impulse of ownership.'
>
> VI: 10

You should always look forward to this period of daily silence, with deep love and longing in your heart. It is this love, this longing that can take you into the depths within, where God waits for us. It is in these depths that the beauteous face of God is revealed to us, and the radiant music of His voice can be heard in the stillness of the mind.

Yes, my friends, God can be seen, God can be felt, God can be touched, God can be heard – in the depths of silence. We can truly experience Him, for He is more real than all the objects of this material world. But for this, effort is needed.

Sri Ramakrishna said to us, "Yearn for the Lord even as a miser yearns for gold. Yearn for the Lord even as a child who has lost its mother yearns for her presence, yearn for the Lord even as a lover yearns for his beloved!"

The *Vedas* describe God as *be-anta*. You cannot reach Him, but He will come to you! He will reveal Himself to you. But to receive Him, you must create a vacuum in your heart. Only when you create that emptiness, that hollowness, that state of *shoonya* in the heart within, will God rush in to fill it – for this is a scientific principle. Nature abhors a vacuum, and it will be filled by God, when you empty your mind of all else!

After you have done your duty, after you have contributed to *lokasangraha*, after you have served someone in need, do find a silence-corner where you can contemplate the *leela* of the Lord; where you can marvel at the glory, the goodness, the infinite mercy that He is.

I often tell my friends, we live in a world of deafening noises. All around us there is noise. Sometimes, you have to stuff your ears with cotton wool, when the decibel level of the noise outside threatens to deafen you. We live in a world of deafening noise. I know of people who, on first getting out of bed in the morning, switch on their TV sets! They turn the volume on so that it keeps blaring in the background, while they carry on with their daily routine. Before they even wash their face or brush their teeth, the TV is turned on!

Oh yes, we live in a world of deafening noise. Even as particles of dust cling to our clothes, particles of noise cling to our minds. We wash away dirt and dust from our clothes with soap and water. So too, our minds must be washed, our minds must be cleansed in the fresh, pure waters of silence. It was a great Christian mystic, Thomas Merton, who wrote a book called *The Waters of Silence*. He says silence is a beautiful and ever-flowing river, in which you must take dips again and again. Silence purifies the mind. Silence heals the heart. Silence reaches the very depths of the soul within! Sitting in silence, you may repeat the Name Divine — any Name that appeals to you. God is the Nameless One, but the sages have called Him by many names. Pick up any name that you can utter with deep feeling of the heart. It is this deep feeling, this love, this longing of the heart, this devotion that you pour into the repetition of the Name Divine that really makes it meaningful and valuable — without it, the utterance of any name is of no value.

I have spoken to you of Swami Dayanand, the founder of the Arya Samaj. Sadhu Vaswani greeted him as Rishi Dayanand, for he was greater than a swami! Rishi Dayanand used to advise his disciples thus: 'If you wish to grow in interior purification, you should end every breath you take with the Name Divine. When you breathe in, utter the word '*Om*' ... silently. When you breathe out, utter the word '*Ra ... am*' silently. '*Om ... Raam*' silently, as you breathe in and breathe out. You will find your whole being charged with a new energy.

Sitting in silence, you can pray. Prayer is not a complicated matter! Supposing a friend were to come to see you, would it not be the most natural thing in the world for you to talk to him, to share your anxieties and worries with him, to discuss your problems and perplexities with him, and share with him your hopes, desires, and dreams? You must do likewise with God. For He is the friend of all friends. When all other friends fade away, this one remains. Sitting in silence, you can meditate. You can do your spiritual thinking. Meditation is not really difficult. Sitting in silence, you can sink deeper and deeper within yourself until, one blessed day, with the grace of God and the guru, you will be able to see God face to face.

It is only when we have more and more such people — men and women who do their duty, faithfully, honestly, conscientiously, men and women who serve the needy, beholding in them images of the eternal, men and women who have beheld God face to face — that you will have a mighty revolution of the spirit on this ancient, unhappy globe! Then, and only then, will we be able to usher in a new era of peace for which the tortured, wounded soul of humanity has piteously cried, age after age.

Do not pray to cover up your errors; do not ask for forgiveness. Rather, pray for strength and wisdom and understanding, so that you will not fall into error again. Do not ask God to lighten your load, or to evade your duties and responsibilities. Ask God for the ability and strength to bear all your loads lightly. Prayer is meant to make you aware of your true nature, and help you grow in insight and wisdom.

All the religions of the world emphasize communion with

God through prayer. Remembering God constantly is even more important than repeating the Name Divine. Remembering God reminds you that the world with all its objects and all its people, is a manifestation of the Divine.

Hindus believe that when a person dies with the name of the Lord on his lips and, more importantly, the thought of God in his heart, he is led towards salvation and liberation. As the sages and saints of India have constantly taught us, we should not wait till our last breath to utter the Name Divine and think of God! For such a thought cannot come to you as an accident or a coincidence. It is only when you have remembered the Lord constantly throughout your life that you will be able to reach such a deeply charged state in which the remembrance of God becomes natural, automatic, spontaneous. Therefore, amidst the trials and tribulations of daily life, practise remembrance of God.

This is best done, as I suggested, by the *sadhana*, the *abhyasa* (the discipline and practice) of daily silence. Meditation and silent prayer enable you to drink deep at the fountain of Divine Love. This will transform your life and help you live in God's presence and move with Him wherever you go, whatever you do. When you have attained this enviable state, you have crowned yourself with success!

Sadhu Vaswani taught us: 'By a triple process may the Lord be worshipped:

1. *Nishkama karma*, selfless activity;

2. *Saranagati*, taking shelter in the Lord, dedicating all secular duties to Him; and

3. *Prema bhakti*, Love Divine.'

Therefore, Sri Krishna tells Arjuna:

> 'Fix thy mind on Me; be devoted to Me; worship
> Me; bow down to Me. Thus having controlled
> thyself, and making Me thy goal supreme, thou
> shalt come unto Me.'
>
> IX: 34

And, even more forcefully:

> 'Listen thou again to My supreme word, the
> most secret of all. Well-beloved art thou of Me,
> therefore shall I speak for thy good.
>
> 'Fix thy mind on Me; be devoted to Me; sacrifice
> to Me, prostrate thyself before Me. So shalt
> thou come to Me. I pledge thee my troth; thou
> art dear to Me!'
>
> XVIII: 64-65

The *Gita* tells us too, that there are four types of devotees
who engage in communication with the Lord, all for a
variety of reasons. This in itself is noble – for birth after
birth, *janma* after *janma,* they must have done noble deeds
and developed good *sanskaras*; thus have they developed
vishvasa (faith) in the Lord. Thus have they been born
bhaktas of the Lord in this life.

> 'Of four kinds are the virtuous ones who
> worship Me: the man who suffers, the man who
> yearns for knowledge, the man who seeks wealth,
> and the man of wisdom, O Arjuna!'
>
> VII: 16

The four types of *bhaktas* are:

1. The *artah bhaktas* : they are the afflicted ones. They seek the Lord's protection in distress. Think of Draupadi: when she is insulted and humiliated and about to be disrobed by Dushasana, she lifts her heart up to Sri Krishna in affliction. Mira captures her predicament memorably:

   '*Tum bin meri kaun khabar le, Govardhan Giridhari!*'

   In the *bhari sabha* of the Kauravas, this princess, wife of the valiant Pandavas undergoes the vilest humiliation. She cries: 'Govinda! Keshava! O Thou who can destroy all affliction, save me! I have taken refuge at Thy holy feet! Come to my help! Guard me in this hour of deep distress!'

   And Krishna heeds her call! He hastens to her aid. He performs a miraculous *vastra-leela*. As Dushasana pulls and pulls at her saree, Draupadi continues to remain robed. The evil prince falls down in exhaustion, and Draupadi's honour is saved!

2. The *artharthi bhaktas*: they seek success in their undertakings. Some of them want wealth; some of them want salvation. But they do not beg or plead: they depend on the Lord, nay, they expect Him to grant them success. Such is their *shraddha* (reverence), such is their faith, that they will not look to the world for anything. He, Sri Krishna, is their assurance. He is their anchor.

   Think of Dhruva. He is a prince, the eldest son of his

father Uttanapada. But the king has two wives, and Dhruva's stepmother will not allow him to play with his father. Dhruva runs to his mother weeping, and she tells him, 'You must go and pray to Lord Hari.' Dhruva makes straight for the forest, Madhuvana, on the banks of the river Jamuna. Here he meets Rishi Narada who gives him the sacred *mantra*, '*Om namo bhagavate Vasudevaya.*'

Dhruva repeats this *mantra* in the dark forest, he casts out all fear of wild animals, and all fear of solitude. This mere child is granted a vision of the Lord, who assures him that he will inherit his kingdom. Dhruva is granted the *artha* he seeks, by the Lord Himself.

3. The *jignasu bhakta*: he is special. He is a seeker after light. He seeks the Truth. He prays to the Lord for illumination. Ancient India was the land of such *bhaktas*; they travelled far and wide in search of a guru, who could speak to them of *tatva*, the essence of the universe.

    Think of Nachiketas. Offering himself as a sacrifice to the Lord of Death, he willingly leaves the world behind. But even when he is released from his bond, he refuses to return, until he has been taught the secret of life and death.

4. The *gnani bhakta*, the wise devotee, who seeks nothing less than God-realisation. He seeks the One Lord in all objects, all men, all creatures, all countries, all races, all religions, all scriptures, in all the prophets and saints.

    Think of Prahlada. He is tormented, ill-treated, tortured

by his father Hiranyakashipu, who expects all his people to worship *him* as God. Prahlada refuses. 'Father,' he says, 'Hari is real and Him will I worship.'

The annoyed king orders Prahlada to be flung amidst serpents. But they do not harm him, for he sees the Lord in them! The king orders the boy to be trampled upon by an elephant. But the elephant refuses to move, for he sees the Lord in the elephant! He is thrown from a steep cliff. The earth receives him lovingly in her arms unharmed. He is flung into the sea, the waves refuse to drown him. He sees the play of the Lord in the rise and fall of the waves. He is thrown into a roaring fire. In the flames he beholds the face of the Lord and, of course, the flames do not burn him!

"Where is thy Hari?" roars his infuriated father.

"I see Hari everywhere" replies the child. "He is behind me, before me, above me, around me. He is in the speck of dust. He is in this mighty pillar!"

In anger, Hiranyakashipu strikes the pillar, and out of the pillar Sri Hari appears as Narasimha, to protect His beloved devotee Prahlada!

The first stage, *artah*, is one in which we seek God in distress. Most of us are familiar with this type of devotion. As Sant Kabir sings, 'Everyone turns his mind to God when they are in a state of distress. But when there is happiness and prosperity, people forget Him.'

If one were to worship God in prosperity why should there be any adversity for Him?

2432436243243624365243652436243243243243242424324324324324324243652436524365243652436522436524365243652436524324365243652436524365243652436524365243652436524365243652436

Recently there was an earthquake in Kashmir. A TV show was being aired live, and a VIP was being interviewed. As the quake hit, and the TV studio began to rock, with tables and chairs swaying, the VIP began to pray loudly, and the compères of the show joined him in his prayer. People in unaffected areas, watching the show, began to be concerned. "What's wrong? Why are they praying? Something must have happened!"

Why should we confine prayer to such desperate situations? I agree, it is the most natural thing for us to turn to God in distress, but we must train our minds to remember God always, in all situations. The highest form of *artah* devotion is when you pray to God with compassion for all of suffering creation. This is, indeed, a step in the right direction, a movement towards *bhakti yoga*.

The *artharthi bhakta* asks God for material objects and conditions; this too, is natural, for God is our loving Father, our loving Mother, and to whom can we turn, if not to Him, to fulfil our needs? And so people pray for financial security, success in examinations, welfare of their children, etc. As long as these are used as means for one's spiritual evolution, this form of prayer has value. The grant of these gifts must turn your mind Godwards, and help you to serve Him by serving suffering humanity.

The *jignasu bhakta* seeks knowledge, wisdom, and truth. He asks for greater clarity, greater understanding. However, intellectual knowledge must become a stepping stone to spiritual knowledge. Your intellect must help you probe the purpose of your existence; it must promote in you the awareness that you are an aspect, a part of the Universal

Soul.

Sri Ramakrishna reached such a profound understanding of truth. When his doctor who was treating him for cancer, exhorted him to pray to the goddess to save his life, the saint of Dakshineshwar replied, "I have lived through so many births, so many personalities, even as a tree *lives* in all its branches, through all its leaves. If a few of the leaves should fall to the ground, why should the tree be affected? If this, my physical body, should drop down dead, how is the Universal Self in me – the real I – in any way affected?"

Here was a great devotee who had mastered true knowledge, and risen above identification with the body!

The devotion of a *gnani bhakta* is indeed special. Such a one has become a total *bhakta* in whom all aspects of personality – prayer, devotion (*bhakti*), duty, action (*karma*), wisdom, and knowledge (*gnana*) – are all integrated.

Some scholars associate *artah* with devotion of the heart; *artharthi* with devotion through the hands; *jignasu* with devotion through the intellect. When all these are integrated, indeed is your devotion integral devotion! Your entire personality, your entire being, body, mind, heart, and soul are established in Divine Consciousness, and you realize the truth of the saying of the *Vedas*: '*I am the Divine Self*'.

Scholars think that the word *bhakti* is derived from the root *bhaj* which means adore, honour, worship, and the suffix *kti* which means action. Thus *bhakti* can be taken to signify devotion, loyalty, worship, homage.

The *Narada Bhaktisutra* defines eleven different components, or eleven different aspects of *bhakti*, such as adoration of the Lord's quality (*guna*), His form (*rupa*), His ritual (*puja*), meditation on Him (*smarana*) etc., but it talks also about five different *bhakti bhavas* or attitudes. These are:

1. *Santa bhava:* in this attitude the devotee is at peace. He is not emotional. He does not shed tears, or weep or sing or dance in ecstasy. His heart is full of intense devotion. We may cite Bhishma Pitamaha as a wonderful example of this attitude, for he adored the Lord without any outer form of expression. In modern times, Sri Aurobindo is said to have exemplified this aspect. Many renunciates (*sanyasis*) have this attitude.

2. *Madhurya bhava:* in this, the devotee loves the Lord even as a lover adores his beloved. Even today, in Mathura, Brindaban, and Nadiad, you will find devotees with this attitude. The *Ashtapadi* of Jayadev captures this attitude beautifully, dwelling on the *ras-leela* of Radha and Krishna.

3. *Sakhya bhava:* in which the devotee sees himself as the Lord's companion. Arjuna was fortunate enough to be the Lord's friend, in deep devotion.

4. *Vatsalya bhava:* in which the devotee loves God as his own child. This attitude is unique to the Indian *bhakti* tradition. The saints and *alwars* imagine themselves to be Maa Yashoda, holding Sri Krishna in her arms, even while she enjoys His divine *leela*.

5. *Dasya bhava:* in which the devotee regards himself as a servant to the Lord, who is his Master. In such a spirit did Mira sing: '*Chaakar raakho ji, prabhuji mane chaakar raakho ji!* Take me as Your servant, O Lord!'

Our sages have also identified different stages by which one may attain *bhakti*. This requires certain spiritual practices.

1. *Shravana* (listening). For the aspirant, *satsang* is vital, because it enables him to listen to the voice of enlightened ones, like readings from the scriptures. Listening to *satvishaya* (good teachings) repeatedly sets him on the spiritual path easily.

2. *Kirtan* (singing) is the next step. I have always maintained that singing the Name Divine is the shortest route to God. Sri Chaitanya Mahaprabhu was a great exponent of this practice.

3. *Smarana* (constant remembrance) of the Lord is the next step. In this stage, you become aware of the divine presence in everything you do or say; you feel His presence in every breath you take. Your life is enfolded in His presence.

4. *Archana* (offering flowers) is not just a ritual. Symbolically, it implies that we offer good qualities, virtues like humility, compassion, and goodness to the Lord.

5. *Padasevana* (serving the feet) symbolizes the spirit of service. This is what Sadhu Vaswani meant when he described service of the poor as the best form of worship to God.

6. *Vandana* (bowing down). Within the heart, the devotee reveres the Lord; outwardly, he reveres all creatures, all objects which are, after all, manifestations of the divine.

7. *Atmanivedana* (absolute surrender). This is the ultimate

goal of spiritual attainment, to live in total surrender to the Lord.

Bhakti yoga, the path of devotion to the Lord, is in essence, the path of love — love that is unconditional, whole-hearted, selfless, and completely fulfilling. Alas, human love is frittered away on worldly objects and goals that are perishable, mortal and therefore, utterly futile. But when our love is bestowed on God, we find complete and absolute fulfillment. We transcend the ego, and commune with the divine.

Sage Yajnavalkya tells us in the *Brihadaranyaka Upanishad*:

'*Atmanastu kamaya sarvam priyam bhavati.*' In other words, "Everything becomes dear to us for the sake of the Self alone."

Everything in the world is dear to us, only because we find ourselves, our interest, reflected in it. Otherwise it is meaningless to us. So too, we seek to find our self ultimately reflected in the Divine Self. This is the perfect object of love that we have been seeking in several embodiments, several births. In *bhakti yoga*, this sublime attainment is reached in the highest state of complete and utter surrender. Each step that you take towards this goal is blessed; for it has truly been said that the person who grows in the spirit of *bhakti* does good not only to himself, but to all humanity.

The story is told of a seeker who sat down to pray and meditate on the banks of the holy River Ganga. His aim was to find God and seek union with the divine. But the more he prayed, the farther he was from his goal. After several days of futile devotion, he arose from his meditation, crying out bitterly, "O Lord, Lord, where are You? I seek You and find You not! My devotion has been in vain. I can only reach the sad conclusion that You do not exist!"

At that moment, a fish jumped up from the river, crying, "Water, water! I have looked for water in vain. Where is the water? All my swimming and searching has been in vain. I die of thirst, and I can only come to the sad conclusion that water does not exist!"

"You are indeed stupid," scolded the seeker. "You are living in water, moving in water, breathing in water. There is water all around you. How can you die of thirst?"

"So is it with you, O seeker," said the fish. "You are of God. God is within you and outside of you. He is manifest in the whole wide world, and yet you say you cannot find Him! Open the eye of the spirit and behold Him everywhere!"

So saying, the fish leapt back into the waters. He had taught the seeker a valuable lesson: God is everywhere. God is within you. All you need to do is purify your mind and heart in order to behold His beauteous vision.

Maharishi Patanjali's *Raja Yoga Sutra* teaches us the technique of purifying the mind, which he calls *kriya yoga* (the yoga of purification):

'*Tapa swadhyaya ishwara pranidhanani kriya yoga...*' *Tapa* (austerity), *swadhyaya* (study of scriptures), *ishwara pranidhan* (surrender to the Lord) – these constitute *kriya yoga*.

Truly, these steps subsume all the Seven Commandments of the *Gita*! For the seeker who follows these practices will find that he does his duty with patience and selflessness; he will disengage from identification with the body, and look upon all conditions of life with equanimity; studying the scriptures and uttering the Name Divine, he will meditate upon God, and serve God by serving humanity. Attaining this high state of devotion does not mean giving up on life, renouncing all action.

> 'These bodies of the embodied One, who is eternal, indestructible, and incomprehensible, are said to be passing. Therefore fight, O Arjuna!'
>
> II: 18

Once the mind has glimpsed the reality of our innate identity, there is no cause for grief, pain, or sorrow. Knowing that you are *Brahman*, the Absolute Self, you should fight the battle of life in a heroic spirit.

'Fighting' here does not mean making war! 'Fighting' is Arjuna's *swadharma*. He is a warrior, and he has come to Kurukshetra to fight the forces of evil and darkness. Therefore, he must do what he can do, what he is meant to do, in a spirit of enlightenment, free from confusion.

For many of us, life in this world is like wandering in darkness. How wonderful it is, to find a lighted window when you are lost in the woods, to walk into a welcoming sanctuary and find a bright light burning there! Imagine the warmth, comfort, relief, and joy you experience on moving close to the light!

God is the light of our life. All we need to do is move

towards this light, and we will be free from all insecurity, fear, and anxiety. In seeking your daily appointment with God, you are moving towards this light — slowly, but surely!

We also need to understand the three *gunas* (modes of nature) and how they operate for us. *Rajas* implies a restless, distracted mind. Such a mind is swayed by anger, irritability and other negative emotions. *Tamas* is inertia, insensitivity, caught in the same old grooves of earlier mistakes, becoming narrow-minded. Both *rajas* and *tamas* take us away from God. *Sattva* is the mode of peace and harmony that will help us move Godwards; you are promoting *sattva* when you keep your daily appointment with God, and commune with Him in silence.

Routine is essential to an orderly life. There is a time for everything: when to wake up, when to pray, when to work, when to eat, when to serve, when to relax, when to sleep. This routine should also allow time for your near and dear ones, time for the needs of those around you. But let me repeat: as you allow time for all the activities that are important to you, also allow time for that most important of all tasks, your daily appointment with God.

The mind, it is said, is a monkey. This is illustrated by the story of the dreamy milkmaid. This young woman was carrying a pot of milk to sell in the market. She thought to herself, 'I shall sell this milk and get money; when I have made enough money, I'll buy another cow; soon I shall have a herd of cows ... I shall grow rich and wear beautiful clothes and jewels ... the zamindar will take one look at me and fall in love with me ... I shall marry him and live a life of comfort and luxury ... there will be a dozen maidservants to do my everyday bidding ... and if one of them would be lax in serving me, I shall kick her, like this ..." As she kicked her foot in the daydream, the pot of milk fell down and crashed to a hundred pieces.

The mind is indeed a monkey, and one needs to manage it, control it, by spiritual *sadhana*. I know of nothing simpler, nothing easier than the daily practice of silence.

Just as we take care to eat nutritious food, and do exercises like walking, swimming, and jogging to keep the body fit and healthy, so too, we need to nourish, strengthen and sustain the good health of the mind. For this, there is no need to pay a fat subscription and join a gym! The daily practice of silence and meditation are the most effective techniques for making the mind healthy, stable and focused.

When we schedule regular periods of the day to devote to *naam japa*, *kirtan*, meditation, study of scriptural texts, and prayerful silence, we are revitalizing the spirit. We rid the mind of negative impressions; we overcome many of our anxieties, frustrations, and insecurities; we gain mental strength, and we move closer to God. Even during your working hours, there are periods of inactivity, moments of waiting, when all activity is at a lull. During such periods, I suggest that you renew your contact with God by uttering in silence, the Name Divine, or repeating to yourself the *mantra* that is dear to you.

I often see many of my young friends rushing to 'charge' their cell phones whenever they find a spare plug point. They explain that they had been using their cell phones so much, that the 'charge' is running out ...

My dear friends, we are taxing our minds and hearts with so much useless activity that they too need to be charged, recharged by contact with the greatest of all power-sources – God!

A weak, frightened mind can drag down even a strong body. This is why some old people deteriorate severely with age. Their nerves are shattered, and they have no stamina to face life. On the other hand, spiritually strong people find their minds and intellects sharp, even as their bodies become weaker. A strong mind is one that is tempered by faith, focussed by meditation, and nourished by prayer. Such a strong mind will constantly remind you: *'You are not this body that you wear. You are the immortal soul'*. You are an aspect of the divine. And the source of infinite strength and power is open to you in God-realisation!

Time is the most precious gift that God gives us during our earthly life. Most of us just fritter away time, unmindful of the fact that we can never get back even one second that we throw away! How long do you expect to live? 70 years? 80 years? Multiply it by 365 days, 24 hours, 60 minutes, and 60 seconds – 80x365x24x60x60...

What are you doing, what have you done with so much time at your beck and call? You celebrate each birthday, each new year with such great fanfare as if it were a landmark event in your life. What would be your reaction if you paused to ask yourself, 'What have I done with my life during the year that has just gone? Have I moved closer to my goal? Have I moved closer to God?'

Realise the value of time. If you are to be in the *satsang* by 6.45, do not wait till 7 o'clock to leave home. Rather, be aware of your appointment at the *satsang* by 6.30, so that you can be there, ahead of schedule, eager to keep your appointment. Self-discipline, punctuality, and time-management are very important, for life is very short, and every resource you have must be well utilised so that you find enlightenment and liberation – your ultimate goal.

Raja Yoga refers to five states of the human mind:

1. *Mudha* (dull);

2. *Kshipta* (distracted). One cannot concentrate or achieve anything in such a state. The practice of *mauna* (silence) helps us to overcome this state, and evolve spiritually.

3. *Vikshipta* (partially distracted) is where most of us are. We are able to concentrate to a certain extent, but this may change when conditions become unfavourable.

4. *Ekagrita* (one-pointedness) is attained by an advanced aspirant, in whose personality *sattva* (purity) has been increasing steadily. He is able to concentrate in a state of mystic silence.

5. *Nirodha* (a controlled mind) is attained in the period of *samadhi* – a state of profound communication with the divine.

Truly has it been said: speech is silver, silence is golden. Silence (*mauna*) is a good spiritual *sadhana* which can lead you on towards deep, mental silence. Therefore, observing silence is strongly recommended by all spiritual elders. When you observe silence, keep your mind relaxed; focus on prayer, a *mantra* or a name dear to you. This will enhance the power of the silence. You will feel the spring of peace beginning to flow in the depths of the soul.

Sages and wise ones tell us that there are three types of occurrences in human life:

1. *Anichha prarabdha*: These are acts of God, events over which we have no control whatsoever. Think of the tsunami that struck South Asia in December 2004; think of Hurricane Katrina which devastated New Orleans; think of the earthquake that killed thousands of people in Pakistan and J&K (India). These are occurrences which we have no power to stop or inhibit. Such natural disasters teach us to let things rest in divine hands for God knows best.

2. *Parechha prarabdha*: These are things you do under compulsion, because others around you force you to act in such a way. Many people find this the most difficult to bear.

    They curse and fret and complain; they try to hit out at others whom they regard as their enemies. Such an attitude is both unwise and uncultured. What we need to realise is that all of us are inter-dependent, and that there is a divine power operating over all of us, using us as His instruments, His puppets in His divine *leela*. When we understand His divine plan is in operation at all times, we will no longer be agitated and distracted by such events.

3. *Swechha prarabdha:* These are events that are caused by your own will.

You are apt to imagine that whatever happens according to

your will, must surely be pleasant and acceptable to you.
But it is not so simple! Often we act as we wish but this
leads to undesirable results. Thus we wallow in regret and
self-reproach. 'If only I had done this ...' or, 'If only I had
not done such and such ...' In other words, we don't really
learn our lessons, but indulge in futile regret, intensifying
the ego.

Here too, the important thing to realize is that it is not
our will that operates but God's will which controls our
life. The idea therefore, should be to harmonize our will
with the Divine Will. Then we will grow in the
understanding that the world operates according to His
will, and that your safest option is to let yourself relax at
His Divine Feet, in His Divine Hands! Thus, we come
closer to God! Sant Kabir was once walking along the
banks of the Ganga, when he saw a *chatraka* (rain bird) fall
into the river, with lack of water.

The rain bird, no matter how thirsty, and no matter how
much water is available, only drinks pure drops of rain. So
too, this bird, struggling on the river on this hot summer
day, would not drink the water of the Ganga!

On seeing the bird, Kabir sang:

> 'As fish cannot live out of water; as the thirst of
> the chatrak can be quenched only by the rain;
> with a like intensity, the saints yearn for the
> Lord; only the sight of Him can slake their
> thirst for Him!'

When Guru Nanak was in Mecca, a renowned qazi once
asked him: "Can you describe to me the palace of God?

How many towers does it have? How many turrets and
how many doors?"

The great guru smiled and said in reply: 'Know thou, that
the palace and the temple of God are the human body. Of
towers, it has twelve — hands, forearms, upper arms on the
right and left (six); similarly feet, legs and thighs, each on
the right and left (six). The palace has nine doors — two
eyes, two ears, two nostrils, the mouth, and the two lower
apertures."

Guru Nanak continued: "But God's palace of light (the
spiritual realm) is beyond the fifty-two turrets, nine doors,
and twelve towers. From this palace of light an everlasting
fountain of nectar, ever flows. From this palace of light,
God constantly calls to us from above. But alas, we are
asleep, and we hear Him not.

'The way to the palace of light is through this human
body, the living temple of the Lord. The *satguru* awakens
the disciple, and teaches him how to go inside the body,
and through it find the way to God's great palace."

It was King Pipa who sang:

> 'He who pervades the universe also dwells in the
> body. Who seeks shall find Him there. Saith
> Pipa: God is the Primal Being. The true guru
> shall reveal Him.'

During his daily walks in the city of Benaras, Kabir saw a
man relaxing in his garden. Often, Kabir would stop and
tell him, "Sir, why don't you spend your time in spiritual
meditation, instead of sitting idle here?"

"In good time," the man would reply. At first his excuse would be his children. "They are still very young. They need my attention now. I will take up spiritual practices only after they are grown up."

A few years later, Kabir asked him, "Do you now find time for spiritual meditation?"

"The children are about to be married, I must see to their welfare," the man replied. "After that I will have time for *sadhana*."

Later, when Kabir met him, he said, "Now all your children must be married and settled! Are you ready to take on your *sadhana*?"

"I am eager to spend time with my grandchildren, see them grow up and get married." In good time, this too, came too pass.

"What is your position now, friend?" Kabir asked the man.

"Alas, my children are all careless. I have to take care of the house, my wealth, and my business, so that I may leave it all behind for them," the man sighed.

Some years later, Kabir passed by the garden and found the man missing. On enquiring, he was told that the man had passed away. He had spent his entire life wallowing in his worldly cares and concerns. He was chained down by his attachments, but even a few moments of love for the Lord would have helped to liberate him from his bonds!

The world today does not need words; it cannot be satisfied with abstract philosophy; nor is it seeking a new

theology. People are seeking God, they are hungry to feel
Him, to experience Him, to make Him a part of their lives.
And God is best discovered in silence. Silence is as much a
discipline of the ear, as it is of the tongue. And in silence
alone can we hear His Divine Voice — not in the noises of
the world.

Unfortunately, people find it difficult to rest in silence. I
see motorists and drivers talking on cell phones, even
while they are negotiating through heavy traffic. I see men
and women taking walks on the seashore and on the hills,
with stereo headphones in their ears, listening to music! I
think music is delightful; and human conversation is
definitely one of life's great pleasures. But they have their
place in our lives, as does silence! We can never be really
happy and peaceful until we are able to touch the depths
within us, in our own spiritual solitude.

Outer silence is essential, if we wish to attain the inner
silence in which we can hear God speaking to us. "If you
wish to be happy, keep your mouth shut!" said Sadhu
Vaswani. How can you hear the sweet, subtle voice of God
if you do not keep silent?

The Syrian monk, Isaac of Niniveh, said: "Many are
continually seeking, but *they* alone find Him, who remain
in continual silence ... If you love truth, be a lover of
silence. Silence, like the sunlight, will illuminate you in
God and deliver you from the phantoms of ignorance;
silence will unite you with God Himself."

God communicates with us in silence but this does not
mean that we can adopt any posture, any position we like
in prayer.

A preacher once found a man slouched on an easy chair, smoking a cigarette, legs crossed over each other on a stool before him, his eyes half-closed.

"You are immersed in deep thought, my friend," the preacher said to him.

The man took a deep puff of his cigarette before he replied, "Actually, Reverend, I'm praying."

The preacher was taken aback. "Tell me, friend," he said. "If the Lord is with you in His radiant presence, would you slouch before Him as you do now?"

"I imagine I wouldn't," drawled the man.

"In that case," said the preacher, "you cannot be praying now, as you say. You do not have the consciousness of His presence."

Reverence and devotion should be expressed in your attitude as well as your posture; for your heart and mind can only express what your body expresses.

As I said to you earlier, God gave man a body, mind, and five senses so that he may perceive the finite world and live in it. However, man is much more than body or mind; his true nature is the immortal Self, the *Atman*. It is only when body and mind are quietened and still, can he hope to know God and be in touch with Him. God is infinite joy, love, wisdom, bliss. He is the Absolute. And the first proof of His presence with you is peace — the peace that passeth, surpasseth understanding.

What are the qualities of a devotee who seeks to find

God's presence within?

The first, as Sri Ramakrishna tells us, is a sincere and deep yearning for God. It was the saint of Dakshineshwar who narrated to us the parable of the seeker who went to his guru and insisted on God-realisation. The guru took him to the river for a holy dip. When they were nearly neck-deep in water, the holy man grasped the seeker's head firmly and pushed it under water, and kept it there, until the man struggled desperately to release himself.

"Why do you resist my efforts?" the guru asked him.

"I was gasping for air!" cried the man. "I would have died if I hadn't managed to push your hands away!"

The guru smiled. 'The day you desire God as desperately as you desired air, the day you yearn for God with the same degree of longing and intensity – you will surely find Him!"

- Yearning must be followed by sincerity and dedication. Dedicate yourself to God first, and to the guru whom He has sent for you. When you seek God and the path of truth, God is sure to send you a guru who will guide you on the path. So serve the guru with loyalty and devotion, in order that He may inspire you to achieve God-realisation.

- As we proceed on the path, we must practise virtuous conduct. The spiritual qualities that we feel in the heart within must be manifested in our outward conduct, so that we may be an inspiration to other people.

- We must practise the virtue of humility, for it helps us to conquer the ego. As the ancient Hindu scriptures tell us 'When the false *I* shall die, then will I know who *I* really am.'

- The last and most important mark that distinguishes a true devotee is what I have been talking about all along — he never ever misses his daily appointment with God. You deceive yourself when you are too busy, too involved in your work to find time for God! The seeker must overcome this serious misconception before he can make progress on his chosen path.

Do not wait for bitter experiences, serious reversals of fortune, and major illnesses to afflict you before you decide to turn to God. Turn to Him in your period of prosperity and peace, put Him first in your life always!

It was William Penn who said, "In the rush and noise of life, as you have intervals, step home within yourself and be still. Wait upon God and feel His good presence; this will carry you evenly through your day's business."

In England, they have an ancient musical instrument called the Aeolian harp which they leave outside in the garden, or before an open window. The wind plays upon the strings of this instrument, producing unearthly, lovely music. When we seek our daily appointment with God, we too, become like the Aeolian harp, allowing God to play His Divine Music upon us. But remember, we can hear this exquisite music only in stillness and silence!

It is said that at the foot of a high cliff, under the windows of the Castle of Miramar, which was the residence of the Emperor Maximilian of Mexico, at a depth of a hundred feet in the Adriatic Sea, experts had designed an iron cage fixed to the rocks on the sea-floor. When this cage was discovered by divers, centuries later, they found some of the most magnificent pearls in existence. How had they come to be there, in the depths of the clear sea waters?

It was said that the pearls had belonged to an empress. Having been left unworn for a long time, they had lost their lustre and their splendour. Experts had declared that the only means by which they could be restored to their original brilliance was to submit them to a period of prolonged immersion in the depths of the sea, from where they had come in the first place. Lying in the crystal depths, they gradually regained all their lost beauty and splendour.

Our soul too, is a priceless pearl, unrivalled in its splendour and glory. If we wish to capture its lustre and magnificence, all we need to do is to allow it to repose in those blessed depths where it can retrieve its divine touch!

The Fifth Commandment:
'Whatever Thou Doest, Do It for the Love of God'

In one of the most beautiful *slokas* of the *Bhagavad Gita*, the Lord tells Arjuna:

> 'Whatever thou doest, whatever thou eatest, whatever thou offerest, whatever thou givest away, whatever austerities thou dost practice — let it all be done, O Arjuna, as an offering unto Me.'
>
> IX: 27

Whatever you do, do it not to please men, but to be blessed by the Lord. Indeed the joy of life is known only to him who acts not for the purpose of gain or fame, but to reflect the Life Divine. Indeed, as Sadhu Vaswani said, to act this way, to walk this way is to be like the little child who thinks only of his mother. Like the little child, we too, must think only of our Divine Mother. Thus the teaching given in the holy books of Tibet is, "Be not distracted!"

Sri Krishna makes it clear to us that the way of work, the way of activity, *karma marga*, starts with duty and ends on a note of adoration of the Eternal, of worship of the Lord. In other words, dedicated work is worship.

Alas, the way of the world is different! When I am given any work to do, my first question is: 'What do I get out of it?' This is the attitude that we must overcome. Don't think of wages; don't think of the reward; think of offering your work at the lotus-feet of the Lord, and you will be richly blessed! Work not for wages — work for the love of God! *Karma Yoga* entails that you develop the attitude of worship to God through the duty and work that you perform.

For the spiritually evolved, all actions become worship of God. Until we reach that stage, we need to promote selflessness in all our actions. Think of others; think of all that you can do to help and serve others. Utilize your God-given gifts and talents to benefit others. When this attitude grows, you will find it easy to sacrifice all your actions, all your labour to God. This is the true spirit of *Karma Yoga* — the attitude that offers every action as a form of worship to the Lord. The lowliest among us is free to approach the Lord in this fashion. Even the simplest offering is acceptable to Him, provided it is made with love and devotion.

This is what Sadhu Vaswani called 'the little way,' the way to the life beautiful. *Pattram, pushpam, phalam, toyam* — a leaf, a flower, a fruit, a little water — no matter how poor or simple your offering, it is acceptable to Sri Krishna provided it comes from an earnest soul with a sincere longing. The Lord does not ask all of us for great things. Little things are enough; in little things, remember Him each day — for every trifle, every moment, every raindrop, every blade of grass, and every ray of the sun reflect Eternity, His power and grace.

'He who offereth to Me with devotion a leaf, a
flower, a fruit or water, that gift of love I accept
as offering of the pure of heart.

IX: 26

Be dedicated to the service of God! Consecrate to Him all
your acts. Let all the common tasks of daily life be your
worship to God; let them be an expression of your love for
God. But remember, not your words, but your *deeds*, should
be dedicated to Him! This is exactly what Sadhu Vaswani
meant when he exhorted us: "religion? Let us *talk* of it less,
practise more!'

When you dedicate all your actions to God, when you root
your life in the Lord's presence, you will find your life
transformed. It is not a question of degree or quantity or
effort that makes the difference – it is the devotion, the
cheerfulness, the enthusiasm, and the selflessness that
makes our offering acceptable to God.

In one of his immortal *dohas*, Sant Kabir tells us:

'The lane of love is so narrow that it cannot contain two.

If I am, He is not;
if He is, I am not.'

The love of the Lord should supersede all other loves, all
other desires of life. If we clamour after riches and power,
our soul cannot advance; indeed, the doors of heaven
cannot open for us. But selfless love and devotion will
form a ladder that will take us straight to the world where
the Lord resides!

I wonder if you have heard of the story of the milkmaid

who was selling milk. Each buyer came up to her, paid her an anna, and obtained a measure of milk, carefully poured out — not more, not less. But when the young man whom she loved came to buy milk, it was a different story! Money and measure were both forgotten. Her eyes shone, her heart leapt with joy, her whole countenance sparkled as she poured out measure after measure of milk into his bowl. Her mother, who was keeping an eye on the girl, was horrified. She began to scold the girl for giving away, or rather, throwing away, good milk in this fashion.

"Mother!" cried the girl, "how can I keep account with the one I love?"

That, of course, is earthly love. Think then of divine love: God too, will forget all our 'accounts' if we offer our true love to Him.

This is the promise made to us in the *Gita*. God condemns no one, favours no one. He is the same to all living creatures. But those who worship Him with faith and love are special to Him. They who offer Him their love, in turn win His love:

> 'I am the same to all beings. To Me there is none
> hateful nor dear. But those who worship Me with
> devotion, they are in Me, and I also am in them.'
>
>   IX: 29

Sinners need not despair, for in them too, is the Sinless One; the Lord pursues them, like the 'Hound of Heaven'! And when the sinner turns to God with a single heart, and resolves to sin no more, he grows in spiritual strength and vision.

'Even if a man, deep-sunk in sin, worships Me
with single heart, he, too, must be reckoned as
righteous, for he hath rightly resolved.'

IX: 30

Through *bhakti* (devotion), through *Krishna arpanam*
(offering our all to the Lord), everyone can attain Him.
For He belongs to all. His love is open to all men and
women, all seekers, all aspirants who turn to Him. The way
is clear: the way is the path of utter surrender and pure
devotion.

'Fix thy mind on Me; be devoted to Me; worship
Me; bow down to Me. Thus having controlled
thyself, and making Me thy goal supreme, thou
shalt come unto Me.'

IX: 34

Can there be a greater assurance than this? Can there be a
better option for struggling human souls caught in the
wheel of birth and death? "Thou shalt come unto Me!"
the Lord promises us. By giving your whole heart to Him,
by loving and adoring Him, by worshipping Him always,
we will find Him – the Lord of our life and destiny!

Therefore let us resolve, right away, to live and work for
the love of God, and for that alone! We do not know how
many days yet remain to us. We may be called away any
time. We live in a world of uncertainty, we live the kind of
life in which the only certainty is that we shall all die one
day! Sadhu Vaswani spoke of human life, life on earth as a
volcano which might erupt any time. Therefore, let us
devote our life to God. Whatever we do, let us do it for
the love of God.

Raja Yoga tells us of five *kleshas* (afflictions) that affect us:

- *Avidya* – ignorance
- *Asmita* – egoism
- *Raga* – attachment
- *Dwesha* – hatred
- *Abhinivesha* – clinging or attachment.

I find people are often confused about the idea of true detachment. Detachment does not mean neglect of your loved ones. It means that you withdraw your focus from the world and concentrate it on God. Narrow, selfish love then gives place to a more profound, universal, selfless love – you begin to love and serve God, in loving and serving others.

When we dedicate all our actions to the Lord, we grow in the spirit of perfection. As I said, there are a hundred and one ways of doing the same thing – even a simple thing like laying a table, driving a car or peeling vegetables! There are many ways of doing these things, but there is one way which is *the best*. We have to do it in the very best way possible, because it is our offering at the lotus-feet of the Lord – nothing less will do for Him.

You may be a professor teaching a class of students in a college or a university; you may be a doctor treating patients in a clinic or a hospital; you may be cooking for five or ten or a hundred people; you may be serving food; you may be sweeping, cleaning, or washing dishes; you may be an office assistant or labourer. Whatever you do, give it your best; do it in the best way possible, for that is your offering to the Lord! Therefore, work not for wages! Work for the love of God! Work for the love of suffering humanity – for these are one and the same.

Alas, people work only for wages today. "What is in it for me?" "What do I get for this?" they want to know. They have forgotten what it is to work with joy, what it is to make their work a source of delight. No wonder then, that to many people today, work has become a cause of so much boredom and frustration! Work for the sheer joy of work! Work for the love of God! Many of you will turn around and ask me, "But what about our wages? How can anyone live without wages in this world of growing needs? What about our families who depend on us?"

So let me tell you, that wages and work go together. They are but two sides of the same coin. Whether you work for wages or otherwise, wages are sure to fall into your lap. What I stress is this: it is your attitude to work that counts! Those of us who work only for wages, will never experience real joy! But when you work with love, and make your work an offering to the Lord, you will find it a joy for ever!

A rich, young girl volunteered to serve the poor men and women in the Home for the Aged which was being run by her guru. On her very first day, she was sent to nurse an old woman who was on her deathbed. For four hours, she sat with the old woman, holding her hand, stroking her head, and offering comfort to her. When the old woman fell asleep at long last, the girl tiptoed away from the room, with a radiant face.

"What have you been doing?" one of her friends asked her.

"I have been holding God's hands," was the reply.

Tetsu-jen was a deeply devoted and committed Buddhist monk. It was his dearest wish to undertake the monumental task of translating and publishing the great Buddhist scriptures into the Japanese language. He was convinced that this was the only way by which the Buddhist religion could reach the masses. He knew that the project would entail great expenditure. But with undaunted spirit, he set up a public fund and zealously began to collect the money required. At the end of ten long years, when he had enough money to start his task, a terrible flood ravaged the district where he lived. Spontaneously, Tetsu-jen gave away the entire fund to be spent in the service of the victims of the flood.

However, he was not going to abandon his original mission. He started afresh with his collections which, again, took another ten years. This time too, another calamity struck the people, and Tetsu-jen gave away his huge collection to help the victims. But Tetsu-jen was one of those rare people who never, never, never gave up! He started a collection for the third time, and took more than a decade to reach his target.

Now, at long last, the Buddhist scriptures were available to the Japanese people in their own language. They fondly called the publication, 'The Third Impression', for the previous two 'editions' had actually been scriptures in action!

As for Tetsu-jen, he was a true *karma yogi* who had done whatever he had done in the spirit of utter devotion to the Lord!

When we dedicate our actions to the Lord, when we begin to do all we do in the spirit of love and devotion to the Lord, we see the Lord everywhere! It was Swami Vivekananda who said: "Serve the Lord who comes in the shape of the lunatic, the leper, and the sinner."

When Ramana Maharishi's following began to increase, it angered his antagonists who wished to discredit him.

"You are a hoax and a fraud," they said to him.

"You claim to see God and converse with Him. If this be true, we demand that you show your God to us!"

"Otherwise," one of them added threateningly, "we will dispatch you to His presence."

Ramana Maharishi was calm and collected. He said to them, "Come with me tomorrow morning, I will show God to you."

The next day, he led the people to a dark and neglected part of the woods, where a dilapidated hut stood. He went inside the hut and told them to follow him. Inside the hut, on a pair of rickety cots, a couple afflicted with leprosy was lying helplessly. The maharishi's enemies withdrew hastily and watched from a distance, as the great sage washed and bandaged the wounds, and made the old couple as comfortable as he could. He then offered food to them, and spent some time talking to them. All this took more than three hours.

He then said to his enemies, "I see God in them. I talk to Him and I serve Him through them." His antagonists were ashamed. They bowed down and apologised to him.

Indeed, to serve the sick and the lowly is the noblest duty one can perform in this world, for such service is the highest manifestation of humanity. Again, it was Swami Vivekananda who said, "Man is nearest to God when he does good to others."

We are told that in his youth, Sant Tulsidas was passionately fond of his newly-wed wife. Such was the intensity of his love for her that he could not bear to be separated from her even for an instant. Once, she had to be away for a few days, but she was recalled soon after she left, because Tulsidas had fallen ill after her departure. From then on she resolved never to go anywhere without him. But there arose an occasion when she had to visit her parents' home, which was a few miles away, in a village across the river. She went, and Tulsidas somehow managed to pass the day without her. But when dusk fell, he felt so lonely and lovelorn that he decided to go to his wife's village on foot. By the time he reached the riverbank, it was pitch dark. The river was in spate, its swirling, muddy waters flowing with a loud, rushing noise. Naturally, the boatmen refused to ferry passengers across, even at four or five times the normal cost.

"You can keep your money," they said to him. "We value our lives far more!"

Tulsidas was not prepared to go back. Desperately, he looked around for a floating barrel or log which he could latch on to, and cross the river somehow. How was such a handy object to be found on a night like that? So he decided to swim across the flooded river. Barely was he halfway across, when the waters began to overpower him. As he struggled to keep afloat, something hit him – an object floating down the river. He clung on to it tightly and managed to cross the river, only to discover that it was a dead body!

Unfazed, he walked barefoot to his father-in-law's house, where everybody had gone to sleep, with the doors and windows shut tight. Frustrated and exhausted, he sank down below the lighted window of his wife's second-storey bedroom. He had to get to her somehow or the other! As he sat there, wondering how he could manage to clamber up to the second floor, something fell down from the second floor window: it seemed to be a sort of rope! Delighted at his happy chance, he grabbed hold of the rope and climbed up to his wife's room!

Ecstatically he embraced her and thanked her for letting the rope down to help him.

"What rope?" she asked mystified.

"The rope I climbed up with," he said, pointing to the window.

They both looked out and she saw to her horror that it was a long, fat snake, which he, in his blind infatuation, had taken for a rope! Laughing and crying at the same time, he told her of his adventure – how he had caught hold of a dead body to cross the river.

Overcome with emotion, his wife said to him, "O my dear husband! How intense and powerful is your love for me – a mere creature of flesh and blood! If only you had even one-tenth of this love and longing for the Lord, what would He not do for you! Why, He would have opened the gates of heaven to receive you into His presence! Alas, what can I offer you, but this perishable body? I beg you to turn your love towards the Lord, so that both of us may be liberated from the bonds of our *karma!*"

In a blinding vision, Tulsidas saw the profound truth that lay behind his wife's words. His life was transformed at that very moment! He fell at the feet of his wife, a young, innocent, simple village girl. "You have shown me the light, you have shown me the way!" he wept. "You are not just my spouse, but my guru."

He took leave of his wife, never to see her again.

God blessed Tulsidas with His special grace, when the saint's heart and soul turned to Him in love. As you all know, Tulsidas composed the Hindi version of the *Ramayana*, which is still sung with deep devotion in the villages of Northern India. Before we aspire to submit our will to the Divine Will, it is necessary that the ego should be conquered.

Ego — the *Guru Granth Sahib* calls it the *houmai* ; the Islamic mystics call it the *ananiat* — it is the consciousness of one's existence as separate from God's. This gives rise to *ahankara* — the pride of *I, me, and mine*. This in turn, is the cause of human bondage to the wheel of *karma*.

The I-me-mine syndrome feeds and waters the instinct of possession. When we wish to possess more and more, make everything 'ours', there is strife, greed, competition, and violence. And the deadly sins of envy, jealousy, lust, greed, and anger are aroused in our hearts.

Our great saints and sages tell us that, once upon a time, our souls dwelt in bliss, in the land of truth, the ocean of light — *Sach Khand*. This was the state of oneness with the Divine, with *Brahman*. But as the soul departed from *Sach Khand*, it sang the song of separation — *'Soham* — I am that'. In *Sach Khand* there was no 'I', no 'That' — it was all one. But in the *Soham Desh*, the great separation began.

The *Masnavi* of Maulana Rumi begins thus:

> 'Hark! What a sad story tells the flute!
> It deplores its sorrowful separation.
> Its plaintive notes bemoan that
> Since the day it was separated from me forever,
> It has done nothing but sigh and weep.

The soul too, weeps, for its 'separation' from the One has been the cause of all its misery, pain, and suffering.

You were *'That'* when 'you' were not! Your 'being', has taken you away from the One, made you the slave of desire, and forged iron fetters out of your own ego to bind you to this earth! Therefore, the great sufi mystics tell us, 'Egoism is opposed to the Holy Name; the two cannot dwell in the same house.' Cast the ego out, and cry to the Lord, "O Lord, I desire Thee and Thee alone!" When pride and vainglory drop away, then one is face to face with the Supreme Self, and naught abides except His love!

There is a beautiful parable that emphasizes the illusory, restricting nature of human attachment. A king had a pet falcon which he loved dearly. Every day he took the hawk with him as he went out for a ride, or went to the forest to hunt. In the forest, the falcon saw the cottage of an old woman, and peered inside out of curiosity. He found a cosy room with a glowing fire in the oven.

'Come, come, sweet bird,' the woman called lovingly, offering him tasty morsels to eat, as he perched on her window.

It became the habit of the falcon to pay a visit to the old woman every day. How wonderful it would be to live with her in the cosy cottage, he thought to himself. One day, he ventured inside the hut, determined to enjoy its warmth all the more. The moment he went in, the old woman seized him firmly and clipped away the feathers that enabled him to fly and soar.

"I love you dearly," she cooed in the bird's ear. 'I want you to myself. Therefore, I shall imprison you here in this little hut, and I shall never ever let you go!'

And so the falcon was caged, imprisoned; he lost his freedom to fly and soar – all in the name of love! When love is tainted by attachment, it only creates bondage! Deeper love for God frees you from attachments. Such a love liberates you!

Long ago, a poor juggler called Francis lived in Paris. His tricks and his jugglery delighted the children and the adults who flocked to see his show. When he took his hat around at the end of each show, people would throw silver coins into it and applaud him. Francis would then go to the nearby cathedral, offer a coin or two as his contribution, and thank the Lord for providing him with his daily bread.

Once, as he stepped into the church after his morning performance, he saw a congregation of senior monks kneeling and praying aloud. As he heard their sonorous Latin prayers, his pure and simple heart overflowed with devotion. With tear-filled eyes, he thought to himself, "Alas, how simple and foolish I am, that I do not even know these prayers! How can I ever hope to please God?' Suddenly an idea flashed across his mind. He waited patiently until the litany was over, and the monks had left the church. Then he closed the doors of the church and took out his bag of plates, knives, and assorted articles, and began his special show for the Lord. After all, people young and old had been delighted with his jugglery. Would not God too, be pleased with his 'bag of tricks'?

And so plates and glasses and knives began to fly in perfect order before the altar. Flat saucers danced merrily on thin sticks; cups and spoons followed each other in a perfect circle. Francis was putting up the best performance that he was capable of.

One of the monks, who happened to come to the church, was astonished to find the doors locked. Peeping through the keyhole, he was taken aback by the strange sight that met his eyes: Francis was standing on his head before the altar, throwing up two lead balls into the air with his feet, while he moved round and round on the floor. And he was exclaiming, "How is that God?" "How do You like this?' and "Does this please You?"

The monk was breathless with rage. How dared this pathetic little juggler treat the sacred premises of the cathedral like a fair ground? What would be the suitable way to punish him and teach him the lesson of his life? But before he could devise a suitable punishment in his mind, the monk was blinded by a flash of brilliant blue light that appeared before the altar. As he continued his scrutiny through the keyhole, he saw the Lord appear before Francis and smile His blessing on him! In rapture, the monk pushed open the door of the cathedral, but the vision had vanished when he stepped in.

Has it not been said, "Blessed are the pure of heart"? And so the Lord's vision was granted to the humble juggler, whose only desire was to please Him.

The Sixth Commandment:
'Thou Shalt Seek the Lowest Place'

Thou shalt seek the lowest place! I wonder how many of us will abide by this commandment in this day and age when there is a scramble for power and greatness. Everyone is seeking the highest place! Governments are toppled; boardrooms have become battlegrounds; sons oust their fathers; coups are staged; fierce rivalry and competition prevail. Everyone wants greatness!

But the true student of the *Gita*, the devotee of the *Gita*, will always seek the lowest place. This has been the witness of the great ones of humanity, and Sri Krishna Himself demonstrates this wonderful ideal to us, by His own personal example.

Think of how Sri Krishna comes to the battleground of Kurukshetra – not as a leader, not as a general, not as the king of Dwarka, but as *Parthasarathi*, Partha's (Arjuna's) charioteer. He comes as the driver – as we would call Him today – of His dear, devoted disciple and friend, Arjuna.

Think of Jesus Christ. At the Last Supper, on the eve of His crucifixion, in the very last hours of His earth pilgrimage, He picks up a bowl of water and a towel, and

He washes and wipes the feet of His own disciples. He also tells them words which we would do very well to heed: 'He that would be the greatest among you, let him be a servant of all.'

This is the witness of the great ones — they seek the lowest place:

> 'He that is down need fear no fall
> He that is low no pride:
> He that is humble ever shall
> Have God to be his guide.'

These are the words of John Bunyan in his book, *Pilgrim's Progress*.

Think of Sadhu Vaswani. One day some of us were sitting in a group, allotting duties for the *Janmashtami langar* which was to be held a few days later. Sadhu Vaswani saw us and enquired as to what we were discussing.

"We are allotting duties to each one for the *langar*, Dada," we said to him.

"What duty are you giving me?" he demanded of us.

One of us said to him, "Dada, it will be wonderful if you could join us during the *langar*. Your 'duty' would be to remain seated at the entrance to the hall where *langar* is held, and to bless each one who enters to take his or her place in the hall. That would really make our day!"

'No,' said the Master. "I will take a different duty. I shall sweep the floor after each batch has eaten, to get the hall clean and ready to receive the next batch."

Sadhu Vaswani always sought the lowest place. The *Gita* tells us to walk the little way, to walk the way of humility. This is the way on which the grace of God will be poured upon us abundantly! God's grace is like holy water, and water, as you all know, seeks the lowest place. If you have occupied the lowest place, the grace of God will flood into your life, and you will not only be truly blessed, but you will also be a source of blessing to many! Holy men and sages tell us that humility is the true mark of the evolving soul. You may be assured that it is not easy to attain, for it involves the utter effacement of the ego.

Alas, for many of us, I'm afraid, the ego is unconquerable. Man has conquered space; man has conquered the sky; man has controlled even the courses of the rivers and the growth of the great forests, but man has not found it easy to control or conquer the ego.

It is the presence of unconscious *vasanas* (subtle desires) in the mind which give rise to ego. Most of our human interactions are based on the ego. In fact, for the vast majority of the people, their ego is their identity. When people are disgruntled or disappointed, their ego begins to rise like high fever. They try to assert themselves, to assert their identity. Little do they realise that ego only blocks the flow of energy and power into their lives. When ego becomes the source of your motivation and initiative, you can achieve little; but when the ego is subdued, the Supreme Self becomes the source of your advancement and initiative. This is what makes the best human achievements possible.

There are very many amusing stories told to us of Birbal, King Akbar's witty and wise minister. Akbar was very fond of Birbal, and Birbal was known for his outspokenness. This made many of the courtiers his enemies, and they planned to draw him away from the King's favours.

They began spreading the notion that the king was like God. They knew this would flatter the king's ego, for he was a man of vanity. They also knew that Birbal would never ever accept this notion, and that would surely make him get into the king's bad books. The king would want everyone to praise him and Birbal would fall from grace. The officers bowed and bent and knelt before the king and said to him, "To us, you are like God Himself. But Birbal does not agree with our view."

The king summoned Birbal and said to him, "I am told that you do not agree with the view of my courtiers, that I am like God to my subjects. Why is this so? Don't you have any respect for me?"

Birbal replied, "How can I agree with them, Your Majesty? In my view, you are greater than God!"

"How so?" asked Akbar, both surprised and delighted.

"It's this way, Your Majesty," Birbal explained: "So many of us make mistakes, commit serious errors which offend God. Yet He does not drive us out of the world, which is His kingdom. We live, we continue to offend Him, and He lets us off. As for you, if someone should do something to offend you, you have the power to banish him from your kingdom. Are you not greater than God?"

Akbar was a wise king. He understood very well his witty minister's implication – when a man develops his ego, he is apt to imagine that he is even greater than God!

How can we conquer the ego? This is only done through constant *sadhana* (discipline) and the complete integration of one's personality. When you have reached this state, you will find that the best in you finds expression your best qualities and talents are unfolded.

Take the example of a young woman who has been asked to compère a grand public function. If she tells herself, "I will show everyone how good I am! I will prove that I'm the best, and that nobody can do it as well as I can!" Then she is only feeding her ego and making her ego the source of her motivation. On the other hand, if she enjoys what she is doing and decides to give her best to the job at hand, she will find that she goes down very well with the audience. They will enjoy what she has to say and will extend their appreciation to her. For when your ego takes a back seat, you find that you are able to communicate better with people. True, out of ego, people achieve great things too, but they surely cannot reach out and touch the hearts of the people. Alas, for most of us in the modern age; complete relaxation of the ego is achieved only during the sleeping state. Ego is then set aside, *not* by a process of conscious effort, but by a biological, unconscious process. This is why we say, 'He/she is sleeping peacefully as a child.'

When you are able to set aside your ego by a conscious voluntary effort, through your own intuition and understanding, you have every reason to congratulate yourself, for you have taken the first step on the path of liberation and enlightenment. Of such a man, Chaitanya Mahaprabhu says:

'One who is humbler
Than a blade of grass
And yet, more enduring than a tree:
One who gives respect to those who lack it,
Such a devotee is fit to sing
The praises of the Lord at all times!'

Many distinguished scientists have said that, when man realises the vastness, the grandeur, and the immensity of the universe we live in, and our own insignificance in the universal scheme of things, it is impossible for us to feel egotistic and proud. Just think, at one time, the universe existed; time existed; creation existed; but the planet earth did not exist; the solar system did not exist; man did not exist; and, in course of time, a day will come when this earth will cease to exist; and the solar system would have disintegrated. And yet, time will live.

It is said that when Emperor Alexander lay on his deathbed, his mother was overpowered by grief. He then said to her, "Mother, do not weep. When I am dead and buried, come to the graveyard on a full moon night and just call out my name. I will talk to you."

Soon enough, Alexander passed away. On the first full moon night after his burial, his mother went to the graveyard where he was buried, and called out, "Alexander! Alexander, my son!"

To her shock and horror, a hundred voices called out from a hundred different graves, "There are a hundred Alexanders buried here. Which one do you want?"

Someone asked Mahatma Gandhi, "Why are you called

Mahatma, or great soul?"

Gandhiji replied, "Because I consider myself the least of human beings."

What he meant was that one had to take the lowest place possible, in order to become truly great in the eyes of God. Therefore Gandhiji always remained humble, always a student, always a servant of others.

"No man is an island," said the great poet John Donne. The concept of inter-dependence is what keeps the world moving. In such a world, we must learn to respect others, value their presence and contribution. Even a spiritual aspirant should not think that he does not need others.

There is a simple fable that illustrates this concept. A merchant was travelling to a distant town, accompanied by his horse and donkey. He himself rode the horse, while the donkey was laden with all the merchandise. The horse skipped along merrily, feeling very proud. The poor donkey was suffering from a chill, and could barely move with the heavy burden on his back. He cried out to the horse, "Dear brother, take a little burden off my back, just for today! Give me some relief from the pain I have to endure!"

The horse laughed haughtily and said, "You are just a donkey and it is *your* lot to carry burdens. As for me, I am the chosen beast of my master. How can I carry your burden?"

The donkey was so broken-hearted by this jeer that it fell down and died on the spot. Shocked by this, the merchant jumped off from the horse's back and tried to revive the donkey. When he realized that he could do nothing, he sighed sadly and loaded all the merchandise on to the horse's back. And then, feeling sorry for the poor donkey which had served him so faithfully, he decided that he would take it with him and give it a decent burial, instead of abandoning it there. So the dead donkey was also loaded on to the horse's back, and the merchant walked sadly beside the horse.

The horse was ashamed of itself and bitterly repented. "I wish I had taken a little burden from the donkey when he begged me to help him,' the horse thought. 'It would have saved his life, and I would have been spared this burden too!"

Let me warn you too, against false humility or superficial humility. I am sorry to say that people often assume false humility for a particular purpose. Thus, subordinates bow and scrape before their superiors. When you assume false humility for a selfish purpose, it is not really humility at all, but hypocrisy!

Akbar was eating lunch with Birbal one day. A delicious dish of aubergines (*baingan* or brinjal) was set before them. Akbar enjoyed the spicy dish and exclaimed with delight, "I tell you Birbal, the brinjal is the best among vegetables."

"Indeed, your Majesty,' agreed Birbal. 'This is why God has put a crown upon it!"

"How true!" Akbar exclaimed, and ate more of the dish.

The brinjal curry gave him severe indigestion due to overeating. The next day, he ate only a thin gruel for lunch.

And he said to Birbal, "I tell you Birbal, that brinjal is an evil vegetable. Why, it is practically indigestible!'

"That is exactly so, your Majesty," nodded Birbal solemnly. "This is why God drove a nail into its head and put thorns around it."

"Yesterday you said it had a crown on it. Today you say God put a nail into its head. What's wrong with you?" asked Akbar angrily.

"O King,' said Birbal. 'Remember I am your servant. I have to agree with everything you say. However, I am not a servant of the brinjal, and I can say whatever I like about it."

In fact, Birbal's 'humility' taught Akbar a valuable lesson – not to succumb to flattery. Even the greatest among us fall victims to the ego.

The *Mahabharata* tells us the story of how the Pandavas were taught valuable lessons in humility, which made them better human beings. Bhima learnt his lesson when Draupadi begged him to bring her a rare flower. She had been captivated by the fragrance of the flower, and wanted more like it. Eager to fulfill his beloved's every wish, Bhima set out to get the flower. As he crossed the rocky paths and thick forests at breakneck speed, Bhima approached a grove, where a huge monkey lay across his path.

"Get out of my way," he snarled at the creature. "I'm in a hurry, so don't keep me waiting."

The monkey opened its eyes and looked at him sleepily. "I am too old and tired to move', it said to Bhima. 'Why don't you just lift my tail and shift it to one side, so that you may pass me?"

Arrogantly, Bhima started to lift its tail with disdain, but to his utter shock and dismay, he could not even stir it! Gritting his teeth, summoning all his strength, he tried hard to push the tail away. He was now perspiring heavily, and his breath was gasping, but he could not budge the tail even an inch.

In an instant, Bhima realized that this was no ordinary old monkey, as he had assumed it to be. Filled with humility, he bowed down to the monkey and said, "Please reveal your true identity to me. I have learnt a valuable lesson from you today."

The 'old monkey' revealed himself to be none other than Hanuman, beloved of Sri Rama. He had come to meet Bhima, test his strength, and bestow his blessings upon him. When Hanuman embraced him and blessed him, Bhima felt a fresh energy, a new spirit, and immense strength flowing into his body – much stronger now than the inflated, egotistic personality which he had asserted a short while ago!

When the Kurukshetra war was over, Arjuna prepared to alight from his chariot. He was proud of his might and valour, which had been the chief factor in defeating the Kauravas. How many *astras*, how many celestial weapons had been directed against him! But he had bravely stood his ground against them. They could not even touch him. Now it was time to leave the battleground, and rest his weary limbs.

Before he alighted, Arjuna said to Sri Krishna, "Please alight now, Lord. You must be tired too!"

"After you, Arjuna," said Sri Krishna with a smile. "I am your *sarathi*. How can the driver alight before his passenger does? You must be the first to get off."

Delighted by the Lord's gracious reply, Arjuna descended from the chariot and prepared to hold the reins of the horses, so that Sri Krishna could alight. But to his surprise, Sri Krishna asked him to go away, and stand at a distance.

When Arjuna was at a safe distance, Sri Krishna alighted from the chariot. In a moment, the chariot was blown to pieces, disintegrating before their very eyes!

Arjuna realised that what had kept him alive and prevented his chariot from utter destruction was not his valour, but the Lord's presence. It was Sri Krishna's grace and power that had stopped all the celestial weapons hurled at Arjuna. If the Lord had alighted from the chariot first, Arjuna would have been blown to bits without His Divine Protection. This was why Sri Krishna had asked him to walk away before He Himself alighted from the chariot, thus making it defenceless and subject to the power of the various *astras* hurled against it!

Many great men of the modern world were men of simplicity and humility. Indeed, their humility served to set them apart and added to their greatness.

Michael Faraday, the great scientist, was a simple soul. His simple clothes and modest behaviour often concealed from others his superior intelligence and genius. Once, a government official wished to meet Faraday. He went to the Royal Society where Faraday often worked, and asked to see the great scientist. He was directed to the lab where Faraday used to conduct his experiments. When the visitor entered the lab, he found it empty except for an old man in an overall, who was washing bottles at a sink.

"Excuse me, are you an employee of the Royal Society?" the visitor asked him.

"Yes, I have served the Society for many years," said the old man. "What can I do for you?"

"Are you happy with the wages you get here?" the visitor persisted.

"I am content," smiled the old man.

"What's your name, by the way?"

"They call me Michael Faraday," came the reply.

The visitor was mortified. He had mistaken the great scientist for a security guard. How could a great man be so simple, he wondered. Or was he great *because* he was utterly simple?

Gandhiji too, surprised people by his simplicity and humility. One day, Richard Cregg, an American admirer of Gandhiji's, arrived at the Sabarmati Ashram to meet the Mahatma. He was told that Gandhiji was in the common dining hall. Cregg wondered if Gandhiji was having a meal and whether he would disturb him by calling on him then.

However, he found the dining hall practically deserted, and entered inside only to find the great-souled leader seated on the ground, peeling vegetables for the morning meal.

"Come in, come in," Gandhiji greeted the visitor cheerfully. "I'm sorry you find me occupied with my duty at the *ashram*, but I'm delighted to meet you! Welcome to Sabarmati Ashram!"

The American was overwhelmed by Gandhiji's utter simplicity. In a trice, he was sitting next to Gandhiji, helping him with the vegetables'

There is an episode in the *Ramayana* which illustrates the need for humility in the life of all aspirants. Hanuman had been chosen as Sri Rama's messenger to go in search of Sita. He had to cross the ocean to go to Sri Lanka. As he began his magnificent flight across the sea, the *devas* wished to put him to the test. Therefore they sent Surasa, the mother-goddess of the *Nagas* to confront him. She blocked Hanuman's path, standing before him in a gigantic form, her huge mouth gaping wide open.

"The *devas* have sent you to become food for me," she said to Hanuman. 'Therefore, I shall swallow you here and now.'

Hanuman recognised that the lady who stood before him was no evil demon. With great respect he said to her, "Dear Mother, I am now on Sri Rama's mission. It is of the utmost urgency that I should find Sita, and convey her whereabouts to Sri Rama and Sri Lakshmana. When this embassage is completed, I shall return to you and offer myself as food to you. But now, I plead with you to let me proceed without delay."

"No way!" Surasa proclaimed. "I have a boon from the gods that no one can get past me. Therefore, I command you, allow yourself to be swallowed by me at once!"

Hanuman realized that he needed to adopt a different strategy to overcome Surasa. He grew in size, so that he became too large to enter her mouth. Not to be put off, Surasa opened her mouth even wider. Hanuman increased his size further. Just as Surasa prepared to open her mouth wider, Hanuman suddenly shrunk himself to the size of a small mosquito. He quickly entered Surasa's mouth and came out in a trice. Then he said to her, "Dear Mother! I have fulfilled your intention by entering your mouth and coming out. Now bless me and allow me to proceed on *Rama-karya!*"

Delighted by Hanuman's shrewd handling of the situation, Surasa assumed her habitual form and blessed him. "May you succeed in your divine mission!" she said to him.

This beautiful incident symbolizes a great truth. When we are confronted by problems and obstacles on the spiritual path, we must adopt the practice of the virtue of humility. This will help us uncover our own hidden spiritual potential, and surmount the obstacles on the path of liberation.

It was Ramana Maharishi who said, "In humility we gain, in arrogance we lose."

A cart laden with sugar had capsized on a highway passing through a forest. The road was strewn with sugar.

Hundreds of thousands of ants were busy swarming over the road. Each ant was carrying as much as he could, which was no more than a microscopic quantity of sugar. But they carried their sweet burden diligently and enthusiastically, and moved along in their ordered, disciplined manner, to and from their destination. It was a tiny colony, busily and fruitfully engaged in their task. Suddenly, there was a great commotion, as a huge elephant strode in. He saw the sugar strewn on the road, and decided to treat himself to a dessert. Arrogantly, he placed his trunk on the ground and sucked in a great quantity of sugar.

It was horrible! He spat out whatever he had sucked; for, along with the sugar, he had also taken in a great quantity of dust and other impurities from the road, and the sweetness of the sugar was hardly noticeable. The humility and the smallness of the ants were their gain as well as their strength.

Truly, we lose out on a lot of things due to our ego and arrogance, and our own inflated idea of who we are, and what is 'owed' to us!

The *Panchatantra* tells us the tale of the lion who so terrorized the jungle, that the creatures living there offered themselves as food for him. Each day, one creature would go to him, to be devoured as his meal. At least this would spare harassment to the other creatures. One day, it was the turn of a rabbit. Now, the rabbit was clever, and decided to teach the lion a lesson. Deliberately, he went late, and found the lion hopping mad with hunger and impatience.

"Why are you late?" he growled in anger.

"I'm so sorry," squealed the rabbit. "I was stopped on the way by another lion, who said he wanted to eat me. I had to evade him before I came to you."

"Another lion?" roared the cruel lion. "How could it be? *I* am the king of this forest, and there is no place for *another* lion here!"

"Well, he is here," said the rabbit, and added, "He is bigger than you, too!"

"Show this lion to me!" roared the angry beast.

The clever rabbit led him to a deep, dark well and told him to peer inside. The foolish lion peered and saw his own reflection. Blinded by rage and passion, he pounced into the well and was drowned to death, freeing the creatures of the forest from his reign of terror. The lion's ego was his undoing. He could not bear the idea of another lion, his equal in the forest. His pride and arrogance blinded him, leading to his fall.

Sanatan Goswami was a devotee and follower of Sri Chaitanya Mahaprabhu. He lived with his followers and his devoted nephew, Jiva Goswami, at the holy Brindavan near Mathura. The Goswamis were great scholars, well-versed in the scriptures. One day, a famous pundit from Bengal arrived at the *ashram* of the Goswamis. He was an exponent of *tarka shastra*, the art of expounding in debate, the great truths of religion and philosophy. He had proved his merit as a sterling debater at several institutions, courts, *gurukuls* and *ashramas*. He carried with him certificates, trophies, and medals awarded to him, and challenged local scholars to enter the debating arena with him, so that he could prove himself superior to all. The very mention of his name filled the hearts of scholars with terror, and they conceded victory to him, not being ready to enter his challenge. He forced them to issue 'certificates of conquest' acknowledging his superiority.

Having arrived at Brindavan, he collected many such certificates of conquest from the scholars there, and enquired about the rest. They said to him, 'Sanatan Goswami and his nephew Jiva Goswami are the greatest scholars here. If you collect their acknowledgements, then all other pundits in Brindavan will follow suit.'

The pundit went straight to Sanatan Goswami. He displayed his trophies and certificates and explained the purpose of the visit.

"Are you prepared to issue a certificate of conquest or shall we both enter into a debate?" he demanded imperiously.

"There is no need for that," smiled Sanatan Goswami. "Your several trophies and the wisdom shining in your eyes are proof enough of your scholarship. I shall sign a certificate for you."

Having collected the certificate, the pundit inquired the whereabouts of Jiva Goswami, and was told he was not in the *ashram* at that time. Therefore he left in his palanquin, very satisfied with his achievement.

On the way, he was told by one of his followers that Jiva Goswami was approaching them from the opposite direction. The pundit jumped out of his palanquin and eagerly confronted Jiva. He displayed his certificates and trophies, and proudly waved before his eyes the latest certificate he had collected from Sanatan Goswami.

"Your uncle and guru has conceded defeat to me," he announced proudly. "I suggest you do the same."

Jiva was incensed at what he perceived to be an insult to his Gurudeva "Sir," he said, "I am not prepared to concede defeat. I suggest that you and I have a debate here and now."

They went to a nearby temple, and the debate began before a small crowd of local devotees and the pundit's disciples. Within half an hour, Jiva had demolished the pundit's arguments, demonstrating his superior skill and knowledge. He took away the pundit's certificates and tore them up, and told him never to show his face ever again in Brindavan. The pundit fled from the scene of his disgrace, having learnt a lesson which he would not forget in the near future.

Jiva returned to the *ashram* and narrated his exploits to his uncle. Sanatan Goswami listened to him wordlessly, and then began to pack a bag, and proceeded to leave the *ashram*. Jiva begged him to explain what was wrong.

"I have failed as a guru and your uncle, because I have been unable to impart to you, the virtue of humility. I think I am therefore unfit to remain here."

Jiva Goswami begged him for forgiveness.

The guru continued, "What did you achieve by heaping shame and disgrace on a scholar? What did I lose by signing a certificate for him? A spiritually evolved person should be above such things. He would never insult or give offence to anyone. It is only he who seeks the lowest place and accepts the lowest place who is beloved of the Lord."

Of what are we proud, I often ask myself. Power, wealth, fame, youth, beauty – all, all are transient. As great ones have continually demonstrated, even world conquerors leave this earth empty-handed.

Sant Dadu Dayal tells us:

> 'When one has abandoned all pride of birth:
> when vainglory has dropped away, then, only
> then, is one face to face with the Creator.'

Of the great emperor, Shah Jahan, we are told, that during a hot summer night, as he was resting in his private apartments, he was suddenly overcome by thirst. He clapped his hands, as was his wont, to call a servant to attend to him, but it so happened that none of the palace servants happened to be nearby.

The emperor arose from his royal couch and went to the pitcher of water which was always kept near his bed. The silver jug was absolutely empty. By now, the emperor was parched with thirst. He went out into the enclosed courtyard which adjoined his private chamber, for he knew there was a well there, from which he could draw water. As he was not used to this task, he hurt himself badly on the crank of the pulley, when he tried to haul the container of water towards himself. The pain in his hand was quite sudden and severe, and he actually cried out in agony. At that moment, the thought flashed across his mind that here he was, an emperor — but he was so inept that he could not even draw water from the well to slake his own thirst.

"O beloved Lord!" he exclaimed. "I thank you for this experience. How foolish and clumsy I am, and yet, in Thy inscrutable grace, Thou hast made me an emperor!"

It was the great Sufi saint Rumi, who said: "When thou thyself shall come to be, then the beloved Lord will thou find. Therefore, O wise man, try to lose thyself, and feel humility." He adds, for further emphasis, "Egoism and self-will are opposed to the Holy Name; the two cannot dwell in the same house. None can serve the Lord without humility; the self-willed mind is worthless."

Humility does not consist in hiding our talents and virtues, or in thinking of ourselves as being worse than we really are; but in realizing that all that we are, and all that we have, are freely given to us by God. Therefore, as Thomas à Kempis tells us, one of the best ways to acquire humility is to fix the following maxim in our mind: "One is worth what he is worth in the eyes of God."

I remember vividly an incident which occurred when I was a child. I was doing my geography homework one evening when a family friend walked into our house. His conversation was always loud. That day he began to boast about the row of buildings which he owned in Karachi.

"They occupy almost the whole street!" he asserted.

In my innocence and simplicity I went up to him with my atlas and said, "Uncle, will you be kind enough to point out your row of buildings on this map of India?"

Our friend was nonplussed. Karachi was indicated on the map by just a dot. How on earth could he mark out his row of buildings on that dot?

Guru Gobind Singh tells us:

> 'Emperors before whom strong, armed kings did meekly bow their heads in countless numbers:
> Who possessed great elephants with golden trappings, proud and painted with brilliant colors:
> Millions of horses swifter than the wind which bounded o'er the world:
> What mattered it how mighty were these emperors?
> All at the last went hence with nothing, bare of foot.'

Guru Nanak, one day, called his son and said to him, "Today I have forgotten to clean the *goshala* (cowshed). Will you please clean it?"

The guru's son was not very pleased at his father's request. Cleaning the *goshala* was a messy business, and he did not want to do it. Besides, he had just taken a bath, and was wearing good, clean clothes which he did not wish to dirty. Aloud, he said to his father, "I am about to go to the temple for morning worship. I have to be neat and clean when I go there. Please excuse me from this duty."

The guru called his dear disciple, Angad, and repeated the request to him. He noticed that Angad too, had bathed and was ready to leave for the temple. But he immediately acceded to the guru's request and went to clean the *goshala*. When he had done this job thoroughly well, he took his bath once more, changed into fresh clothes and went to the temple for the worship.

Shortly afterwards, before a large congregation of his followers, Guru Nanak declared Angad as his successor. This came as a great surprise to many people; for according to tradition, the son always succeeds his father as chief priest.

A few students came to the guru and asked him, "Gurudev, why did you break the tradition and appoint Angad as your successor?"

The guru merely smiled in reply. Guru Angad had sought the lowest place – and was awarded the highest honour!

Graciousness and humility are instinctive to great people. In fact their personalities are only further enhanced, even adorned, by this special quality.

At a grand banquet where President and Mrs. Roosevelt were present, an old man approached Mrs. Roosevelt and greeted her respectfully. She returned the greeting graciously and spoke to him for some time.

Emboldened by her courteous behaviour, the old man said to her, "Madam, may I bring my wife to you? She thinks the world of you, and she will be delighted to have the opportunity to meet you in person!"

"May I ask you how old your wife is, Sir?"

"She is about eighty-two, ma'am," the old man replied. "She is seated just outside this hall, in the ante-room. Shall I bring her here to meet you?"

"No, Sir," smiled Mrs. Roosevelt. "I should go and see her. You see, I'm fifteen years younger than your wife, and it is I who should go to see her, not the other way round!"

Truly, Mrs. Roosevelt was adorned by her humility!

When the distinguished scientist, Sir Isaac Newton lay on his deathbed, a friend said to him, "It must be a source of great pride and gratification to you to know that you have managed to penetrate to the depth of nature's wonderful laws."

"Far from feeling proud," Newton said to him, "I feel like a little child who has found a few bright coloured shells and pebbles, while the vast ocean of truth stretches unknown and unexplored before him!"

All men of true learning are truly humble. There is a couplet found in an ancient text which tells us: "How does a great man resemble a mango tree? Both bend low with their achievements."

Newton was just such a man who recognized that what he had achieved, was largely due to the pioneering efforts of his predecessors, who had, as it were, prepared the ground for his path-breaking work. He once compared himself to a little boy who had climbed up on to the shoulders of a giant, and could see even further, beyond the giant's vision.

A grateful society carved an epitaph for him in the following words, penned by Alexander Pope:

'Nature and nature's laws lay hid in night:
God said, "Let Newton be!" and all was light.'

And yet this great scientist chose to describe himself as a little boy gathering pebbles on the seashore; or a boy who had climbed on to the shoulders of a giant so that he could look further.

Pierre La Place, the eminent French astronomer, also made invaluable contributions to science. When he died at the age of seventy-eight, he declared: "What we know is nothing: what we don't know is immense!"

Abraham Lincoln always shrank from official honours. When people addressed him as 'Mr. President,' he felt uncomfortable. He would refer to his office as "that place", and would speak of his term as president by saying, "Since I have been in this place ..."

When some old friends from his native state called on him and addressed him respectfully as 'Mr. President,' he begged them, "Now please call me Lincoln, and I assure you it will not be a breach of etiquette with me!"

It was John Ruskin who said, "The first test of a truly great man is his humility."

The great Chinese philosopher, Confucius, too, tells us that humility is the solid foundation of all virtues.

Our ancient Indian sages and poets also admired humility as the greatest virtue in man. To illustrate this, they compared a great man with a bountiful tree laden with fruit, which bows down with its load of fresh fruits.

Rahman was a famous Muslim poet who wrote lovely lyrics expressing *prem bhakti*. He also happened to be a very rich man who spent his great wealth not on his own personal luxuries, but for the benefit of the poor and needy. While he gave away alms to *sadhus* and *fakirs*, he always bowed his head low, and refused to look at them.

Noticing this, a friend asked him, "Why do you bow down your head while giving alms to the poor?"

"They praise me for my humble mite which, in reality, is that of the Almighty." replied Rahman. "I am only His agent, the instrument of His Divine Plan. Therefore I bow down my head in embarrassment, for I do not deserve their praise and thanks!"

The friend became speechless with admiration for Rahman's humility.

John Newton once said, "If two angels came down from heaven to execute a divine command, and one was appointed to sweep the streets, they would feel no inclination to change employments." Why not? Because each would be convinced that he was doing the Will of God, and that, however humble his allotted task, he was glorifying God by doing it well.

In the eyes of God, in His Divine Judgement, everything counts! And thus we read an amusing anecdote about St. Peter who once stood at the Pearly Gates of Heaven, reading the judgements that admitted the Blessed Souls to

God's presence. To a rich philanthropist who had spent much of his wealth on feeding the poor, he said, "I was hungry, and you gave me to eat. So enter the kingdom of the Lord."

To a man of service who had dug canals and wells, and installed hand-pumps in remote drought-prone villages, he said, 'I was thirsty, and you gave me to drink. So come in.'

In the line stood a poor clown who had worked in a circus and made people laugh. He trembled as he stepped before the gates of Heaven. With bowed head he waited for St. Peter's judgement. St. Peter smiled and said to him, 'I was sad and depressed, and you made me laugh. Enter the kingdom of Heaven.'

Sri Ramakrishna narrates to us the parable of the poor servant who once came to visit his master. Having entered the master's great house, he stood reverently in a corner holding something with great care, covered with a cloth.

"What is it that you have in your hand?" the master asked him graciously.

With great trepidation, the servant drew a small custard apple out of the cloth. He placed it deferentially before the master and said, "This is the first fruit of the tree I planted near my cottage some years ago. I would be deeply honoured if you accept it."

The master was a large-hearted man. He saw the loving devotion of the servant in the small custard apple placed before him. With great delight, he exclaimed, "What a fine fruit it is! It looks delicious!"

God looks into the heart of the devotee, not at his actions or his words. He is magnificent in His power and grandeur, but He responds to our love and devotion with grace and magnanimity.

There was a rich but miserly lady, who would never willingly part with even a paisa, or a rotten banana, to a beggar. However, she was determined to go to heaven after her death, and she kept praying for that purpose. One day, a hungry old ascetic came to her door and begged for food. She would give him nothing, as was her habit. But he sat down on the doorstep and refused to leave, unless she gave him something to eat. Unable to get rid of him, she threw a half-rotten carrot at him. Years passed by, and the call of death came to the old woman.

The God of Death stood before her and said to her, "Your life on earth is over, and I have come to take you to hell."

"But I wish to go to heaven," cried the lady. "I have prayed for it every day of my life!"

"Of what use is your prayer?" said the God of Death. "You have not done a single good deed in your life. How can you hope to go to the heaven?"

The old lady protested, "That's not true. I once gave a carrot to a hungry monk. If you want you can check your ledgers."

The God of Death checked his account and found that there was a single entry against her name. She had indeed given away a single carrot, and it entitled her to a few hours in heaven.

Almost at once, a carrot appeared before her. The God of Death ordered her to catch hold of it for it would lead her on to heaven. The old lady caught the end of the carrot, and it began ascending the sky. There was a hawker who was watching this, and eager to go to heaven, he caught hold of her feet and began to ascend with her. Another lady who saw this, held on to his feet and soon, there were six people hanging on to the tiny carrot, ascending to heaven.

When the old lady neared the gates of heaven, she looked down, and saw the other five people coming up with her. Her miserliness asserted itself, and she cried out, "Get off! Get off! This is *my* carrot, and *I alone* must enter heaven with it!" To push the others away, she let go off the carrot, and the whole bunch of them fell down upon the earth!

Surely, our ancient *rishis* were right when they said: "*I* and *mine* are the greatest obstacles on the Godward path."

Unfortunately, we cannot shake off the ego; we want the best, the highest for ourselves. We want more and more and we are never satisfied.

The Seventh Commandment:
Thou Shalt Rejoice in Everything That the Will of God Brings to Thee

There is a prayer that is very dear to me, which I pass on to my friends wherever I go. I do not know how many times I have repeated this beautiful prayer – to myself, and to others. With great joy, I repeat this prayer now, to you, my dear readers:

> '*Tum hi sab kuch janat pritam*
> *Teri ichha puran ho*
> *Sukh mein dukh mein mere pritam*
> *Teri ichha puran ho !*

> 'Thou knowest all, Beloved,
> Let Thy Will always be done!
> In joy and sorrow, Beloved,
> May Thy Will always be done!'

Such a beautiful and simple prayer – it contains a valuable and profound truth: that all that happens to us, happens as the result of the Divine Will! In every incident, every accident of life, there is a meaning of God's mercy. We may react negatively to certain events, we may misinterpret them, but they come to us from the spotless hands of the

Lord. How then can they bring us anything but good?

You may ask me: If that is indeed so, why is there so much suffering and misery in this world? Why are people so unhappy? Why do we face defeat, disillusion, and disappointment again and again? Why do good people suffer? Why do bad things happen to good people?

My answer has always been, and will always continue to be: The Lord knows what is best for us! He is too loving to punish, too wise to make a mistake.

I repeat: God is all love; God is all wisdom. He is our loving Father; He is our kind Mother. Which parent would ever like to harm his or her child?

Therefore, every experience He sends us, comes to teach us a valuable lesson that we need to learn. All of us are forced to confront what appear to be bitter experiences. Suddenly, a dear one is snatched away from our midst; suddenly, we fall ill and suffer pain, undergo surgery or hospitalisation; unexpectedly, some of us lose our jobs; suddenly, losses mount up in our business; suddenly, our circumstances change for the worse ...

Each one of these experiences comes to us as a *prasad* out of God's spotless hands! If we think they are harmful to our interests, it is only because we are short-sighted, and we have identified ourselves with the body.

The culmination of all human endeavours is absolute surrender to the Divine Will. Sri Krishna enunciates this doctrine in the *Gita*:

'Fix thy mind on Me; be devoted to Me; sacrifice
to Me; prostrate thyself before Me. So shalt
thou come to Me. I pledge thee My troth; thou
art dear to Me!

XVIII: 65

Mind, heart, sacrifice, reverence, all are required to be
directed to Sri Krishna.

'Abandoning all duties, come unto Me alone for
shelter. Grieve not! I shall liberate thee from all
sins!'

XVIII: 66

Here is indicated the supreme secret which Krishna
imparts to His dear disciple Arjuna. The school of Sri
Ramanuja regards this as the *charama sloka* – the final verse,
the summing up of the *Gita*.

Leave it to God! Believe in God! Trust Him completely!
Know that He will always do the very best for you!
Therefore, cooperate with His Will. Become a willing
instrument in the hands of God. In this connection, the
following suggestions may help you:

1. Greet difficulties with a smile, and meet trials and
    setbacks with love:

    Never forget that the Lord is ever with you –
    protecting you, guiding you, guarding you. In times of
    trial, feel the thrill of His protection. Whisper to
    yourself, "I am not alone. The Lord is holding me by
    the hand: He leads me on. I feel safe and secure!" The
    Lord never fails us! Therefore, let *us* not fail the Lord.
    Trust in Him to the breaking point. Surrender to His

Divine Will, and you will find that the breaking point does not come to you.

2. Let prayer become a habit with you:

Pray, pray, and continue to pray. So many of our prayers are unanswered because we give up praying. We become impatient and lose faith. We feel that, as God is not going to act for us, we must act for ourselves. What we forget is that God acts at the right time. If He has not yet acted, it only means that the right time has not yet come. This applies not only to our material requirements, but also to our mental and spiritual needs.

3. Pray for more and more faith:

He who has faith, has everything. For, as the wonderful proverb tells us, faith can indeed move mountains. The Bible also tells us the same thing: 'Everything is possible to him who believeth'. Therefore, pray for faith as a famished person prays for food, and a thirsty person for water. What is it to have faith? It is nothing but to accept God's plan for you, to surrender to the Will Divine. It is to feel sure that whatever God does is always for the best. It is to grow in the realisation that, when God seems to deny you, His own child, some good thing that you do desire, He designs to give you something better.

4. Be assured that the cure for all ills – physical, mental, spiritual – is contact with God:

From time to time, detach yourself from your surroundings and enter within. In silence, wait upon

God, conscious of His presence. From time to time, whenever and wherever possible, engage yourself in loving converse with God. Offer all your work to Him. Pray to Him for help and blessing, before beginning any work: and give gratitude to Him when it is over.

5. Accept whatever cometh to you:

Do not seek what is 'pleasant' to you; do not shun what is 'unpleasant'. Rejoice in everything that happens. All that has happened, all that is happening, and is yet to happen — all, all is for the best; so turn out all thoughts of fear and doubt and anxiety. Close the windows and doors of your mind against them, as you would against plague germs. Face each trial and tribulation with love and laughter. Meet every situation in life with the favourite prayer of St. Francis de Sales, the prayer which I am never tired of repeating, the prayer which I know to be the most effective formula for inner peace: 'Yes, Father! Yes, and always — yes!' He who lives thus knows what it is to feel the thrill of protection and safety, now and forever. No storm can upset him: no news can shock him. In the midst of the most furious gale, he is composed and calm as a safely anchored boat.

Such a one has controlled his passions. He has eliminated his Self and entered into a life of holiness and harmony — the life of true freedom, peace, and surrender, which is the birthright of every one of us, as children of God. He owns nothing, yet is rich beyond measure. He is attached to no one, yet all creatures — men and birds and animals — are his friends. He thinks of no one as an alien. All are his, his very own. He breathes out benedictions to all — rich and poor, saints and sinners, thieves and profligates, the forsaken and the forlorn ones. To all he gives the service of love, beholding in them the broken images of the Beloved.

God is our loving Father, our ever-protective, ever-caring Mother. He is always ready to answer our prayers, always ready to grant us all that is good for us. But our prayer should be for the right things.

Shambhu was a poor cobbler, known and loved in his village as an honest, hard-working, God-fearing man. He was the earnest devotee of Lord Vithobha of Pandharpur. As he toiled hard all day, mending old shoes or making new ones, his thoughts would constantly dwell on God. One day, the local zamindar passed with his entourage before Shambhu's hut. As he watched the zamindar's rich robes and glittering jewels, Shambhu was overcome by self-pity. "Look at the zamindar," he said to himself. "He owns twenty villages, has two thousand peasants working for him, and has enough money to buy himself a gold mine. Look at me! I work all day, cutting and sewing stubborn pieces of leather, and what do I get out of it? I can barely eke out a living! Why is God so unkind to me?"

His eyes turned to the idol of Lord Vithal kept in a little niche in the wall behind him. "My dear Lord," he said to his Vithobha, "you are my Almighty Father and my Loving Mother. You watch me toiling from dawn to dusk. Have you no pity on me? Can't you be so generous as to give me a comfortable house to live in, a field to grow *jowar*, and a little money to spend on my family? It's not much to ask you and it will make me so happy!"

That night, Lord Vithobha appeared in the zamindar's

dream and said to him, "The poor cobbler Shambhu is a pious devotee of mine. Give him a house to live in; transfer an acre of land in his name; and offer him a pot of gold coins. You will receive my blessings."

The zamindar promptly carried out the Lord's instructions, and Shambhu was beside himself with joy. His life was transformed, and his family were delighted. They moved into their new big house and began farming the fertile land that the zamindar had given to them. Shambhu buried the pot of gold coins in a corner of his garden, and felt that all his problems had been solved at one go.

However, his troubles had just begun. Distant relatives and greedy family friends began to flock to his house, pestering him for financial help. His wife started complaining that the house resembled a wayside inn. He himself began to feel insecure about his pot of gold. The thought that thieves might dig it up and take it away made him lose his sleep. And, as luck would have it, a severe drought made the crops fail that year.

Shambhu lost all peace and joy. He grew depressed and miserable. But he was wiser now. He stood before his beloved Vithobha and said, "My Lord, I realize now how foolish I was to ask you for a big house, land, and money. I find now that so far from adding to my happiness they have only robbed me of peace and contentment. You were right to place me in a situation of hard work and honest living. Give me back my old life, making and mending shoes. Henceforward, I shall do my work sincerely and leave the rest in Your safe hands. You, dear Father, know best! You know what is good for me!"

And so it was that an ancient Greek philosopher said to us: "God looks forth from the high watchtowers of His providence; He sees what suits each man, and applies to him that which suits him." Who are we to dispute Divine Providence?

Rabbi Burnam was once strolling with his disciples. He bent down and picked up a speck of sand, held it with reverence and then put it back exactly where he had found it. "He who does not believe that God wants this bit of sand to lie in this particular place, does not believe at all," he said. Indeed, what is Providence if not the care that God takes of all living things?

There is a beautiful story narrated by Sri Ramakrishna, which illustrates this spirit of devotion. There once lived a pious weaver whose every word, every thought, every action, was devoted to the Lord. He wove with the name of God on his lips. When someone asked him the price of cloth, he would reply: "By the Will of Sri Rama, the yarn costs eight annas; by the Will of Sri Rama, my labour is worth four annas; by the Will of Sri Rama I add a profit of two annas; therefore, by the Will of Sri Rama, this piece of cloth costs fourteen annas." Needless to say, he had several customers, who kept his business flourishing.

One night, unable to fall asleep, he sat outside his house, chanting the name of the Lord. A band of robbers entered the village, having planned to loot the house of a rich man. They required a coolie (labourer) to carry their loot, and they ordered the weaver to go with them. In his innocence, he followed them, uttering the name of the Lord. When they had looted the house, they brought two heavy bags full of gold and silver, and loaded them on to his back.

Just then, the security guards appointed by the king arrived on the scene, and an alarm was raised. Panic-stricken, the robbers fled from the scene. The poor weaver was caught with the stolen loot on his back, and promptly arrested and put in prison.

The next day, when the villagers learnt of what happened, they rose as one to defend the pious weaver. They went to the house of the magistrate and said to him, "Sir, this man would never have committed the crime he is accused of for we know he lives and works and breathes the name of God!"

The man was brought, and the magistrate said to him, "Now my good man, tell me exactly what happened last night."

"By the Will of Sri Rama I had had my dinner, but it was Sri Rama's Will that I could not sleep. So I sat outside the house, chanting His name. By Sri Rama's Will, a group of men came up and asked me to carry a load for them. In Sri Rama's name I consented. By the Will of Sri Rama, we went to a house, and by the Will of Sri Rama, they put a load on my back. At that very moment, the guards arrived, by the Will of Sri Rama. The robbers fled by the Lord's Will. I was arrested and put in prison, by His Will."

"This morning, I have been brought before your Highness, by the Will of Sri Rama. This is all I know."

The magistrate did not need to hear anything more. He ordered the weaver to be released at once.

"What happened?" his family and friends asked him in wonder.

"By the Will of Sri Rama, I was arrested. By the Will of Sri Rama, I was released," was his reply. He knew what it was to live in the Lord and submit to His Will!

Grow in Faith!

Sri Ramakrishna, speaking to his disciples, said again and again, "The man of faith is like a python He moves not in search of food, his food comes to him."

It was an enlightened singer of the spirit, who sang of God thus:

> 'O ye pilgrims on the path!
> Cast all thy cares upon the Lord
> And chant His name
> By day and by night
> And fill the earth
> With the fragrance of Heaven!
> He, the Lord of love
> Doth in love become
> A burden bearer
> Of His *bhaktas* all!'

What a beautiful conviction this — to rest in the belief that He will bear all our burdens! This conviction will not come to us by reading books or listening to lectures. It is not a matter of ratiocination or argumentation. It will not come by intellectual analysis or reasoning of the mind. It will come only by faith!

Faith belongs to those of us who have learnt to love. For, in love, we renounce our little 'ego', and so rise above the cares and worries of earthly existence. In love, we know that we belong to Him who takes care of us as a mother takes care of her only child. The way of faith is not always paved with roses. In its initial stages, it has its difficulties and dangers He who would walk the way of faith must be prepared to accept suffering and starvation, poverty and pain, and in the midst of it all, give gratitude to God.

The way of faith is not easy. Illness may come to you; death may stare you in the face; your dear ones will let you down when you need their support desperately. You will have to face storms of misunderstanding. Disappointments will crowd around you. Your friends may scoff at you, laugh behind your back, and call you a fool. Occasionally, they may even taunt you, "Where is your God?"

And, in the hour of your anguish and misery, you yourself may say, in the heart within, "I can bear it no longer! I am broken in body, mind, and spirit! In this big, wide world, there is *none* whom I can call my own. I feel forsaken as a beaten, battered boat on a stormy sea! Not this, the path for me!"

If you survive this period of despair and frustration – and believe me, you can do so through constant prayer and repetition of the name of God – you arrive at a stage of blessedness. Your struggles will be over. With you, it will no longer be a matter of hope or faith or trust – it will be a matter of knowledge. You begin to *know* that you are in God's hands and that He will provide for you at the right place, at the right time!

Swami Vivekananda was travelling aboard a steamer that was taking him to America to attend the World Congress of Religions. Although the ticket had been purchased for his voyage, no arrangements had been made for his stay in the United States. There would be no one to receive him on his arrival in that strange, new land. He did not know where he would go when he disembarked, nor where he would stay. However, he *did* know one thing for certain: that the Great Providence, who had always taken care of him, would not let him down in that distant land to which he was now being sent.

As the Swami stood on the deck communing with the Lord of love in the heart within, a fellow passenger came to greet him. The swami's radiant face and piercing eyes had fascinated the American, who was eager to get to know him.

"What takes you to America?" he asked Swamiji, when they had shaken hands and introduced themselves to each other.

"I go to attend the World Congress of Religions which is to be held in Chicago," the Swami replied.

"I am from Chicago," the man said. "May I know where you will stay when you are in Chicago?"

This was more than Swami Vivekananda knew. "I do not know," he said, adding, with his dazzling smile, "maybe, I shall stay at your place?"

The words were uttered in such childlike simplicity that they went right to the heart of this wealthy man from Chicago. Without a moment's hesitation, he said, "It will be a joy and privilege to have someone like you staying in my house. I shall endeavour to keep you as comfortable as I can!"

Many of us are willing and eager to lay our trust in God, but only up to a point. Our trust is partial because our experience keeps us tied down to men and material possessions. The body needs food day after day and so we must always have a stock of food in the house. Prices go up and scarcity may arise, so we hoard things which may not be easily available. We need so many other things which can be bought only with money and so we must have savings in the bank. The banks may crash so we buy stocks and shares and gold.

Alas, we forget that all these are unreliable – but there is One who abideth forever. He was, He is, and He always will be, for ever and ever more. He is the giver of all that is. He is the sustainer of all life. Out of Him is all that we see and all that we hold. And it is His Will that works in all the world and the galaxies of planets and stars. Well sang the Sindhi poet:

> 'Wondrous are Thy ways, O Lord!
> In the twinkling of an eye
> Thou dost reduce kings to beggars:
> And Thou dost lift up
> Wandering mendicants from the mud
> And place upon their heads
> Crowns studded with diamonds!'

When Antoinette Foligno left her home at dead of night, in quest of God, she left behind everything – her dresses and ornaments, her goods and possessions. But she took with herself a penny with which to buy bread on the morrow. As she moved on, she felt a heavy load on her heart. She heard a voice saying to her, "Antoinette! Dost thou trust a *penny* more than thou trustest thy God?"

Immediately, she threw away the penny on the roadside and she felt relieved and happy in the heart within. Having renounced everything, she felt truly free. Having surrendered herself completely to the Lord, she found the greatest security of life. She became a saint of God.

The state of utter self surrender in which a man possesses nothing, and himself is God-possessed, is not possible for the majority of mankind. It is too far advanced a stage and is arrived at only after a person has passed through many a trial of faith. The majority of men will tell me: "I have my family to look after; I have to earn my livelihood. I have to provide for the education of my children, I have to pay the doctor's bills, house rent and taxes. What can I do? What must I do?"

Let me pass on to you a few practical suggestions:

1. The first essential thing is a *change of outlook*.

    As it is, we depend too much on ourselves, our efforts and endeavours. We keep God out of the picture. True, human effort has its place in life. But we need to understand that, above all efforts, is His Will. And He is the giver of all that is. So let not our work be egotistic – but dedicated. Let us learn to work as His agents, the instruments of His Will. Our children are His children. We are here to serve them to the best of our ability and capacity. It is His responsibility to provide for them – maybe through us, or others. And His coffers are ever full!

2. The second essential thing is to share what we have with others. Therefore let us set apart a portion – say one-tenth of our earnings – to be utilised in the service

of God and His suffering creation.

To those who are unable to live on their income, this may appear a difficult thing to do. But even they will find that in the measure in which they share what little they have with others, they will be richly blessed. Out of the little that remains to them, they will get more, much more than they expected. This is what we, in the Sindhi language, call *barkat*.

I know a lady in Australia who sets apart a tenth of her earnings for the service of the lowly and the weak, and she has not been the poorer for it. Once, when she sent a certain amount to be spent on the service activities of the Sadhu Vaswani Mission, she wrote to me: "It is with gratitude that I pass on to you this amount from my 'Lord's Tenth' fund. This money has nothing to do with me, except that I send it to wherever the Lord directs. So this gift is from Him and the recognition and thanks are due to Him..."

This is one of the laws of life – the more we give, the more we get out of the little that remains.

3. When there are occasions where we are called upon to help others – the poor, the needy and the deprived – we must believe that the call is made not upon *us*, but upon *God*. It is *He* who is the inexhaustible source of life and the bounties of life. We fulfill our destiny as His instruments, channels, through which help may flow to those in need.

    It is essential that we must not for a moment think that it is we who give. The giver is God Himself.

4. We must contact God again and again. It is necessary
   for us to repeat His name again and again, to pray
   without ceasing. A prayer which may prove helpful is,
   "Lord! Make me a channel of Thy mercy!"

5. To become a channel of His mercy, we must surrender
   all we are and all we have, at His lotus-feet. So may we
   become His instruments of help and healing in this
   world of suffering and pain.

He who hath surrendered himself hath found the greatest
security of life. And he need wander no more! All his cares
and burdens are borne by the Lord Himself. How
beautiful are the words of the Gita:

> *They who worship Me*
> *Depending on Me alone,*
> *Thinking of no other—*
> *They are My sole responsibility!*
> *Their burdens are My burdens!*
> *To them I bring full security!'*

The more we meditate on the Lord's words, the more we
shall grow in that true life which is a life of self-surrender.
It is a life free from the shackles of earthly experience. And
meditation must deepen into knowledge, into realisation,
before this freedom can be achieved. To be truly free is to
be born anew, to become a pure child of God. Such a one
lives with God and walks with God and speaks to Him and
hears Him speak.

Hand yourself over to God!

To the vast majority of men and women, God is a sort of

storekeeper who can only justify His existence by supplying them with all those things for which they send in a requisition — health, long life, jobs, prosperity, sons, sons-in-law, houses, and husbands. So long as God gives them what they want, God is good, God is loving, God is wise, and there is none like Him. But the moment He refuses to oblige, He becomes a cruel God, unjust and unkind. His very existence is denied. I am afraid that the God many of us want is a 'servant' God, ready to do our bidding, eager to satisfy our cravings and caprices the moment they are born. True, we make tall promises to love God and serve God, but most of us do not really wish to be His servants, only to 'serve' Him in an advisory capacity. We repeat the words, "Thy will be done! Thy will be done!" But this too, is mere lip-service. What we really mean is this: "Not *Thy* Will, but *my* will be done!"

In plain words, we do not want God's Will to be done. What we desire is that *our* will should be done. But the more we succeed in the doing of our will, the more restless we grow, the more unhappy, the more miserable. For it is only God's Will that can restore harmony and order. And unless we learn to submit to the Will of God, even if we reach out to the moon and conquer the stars, we shall but continue to wander from restlessness to restlessness.

A young college student met me, many years ago. "I have fallen deeply in love with a girl," he said. "I cannot live without her. But our parents will not agree to our marriage. What shall I do? I feel I may go mad at any time!"

"Don't you believe in prayer?" I asked him.

"Yes," he answered. "But when I turn to Him in prayer and

try to leave everything in His hands, a fear grips me. I do not know what He may do."

So many of us live in this fear. We do not know what God may do if we surrender ourselves to Him. To surrender ourselves to Him is to accept His Will. We are not yet prepared to do so. We still want *our* will to be done. Our prayers, in effect, are something like this: "O Lord, who art all-powerful! Listen to my cry! Rush to my rescue and grant me all that I ask. I want health and happiness. I want a bungalow and a wife. I want wealth and all that wealth can purchase. I want honours and fame. I want a position of power and authority. I want people to dance attendance upon me. I want my name to appear in the papers every day. In short, Lord, I want *my* will to be done by Thee, and by everyone else!"

And so we keep on chasing shadows. Like butterflies, we flit from one sensation to another, in vain search of that true happiness which is not obtained until we return to God and surrender our will to His Divine Will.

O travellers who are weary with your wanderings! There is no rest away from Him who is our refuge. Return to your refuge! Significant are the words of Sri Krishna in the Gita:

> 'Staying thy haste,
> Do thou still stand in Me!
> United with Me
> Thou wilt attain
> To the Peace
> Of the Eternal—
> The Supreme Bliss
> That abides in Me!'

He who surrenders his will to the Will Divine, stands still in the Lord, firm and resolute. He finds everything he needs in the Lord. Those things which he pursued desperately, and which eluded him till now, come running to him now. But he desires them no longer. He seeks them no more. He needs nothing. He has attained to the stage where his hunger has been appeased and his thirst has been quenched. They whose wills are merged with the Lord's Will are happy indeed! They desire naught but what the Lord wills! They have broken the chains of bondage and they are attached to nothing and no one. Such men live in this world free from fear and hatred. They have no fear even of death. Death, to them, is a messenger of God's mercy, a gateway to the Life Eternal.

And so the best thing a man can do is to hand himself to God: to accept everything including disgrace and disease, trouble and tribulation, misfortune and misery, as coming from God. And whatever comes from God is good; it comes to purify us. Therefore let us rejoice in every situation and circumstance of life, giving gratitude to Him whose works are ever the works of mercy!

Conquer Depression!

Surrender to the Divine Will does not crush you, defeat you or bring you down. Rather, it enables you to face life like a true hero, taking everything that comes at your own pace, with a joyous heart. But we need to strive hard, to achieve this state of equanimity.

Most of us find ourselves saddened, depressed about our problems. We do realize that we cannot be happy and cheerful all the time, but still, life's ups and downs make us dejected. How can we triumph over such dejection and keep our spirits high?

1. Practise deep breathing whenever you are depressed. This brings balance and composure to a dejected mind.

2. Take a brisk walk or do some invigorating physical exercise. This is sure to improve your mood.

3. Get rid of negative thoughts which generate depression and self-pity. Replace them with positive thoughts.

4. Remind yourself of the golden dictum *'This too shall pass away'.*

5. Appreciate the fact that God sends problems to you to make you stronger. You are facing challenges that will help you grow wise and mature.

6. Engage yourself in some creative activity like writing, singing, drawing or painting. This will channelize your thinking and energy into something constructive.

7. Try to take your mind away from your problems, by devoting attention to the needs of others. In the words of Sadhu Vaswani, "If you want to be happy, make others happy!"

8. Don't let depression depress you! Learn to take low moods in your stride. Understand that your low spirits are temporary.

Remember, Arjuna's depression was the starting point of the *Gita*! If at all you must be depressed, do not be depressed over trifles — rather, be depressed about higher things, that you lack spiritual awareness, that you have not yet learnt to take suffering in your stride, that you have not become master of yourself and allowed your will to be surrendered to the Will Divine.

When your dejection is, like Arjuna's, ready to lead you on to a higher awareness of the truth, you yourself will find that God is ready to take you by the hand and lead you towards enlightenment and liberation. When you remember that you are not the physical body, but the immortal *atman*, your worldly dejection will seem but a trifle to you. For you realise that the Divine Self is the in-dweller of the spirit within you!

Cultivate Fortitude!

Perhaps the greatest treasure in the spiritual realm is the virtue of fortitude — one of the essential qualities of a seeker on the path. The Sanskrit equivalent of fortitude is *dhriti* and it includes qualities of patience, endurance, faith, and persistence.

Many people who endure long periods of trial and tribulation are apt to imagine that they excel in the virtue of fortitude. However, they do not appreciate the true strength of fortitude — what it entails, and how it strengthens the enlightened mind.

Fortitude has two aspects, physical and mental. Physical fortitude is essential when we have to work in difficult conditions that do not allow us to think about our personal comforts. For example, relief workers and volunteers serving in disaster zones often push aside their own personal needs to attend to the needs of their suffering brothers and sisters. Think of all the service-minded volunteers belonging to agencies like the Red Cross, UN, and others, who rush to flood-affected, famine-stricken, or earthquake-hit areas in Africa, Asia, and other developing regions. They live and sleep in tents alongside the victims; they ignore their hunger, thirst, and sleep to share the problems of the victims; they give up their comfortable lifestyles and their well-furnished homes to rough it out with the victims of famines and floods. Neither do you hear them complain about the loss of their personal comforts; nor do they boast of their fortitude and endurance.

Mental fortitude requires even greater effort. I know very many people who exercise this wonderful quality, unknown, unrecognized, and unhonoured by the rest of us. There are difficult situations in life which demand tremendous psychological strength. People may abuse you, revile you, attack you maliciously — and you are required to endure it all, without yielding to the urge to hit back, to react with tit-for-tat.

There can be no greater example of such fortitude than Jesus. Think of Him — betrayed by His own disciples, denied by His followers, subjected to an arbitrary, unjust trial, abandoned to the 'mercy' of those who were determined to destroy Him, condemned to be crucified alongside common criminals, reviled and ridiculed by His enemies, cruelly crowned with thorns, and finally nailed to the cross to die a terrible, painful death — and He died with those immortal words which teach all of us the cardinal virtue of forgiveness: "Forgive them, Lord, for they know not what they do."

What a great lesson in fortitude Jesus teaches us!

Fortitude is not cowardice – it is moral courage of the highest order. There are very many situations in life where hitting out, struggling against the current, fighting back etc., will prove to be counter-productive.

The best option in such situations is for you to be calm, quiet, and balanced, without giving in to defeat and despair. It is, indeed, a great virtue to take on such situations with dignity and equanimity. This is also a great form of *tapasya*.

How may we cultivate the virtue of fortitude?

1. By repetition of the Name Divine: the continual practice of *naam japa* will give you inner strength and the power of endurance.

2. By *satsanga* or good association: this brings you in touch with vital truths, and enables you to tap the hidden strengths of your own nature. You grow in awareness that you are not the body, but the immortal spirit that resides within.

3. By selfless service: this eliminates the ego, and helps you to transcend external, physical situations. When you have devoted yourself to the ideal of selfless service, you cease to be affected, irritated by trifles. You grow in faith and you realise that it is His Divine Hand which is leading you on in all situations and all circumstances of life.

Cultivate patience!

Closely allied to fortitude is the tremendous quality of patience. When you read about the lives of the great, enlightened souls of East and West, you will find that they all shared the wonderful virtue of patience.

Think of Sant Eknath. He was a picture of patience. He was always unruffled and serene, a saint who never lost his temper. There were some in the town who were jealous of his reputation and were eager to prove to the people that Sant Eknath, too, had feet of clay. They hired a man and promised to reward him richly, if only he could make the saint lose his temper.

Early every morning, Eknath would go to the river for a dip in the waters before spending some time in worship. One day, as he returned to his cottage, after taking a bath in the sacred waters, on the way, the hired man spat on him. Quietly, the saint went back to the river and took a dip for the second time. Once again, as he was on his way home, the man spat on him. The same thing happened the third time, the fourth time, the fifth time. But it made not a dent in the saint's composure. Unperturbed, he went to the river each time to take yet another dip. The man was not tired, nor was Eknath. The thought of the rich reward lured the man and he kept spitting on the saint every time that he passed by him.

Believe it or not, this went on for as many as 107 times! After taking the 108th dip, as the saint wended his way home, the man's heart melted. Falling at the feet of the saint, he sobbed, "Forgive me! I implore you to forgive me! For the sake of God, do forgive me! I have greatly sinned. I was told by some of the wealthy men of the town that if I could only make you lose your temper, they would reward me handsomely. The temptation of a rich reward made me stoop this low! Pray forgive me!"

Lifting him up, the saint smiled and said, "Forgive you, for what? Today is a unique day in my life, when I have had 108 dips in the sacred river! Had you only told me of the rich reward promised to you, I would have gladly feigned anger for your benefit!"

When you study these great lives, you will soon come to realise that it is their patience which makes them great!

Nature is constantly giving us valuable lessons in patience. Day after day, night after night, the sun and the moon and the stars rise patiently. Year after year, the earth keeps on revolving around the sun; the planets and the the stars patiently revolve in their assigned spheres; the earth allows us to walk all over her, dig her soil, cultivate, and mine, and construct, and develop land, and reclaim the sea, as we deem fit. As you grow in the awareness that a Divine Plan sustains life on earth, even as it sustains you, you will grow in the virtue of patience. Patience is essential for our spiritual evolution. For it helps us to overcome irritation, short temper, and anger, which are all detrimental to spiritual growth.

There is a story about a king who once went trekking in a lonely, forested hill. He climbed higher and higher up the steep hill, having only his pet falcon for company. As the day advanced, he became thirsty and began to look for a spring. Soon he spotted a little stream which was flowing from the rocks. He took a small coconut shell lying nearby, and tried to fill it with water, so that he could quench his thirst.

No sooner had he filled the shell, than his falcon knocked off the makeshift cup from his hands. The king filled the cup again, and the falcon knocked it off again. Impatient, he warned the pet not to do so and filled the cup for the third time, and the falcon knocked it off again. Now the king lost his patience and his temper. He drew his sword out and slashed the falcon to pieces.

When this terrible deed was done, the king found himself filled with dismay and regret. He tried to analyze what had happened, and realized that for some reason or the other, the falcon had tried to stop him from drinking water from the stream. But why?

The king followed the path of the stream and climbed higher up the hill, to see where it came from. When he climbed up, he saw that the water was dripping across a rotting corpse which covered the spring-mouth. The falcon, with its instinct, had realised that the water was filthy and impure. Therefore, he had tried to prevent his master from drinking the contaminated water. However, the king had been too impatient to realise the truth. And his impatience had led him to the cruel act of killing his own pet.

God sends us difficulties, trials and other adverse situations to make us spiritually strong. Thus all these obstacles and problems have their own value and meaning in our spiritual life. When we learn to tackle them with patience, tolerance, and understanding, we evolve spiritually. Spiritual advancement is not accomplished by doing great deeds of heroism and courage. It is gained also in the little things of life: in facing daily life and its little ups and downs with patience. You need patience not only to deal with the outside world, but also with your own near and dear ones. Listen patiently to others' grievances and woes. Give them your understanding and sympathy. Exercise restraint in your speech. Do not yield to your temper and shout at others, especially those below you.

Patience is also the attribute of successful people. You become better organized; you develop persistence, and you work hard until success is yours. Without patience, self-realisation is impossible to achieve. Patience enables you to yield to the Divine Will, and to understand that all that happens to you, happens as a result of God's Will. His ways are mysterious and unfathomable. Patience enables you to overcome all the obstacles that stand in the way of your spiritual advancement, enabling you, ultimately, to perceive the truth.

Once, a great king decided to renounce his power and possessions, and seek initiation from Buddha as a monk. The entire assembly of *bhikkus* had gathered around the hermitage to witness the initiation ceremony. The king arrived, dressed in an ochre robe. His head was shaven, and he had dispensed with all his ornaments. He walked barefoot through the assembly of monks and in his right hand, he carried a priceless diamond, as an offering to the Master. In his left hand, he carried a rare and beautiful white lotus in case the Buddha refused to accept the ostentatious offering of the diamond.

Buddha, seated with closed eyes, said to the king: "Drop it!"

The king, aware of the unsuitability of the offering, immediately dropped the diamond. Buddha's voice commanded again, "Drop it!" This time the king dropped the lotus.

Again the voice commanded, "Drop it!" The king was baffled, for he had nothing to drop now. He continued to walk towards the Master.

But Buddha said once again, "I say to you, drop it!"

The king understood. In one of Buddha's discourses, he had heard the Master say: 'Yena tyajasi tam tyaja', "Leave that (the ego or the I-thought) through which you have left everything!"

He understood that he was still in the grip of the ego; he was still entertaining the thought that *he* had dropped the diamond and lotus at the Master's command. At that moment, he surrendered himself totally to the Buddha and dropped his ego. The Master opened his eyes and acknowledged him with approval for at that moment, the king had surrendered himself truly.

A journalist once said to me, "Your engagement diary must be completely filled with all your pressing engagements!"

I smiled and replied, "I do not plan anything. I just let the Will of God guide me."

Truly, I believe that the clock, the calendar, and the telephone are three 'killers' of humanity. I would earnestly advise all of you to leave the 'planning' to God, as you move from one task to another! Reflect God in your daily life! Hand your life over to God!

The Three Gunas (Qualities) according to the Gita

Chapter XIV of the *Bhagavad Gita* is entitled *Conquest of the Three Qualities.*

In this chapter, Sri Krishna speaks of the three *gunas* (qualities), their relation to *prakriti,* and their conquest by the sages. The Lord asserts that in the conquest of the three qualities is the supreme wisdom of life. Having gained this wisdom, enlightened soul — wise men, *munis* and sage — attain to *nirvana.* Taking refuge in this wisdom, they are changed into Krishna's nature. They grow into the image of Krishna. They live a life of fellowship with Krishna. They become one with Krishna. Becoming one with the Lord, they win release from rebirth.

> 'Once more will I declare to thee that supreme wisdom, of all wisdom the best, having known which, all sages have gone hence to the highest perfection.'
>
> XIV: 1

Great *Bramha* (*Mahad Bramha*) or *maya* is the womb. In this womb, Krishna sows the seed of all life, thus causing the birth of every individual. Thus the seed of God is in each of us.

Of *prakriti* (nature), there are three strands or ropes. They
are the three *gunas*. All actions are performed through the
three *gunas* (qualities). They bind the soul in the body.
They fetter the *jiva* in the body. What are the three *gunas*?

'*Sattva, rajas, tamas,* the three qualities (*gunas*) are
born of *prakriti* (nature, matter). They bind fast
in the body, O Arjuna, the Imperishable that
dwelleth in the body.'

XIV: 5

'What are these three qualities, then? Of these
sattva, from its purity, brings illumination and
health. It bindeth by attachment to happiness
and by attachment to knowledge, O Arjuna!'

XIV: 6

'*Sattva* is purity or light. It makes the *jiva* eager
for knowledge and virtue. But even light binds
jiva to the body, the flesh, when it causes
attachment. Know thou, O Arjuna, that *rajas*,
which is of the nature of passion, is the source
of attachment and thirst. And *rajas* bindeth the
embodied soul by attachment to action.'

XIV: 7

'*Rajas* is energy, mobility, passion. *Rajas* is also *trishna*, a
thirst for life. *Rajas* is passionate energy. It is the child of
strong desire and attachment. It binds the soul to *prakriti*
by activity.

'When external, restless activity predominates, it means
rajas prevails. Therefore, zeal for work is a mark of the man
of *rajas*. But bondage to work also binds the soul!

'But *tamas* (all bewildering darkness), know thou,
is born of ignorance and is the deluder of souls.
It bindeth by heedlessness, indolence and sleep,
O Arjuna!'

XIV: 8

'When darkness and inertia predominate, you have a sure
sign that *tamas* prevails. In the man of *tamas* the forces of
matter predominate. He eats, drinks and sleeps: he lives
from moment to moment.'

The Lord explains further:

Sattva bindeth to happiness, *rajas* to action, O
Arjuna! And *tamas*, having shrouded wisdom,
bindeth to heedlessness (negligence).'

XIV: 9

And further:

'Of *sattva* is born knowledge; of *rajas* is born
greed; heedlessness, inertia and *agnana*
(unwisdom) are born of *tamas*.'

XIV: 17

What must the wise man do? He must "cross over" the
three *gunas*, control them, conquer them, so that he may
move beyond them and seek Krishna. The man who knows
this is freed from birth and death, and drinks the waters of
immortality. "Conquer the three *gunas*, Arjuna!" the Lord
tells His dear, devoted disciple. "Be a seer!"

It is essential for us to understand the three *gunas* and
their relation to the human personality. It is only when we

have understood them that we can conquer them, rise above them, and thus advance on the spiritual path.

Tamas

'When darkness, inaction, heedlessness, and delusion are conspicuous, know that *tamas* predominates, O Arjuna!'

XIV: 13

Tamas is neither light nor energy, but lethargy, listlessness, delusion; *tamas* is darkness: it is a delusive child of ignorance. It binds the soul to *prakriti* by heedlessness, indolence, and sleep. When darkness and inertia predominate, you have a sure sign that *tamas* prevails. The *tamasic* man manifests negative qualities such as anger, greed, falsehood, violence, deception, hypocrisy, languor, discord, grief, delusion, gloom, wretchedness, sleep, negative expectation, fear, and inactivity — this is according to *Srimad Bhagavat Purana*.

These negative qualities are obviously hindrances on the path of spiritual evolution. They also impede progress and personality development in earthly life. Therefore, when expressions of *tamas* impede our progress, we must remove them from our personality. *Tamas* can dominate the unconscious (*chitta*), the mind (*manas*), and the body.

The *tamasic chitta* is filled with negative impressions like greed and hatred. Meditation and repetition of the Name Divine can help cleanse the *chitta*.

The *tamasic* mind makes us dull and aimless, bonded with

obsessions and prejudices. *Satsanga* (good association) and *seva* (service) will get rid of this mental dullness.

The *tamasic* body is characterized by dullness, boredom, gluttony, and laziness. This can be overcome by good work and activities, as well as by regular physical exercise and *yogasanas*, as well as *pranayama*. Intake of *sattvic* food will also help to revitalise the body.

Tamasic food is stale, rotten, and impure. This includes all foods of violence as well as food left overnight. In the modern context one should also include the intake of alcohol, hallucinogenic drugs, as well as smoking, as *tamasic*. The *tamasic* person derives pleasure from such habits.

Tamasic faith make a man worship dark forces such as spirits, ghosts, and vampires. *Tamasic* renunciation makes a man turn his back on his ordained duty and allotted work. Such a person is given to sloth and sleeps too long. *Tamasic* charity is selfish and motivated. The *tamasic* man does not give anything out of the goodness of his heart — but only under pressure, or to fulfill evil desires. If death should come to a person in the *tamasic* state, he is reborn in *tamasic* embodiments, which are subhuman, or in gross, uncultured families.

How can *tamas* be overcome?

1. Substitute positive qualities, positive thoughts, positive vibrations for the negative ones in your mind. *Raja yoga* describes the process of *pratipaksha bhavana* or adapting the mind to positive qualities. This involves three stages:

- Suppression: Recognize the evil effects of the quality, and restrain this feeling to the best of your ability.

- Substitution: Replace the negative quality with thoughts and feelings that are positive and valuable.

- Sublimation: Continue this effort until the negative quality is overwhelmed by the positive one.

For example, if you are given to jealousy, try to understand how harmful and poisonous it is to you, and to others. Develop a disgust for it; realize that it degrades you.

In the second stage, substitute thoughts of love, understanding, compassion, and tolerance, all of which are contrary to jealousy. Assert to yourself constantly, "I am the divine *atman*; I am intrinsically pure, good, and divine."

Continue with these positive self-assertions until the *tamasic* quality, whatever it may be − jealousy, anger, greed, lust, slot − is completely conquered and replaced by the positive one. By having recourse to *pratipaksha bhavana* you will overcome *tamasic* qualities. Your pride will turn to humility; your ignorance will turn to knowledge; your pessimism will turn to optimism; your laziness will be replaced by energy. In due course, you will find that the elements of discord, disharmony and strife are replaced by harmony and universal love.

2. Avoid the habit of procrastination or postponement. Do not give in to indulgence and ease: *alasya* (laziness) and *pramada* (inattention or heedlessness).

3. When you fail to attend to your duty, you will continue to feel restless, disturbed, and tense. Relaxation and ease only come to you with the successful completion of your allotted duties.

4. Devote your full attention and concentration to the task at hand. Do not make half-hearted attempts at anything you do.

5. Turn your energy to the three s's — *seva, satsang* and *sadhana*.

Seva is serving God through humanity. It purifies your mind and action.

Satsanga is perhaps the best remedy to cure *tamasic* effects. Elsewhere, I have spoken about the positive, purifying, transforming effects of *satsang*.

Sadhana is a spiritual discipline which enables you to pursue the practice of *japa* (repetition of the Name), *dhyana* (meditation), and *swadhyyaya* (study of the scriptures), on a regular and systematic basis under the guidance of the guru.

These practices will help you conquer *tamas*, and in the words of the great *Vedas*, lead you "from darkness to light."

Rajas

'Know thou, O Arjuna, that *rajas*, which is of the
nature of passion, is the source of attachment
and thirst. And *rajas* bindeth the embodied soul
by attachment to action.'

XIV: 7

Rajas is energy, mobility, passion. *Rajas* is *trishna*, a thirst for
life. *Rajas* is passionate energy. *Rajas* is the child of strong
desire and attachment. When greed, external activity,
restless activity, predominate, it means that *rajas* prevails.
In fact the man of *rajas* is marked by a zeal for work. The
man of *rajas* is always in the midst of struggle and work.
He has a strong desire to assert and achieve. He struggles
hard to show, to establish his superiority over others. He
goes about in life, not as the servant of the Lord, but
imagining himself to be the Lord of all he surveys. The
man under the influence of *rajas* is the man of action, of
initiative, of inordinate ambition, and restlessness.

'When greed, external activity, zeal for work,
restlessness, envious desire are conspicuous,
know that *rajas* predominates, O Arjuna!'

XIV: 12

The *rajasic* man is thus characterised by the following:
restless activity, uncontrolled desires, and various
impurities of the mind.

Rajas and *tamas* dominate the average man, who is tossed
about from one tendency to the other. While *tamas* keeps
him in the darkness of ignorance, *rajas* leaves him
entangled in his *karmic* residues.

The *Gita* describes three doors to darkness – three gates of hell:

> 'Triple is the gateway of this hell, destructive of the self, lust, wrath, and greed. Therefore, let men shun these three.'
>
> XVI: 21

Lust (*kama*), is the desire for blind satisfaction of the senses. Anger, wrath, or hate (*krodha*), is the desire to oppose those who stand in the way of the satisfaction of those desires. Greed or covetousness (*lobha*) is the desire for inordinate accumulation of worldly goods.

Kama, krodha, and *lobha* are manifestations of *rajas* blended in different degrees with *tamas.* According to *Srimad Bhagavat,* the following qualities are expressions of *rajas:* desire, lust, selfish activity, pride, craving, rigidity, stubbornness, creating disharmony, indulgence in sense-pleasures, love of fame and pride, excessive attachment, frivolity, selfish exertion, and egotistical strength. When a man is unable to cope with his own excessive energy, he falls a prey to restless desires. This makes him prone to agitation and distraction. He is unable to focus his abundant energy on any single, meaningful, creative task. He is unable to integrate his mind and his senses, and thus falls prey to excessive indulgences.

Sense-pleasures attract such a man inordinately, as his distracted, restless intellect is unable to analyze and discriminate good from bad, right from wrong. Thus he is unable to see the *karmic* entanglements in which he is caught, as he falls a prey to the surface charms and superficial attractions of worldly pleasures. Thus, he is trapped in the bonds and fetters of *maya*.

The *Gita* has a lot of valuable insights to offer us on the various aspects of the *rajas*:

1. *Rajasic* knowledge sees the many as the many. It fails to perceive the One behind the many. *Rajasic* knowledge is awareness of difference. By differentiation, it sees all creatures as separate and distinct. It sees *jivas* in the different bodies — heavenly, human, sub-human — and focusses on their qualitative differences.

   Rajasic knowledge knows the name (*nama*) and the form (*rupa*), but does not know the Essence. Thus it knows the earthenware pot — but not the earth of which it is made; it knows the lamp — but not the light that shines therein.

   'The knowledge which sees multiplicity of beings in many creatures, all various, each apart from his fellow, that knowledge know thou, as *rajasic*.'

   XVIII: 21

2. *Rajasic* action is vain, passionate, self-seeking.

   'But that action which is done under great strain by one who seeks to gratify his desires, and is prompted by *ahankara* (sense of self), is declared to be *rajasic* (passionate).'

   XVIII: 24

   Rajasic action has the following marks:

   • They are actions done in spite of nature, "against

the grain", in great stress, strain and with undue exertion.

- They are done under the whip of *kama* (lust) – desire for women, wealth, power, property, position, or office.

- They are impelled by the will of the ego (*ahankara*), selfish pride, conceit, and vanity.

3. The *rajasic* doer acts with desire:

'He who is swayed by passion, who seeks the fruit of his actions, who is greedy, harmful, impure, who is swayed by joy and sorrow, he is pronounced a *rajasic* doer.'

XVIII: 27

The marks of the *rajasic* doer are as follows:

- He is sunk in worldly *vasanas*, attached to sense objects.

- He is moved by lust of gain. He is anxious for fruits, and is eager for the prize of vainglory.

- He is motivated by greed.

- He is brutal and violent: his nature would embarrass others and cause them pain.

- In victory, he is quick to rejoice, and in failure, he gives in to despair.

4. *Rajasic Shraddha* is also the faith of energy. It is the faith of men who want power, wealth, success, and to

this end, they worship *yakshas* (demi-gods), even *rakshasas* (demons).

Of such men, Sri Krishna says:

'The men who practise dreadful austerities, not sanctioned by the scriptures, who are given to hypocrisy and egoism and are carried away by the force of desire and passion, such men are witless. They torment the group of elements in their body and Me who dwells in the body. Know these to be demoniac in their resolves.'

XVII: 5-6

5. *Rajasic* sacrifice is insincere for it is offered for the sake of displaying wealth and power, or to earn fame. It is offered with a view to fruit.

6. *Rajasic tapas* (austerity) is also performed for proud display and for the sake of gaining respect, honour, and worship. Its motive is insincere, and it focuses on ostentation or vain show.

7. *Rajasic dhana* is also made with the desire for returns, such as honour, applause, business success, or attainment to heaven. Sometimes it is offered with a grudging heart.

'When a gift is given with a view to receiving something in return, or with expectation of a future reward, or when it is given unwillingly, such a gift is *rajasic* (passionate).'

XVII: 21

8. *Rajasic tyaga* does not lead to *mukti* (liberation).

'He who abstaineth from an action as troublesome, or from fear, or physical suffering, does *rajasic tyaga*. And he obtaineth not any benefit from such *tyaga* (relinquishment).'
                                                    XVIII: 8

Thus we have men who "renounce" the world and turn to the lonely hilltop or the secluded forest, only to escape their duties and responsibilities. This is not true *tyaga*.

9. The *rajasic buddhi* is distracted and restless; it is often confused; it cannot discriminate between right and wrong: it confuses rights and duties. It confounds duty with pleasure, and sees values awry. It is filled with impressions of excessive attachment and illusions.

'That by which one knows awry, erroneously, *dharma* and *adharma* (the right and the wrong), what should be done and what should not be done, that understanding, O Arjuna, is *rajasic*.'
                                                    XVIII: 31

10. *Rajasic dhriti* (determination) is in pursuit of reward. It is a selfish, personal, gain-greedy will. The man of *rajasic* determination may hold on to virtue, custom, duty, etc., but does so only for love of gain or personal advantage.

'The determination by which one, desiring the fruit, holdeth fast to *dharma* (duty), *kama*

(pleasure), and *artha* (wealth), that determination, O Arjuna, is *rajasic* (passionate).'

XVIII: 34

11. *Rajasic joy* is sheer sensual pleasure. Sweet as nectar at
first, it turns bitter as poison. Socrates spoke of the
"pleasure of wisdom", but what he really meant was
"the joy of wisdom". The *rajasic* man, on the contrary,
seeks wisdom in pleasure, and is sooner or later,
disappointed in his quest. He pursues pleasure, only
to find that it devitalizes him, resulting in physical
depression and moral degeneration. He gorges himself
in haste, and repents at leisure. He is a man who
makes desire his deity. He spends his time in drinking,
revels, feasts, and luxuries.

'That which from the contact of the senses and
their objects (*vishaya*) is, at first, as nectar, but in
the end is like poison, that *sukha* (pleasure) is
accounted *rajasic* (passionate).'

XVIII: 38

12. *Rajasic* food is the food of passionate men – men who
are energetic, worldly-minded. These foods are bitter,
sour, salted, hot, pungent and dry, eg., opium, tobacco,
tamarind, chillies, parched grain, rye, etc.; such foods
produce pain, grief, and sickness.

In general, *rajasic* foods are over-cooked, over-spiced,
laced with artificial colours and preservatives. Such
foods lose their vitality. Excessive use of salt, sugar,
onion, garlic, and other spices also makes food *rajasic*.
Such food may please the palate, but it cannot keep
the body healthy. They produce excessive toxins,

leading to various ailments. Such, foods are also not conducive to the practice of meditation, reflection, or spiritual inquiry.

Should a man die when *rajas* dominates, he is reborn among those who are attached to, bound by, action.

A distracted, restless mind can never really enjoy the pleasures of the serene mind that concentrates on the Self Supreme. This is why a *rajasic* man's life is dominated by the senses. He is bound by his passions to repeated experiences of pleasure-turning- to-pain, until he evolves towards *sattva*.

The story is told to us of a man of renunciation who saw a shining piece of fur floating down a river. He jumped into the river to get hold of it. When he grabbed the fur stole, he discovered to his horror that it was, in fact, a wild and hungry bear, whose body was hidden in the water, while only its glittering fur was exposed above the surface. So too, to the distracted, restless man of *rajas*, sense-objects and worldly pleasures appear to be attracting and alluring, because he is unable to discriminate and analyze them from all angles. He sees only the surface glitter and is entrapped in the entanglements of *maya*.

How may we overcome *rajas*?

1. By *vairagya* – detachment, indifference to pleasure and pain. *Vairagya* comes with the realisation that desire, which afflicts all human beings, is nothing but a kind of madness which drives us from birth to birth in the wheel of life. Desire, in fact, is no better than a shadow of death.

The man who wishes to conquer *rajas* should realize that sense-pleasures are only delusions, leading ultimately to pain. Power, wealth, youth, and beauty are all transient, and they should constantly remind us of death, disease, and old age, to which all of us must be subject, birth after birth, when we are caught in the wheel of *karma*. If one is to avoid repeated rebirths, one must seek self-realisation, enlightenment, and liberation.

2. *Satsanga* — good association. Fellowship with a *satpurkha*, a pure-hearted, love-illuminated one can lead us on the right way forward. When a true spiritual leader shelters a disciple under his grace and guidance, there is the birth of new life in his heart — he is born into desirelessness and detachment.

    Satsanga also helps you to avoid negative associations with people who will drag you back into *rajas* and *tamas*.

3. *Swadharma* — or the performance of one's own duty. The Lord urges us not to neglect our own duty for any other task, however pleasant or superior it may appear to be. Never abandon your own duty for this is what will lead you to *moksha* (liberation). In doing your duty, however humble it may be, you are not bound by action: your work will be as no-work. Go on doing your duty, however imperfect it may be at the start. This will purify your heart and will draw you nearer to the Divine.

    When one acts, freed from the terrible strain of greed and desire, one finds that he is in harmony with the Self. He is not pressurized by expectations, and therefore finds true fulfillment in what he does.

Swadharma thus becomes the first step towards *nishkama karma* (desireless action). Gradually, his actions will be directed towards *loka sangraha* (service of humanity), and he will become a true *karma yogi*.

4. *Japa*, *dhyana* and *vichara* are also methods of overcoming *rajas*.

The aim of the seeker must be to fill his mind with *sattva*, so that he becomes a truly integrated, harmonious soul. Filling the mind with *sattva* does not mean giving up all action.

What is needed is that we must undertake all activity in a *sattvic* temperament, with a *sattvic* attitude, and *sattvic* determination. This will lead us on the path of *dharma* (righteousness.) Let us channelize the excessive energy of *rajas* into *sattva*. Let us conquer the restlessness and distractions of the mind. Let us root our intellect and heart in the Divine, and act with dynamism, desirelessness, and detachment, for the welfare of all creation.

Sattva

Of these, *sattva*, from its purity, brings illumination and health. It bindeth by attachment to happiness and by attachment to knowledge, O Arjuna!

XIV:6

What is *sattva*? It is purity or light. It makes the *jiva* eager for knowledge and virtue. *Sattva* is the principle of truth, beauty, and harmony. The *Srimad Bhagavat* tells us that *sattva* manifests itself in the qualities of serenity, self-control, austerity, truthfulness, compassion, endurance, pure memory, contentment, renunciation, non-covetousness, faith, repugnance for sin, etc.

In the *Gita*, Sri Krishna tells us:

> 'When the light of wisdom streameth forth from all the gates of the body, then it may be known that *sattva* predominates.'
>
> XIV: 11

Sri Krishna also mentions the qualities associated with *sattva*: fearlessness, purity of mind, steadfastness, control of the senses, sacrifice, study of the scriptures, non-violence, truthfulness, freedom from anger and freedom, from envy, malice, and pride.

Sattva elevates the mind, expanding our consciousness. The *buddhi* becomes radiant, and the whole personality becomes vital and joyous. One is able to rise above the narrow, restricting circumstances of the material world, and adopt a tranquil, serene, balanced attitude to life.

Unfortunately for many people, we are able to attain *sattva* only for a very short while. Our great spiritual elders say that when our good *karma* of the past fructifies, it manifests itself as *sattva* in our personality. At such times we become serene, joyous, and tranquil; we radiate pure vitality and happiness. But when the effect of good *karma* ends, we are back in the clutches of *tamas* (dullness) and *rajas* (passion). Thus, we lose our equanimity and serenity, and we are distracted by the troubles, sufferings, and sorrows of this life.

Whenever we experience true happiness, it is because *sattva* predominates in our life and character. Unable to realise this truth, we attribute happiness to external objects and circumstances. When we lose our sense of joy, we attribute it to the loss of these objects and circumstances. Whereas, if we knew the truth, we would work constantly to cultivate *sattva*, so that we may always feel true joy, the peace and bliss that surpasses understanding, and move forward on the path of liberation.

How can we make *sattva* an abiding aspect of our life and personality?

1. By association with the good and the holy *satsang*. This enables us to practise meditation; it promotes spiritual enquiry, and develops virtuous qualities in us.

2. By cultivating the quality of *samattva* (equanimity). This means that we must learn to take joy and sorrow in the same spirit. We must learn to keep our mind balanced in pain and pleasure, rising above what the *Gita* calls the *dwandas* or pairs of opposites, like loss and gain, pleasure and adversity. Obviously, such a state can be achieved only through the conquest of the senses, thus overcoming the desires, affections, passions, and attachments, which bind us.

3. By learning to be in a state of contentment (*santosha*). According to *Raja Yoga*, "contentment gives rise to incomparable bliss". But alas, many of us are given to constant complaints about our lives. We look at our friends and neighbours, and feel that they are better off than we are. We grow discontented. When we grow in *sattvic* knowledge we realize that wealth and comforts cannot bring us true happiness. We will realize that the source of real happiness is in the soul within.

4. By spiritual reflection and enquiry (*vichara*). We grow in purity of mind, and our intellectual energy is devoted to the understanding of the truth. '*Om tat sat*'. This leads to the realisation of the great utterance, *Tat twam asi*, That art Thou!' By this we gain awareness that we are essentially an aspect of the Supreme Self. *Satsanga*, *samattva*, *santosha*, and *vichara* – good association, equanimity, contentment, and spiritual reflection. These are described as the four 'gatekeepers' of *mukti* (liberation) in the *Yoga Vashishta*. They are also dynamic aids in the cultivation of *sattva*.

The Gita also tells us about the different aspects of *sattva*:

1. True knowledge, or *sattvic* knowledge is the perception of One in all. The One is in the rich and the poor; the One is in the saint and the sinner, the sage and the criminal; the One is in all *jivas* – all creatures that breathe the breath of life; the One is also in the stone, the mineral, the tree, the plant, and the soil. The *jiva* itself is immortal, though it resides for some time in the mortal coil; the individual *jivas* may be very different, but in their essential spiritual nature, they are identical. This knowledge is true knowledge.

'The knowledge by which the One Imperishable
Being is seen in all beings, inseparate in the
separated, know thou that knowledge as pure
(*sattvic*).'

XVIII: 20

Pure (*sattvic*) knowledge is the perception of this One
Essence in all. This One is *avyayam* – imperishable,
deathless; it is *avibhaktam* – entire, inseparable. In other
words, *sattvic* knowledge enables us to realize the
spiritual unity that underlies the world of multiplicity.

2. *Sattvic* action – pure, right deeds – is action which is
   obligatory: such as earning a livelihood, or as when a
   mother looks after her child, or those actions enjoined
   by sages and the scriptures, such as *yagna* (sacrifice),
   tapas (austerity), and *dana* (charity). It is:

   • devoid of attachment or a sense of 'doership', that
     is utterly without egoism.

   • performed without a desire for fruit or gain, that is,
     nishkama karma.

   • performed passionlessly or impersonally, for the
     sake of duty, not out of desire, pleasure,or hatred.

   'An action which is obligatory, which is devoid of
   attachment, which is done without a desire for
   fruit, and which is performed without love or
   hate (*raga* or *dvesha*), that is called *sattvic* (pure).'

XVIII: 23

3. The *sattvic* doer is the man who truly acts. He is
   impartial, impersonal, and without vanity. He remains

unmoved in joy or pain. He acts without desire. He has no attachment to action or its fruits. He does not covet honour, fame, or earthly greatness. He is totally free from ego and vanity. He does not boast of his doings. He does not say, "I am the doer" or "I am the agent". There is no egoism in his speech. He does not say, "Without me, this would be impossible." He is full of patience and courage. Even when faced by obstacles, he remains resolute and enduring.

He is *sama*, balanced in gain and loss, pleasure and grief. Unaffected by triumph or defeat, he remains untroubled by the outcome. This is how Sri Krishna describes the *sattvic* doer:

'The doer who is free from attachment, whose speech is devoid of egotism, who is full of resolution and zeal, and who is unchanged by success or failure, he is called the *sattvic karta* (pure or rightful doer).'

XVIII: 26

4. *Sattvic shraddha* (worship) is the faith of purity. It is the faith of those who worship God. They are men of purity and knowledge, who ultimately attain to *nirvana*.

5. *Sattvic* renunciation or sacrifice is offered in the spirit of duty, trusting in God and the holy law, and with no desire for reward or fruit of selfish gain.

6. *Sattvic* austerity (*tapas*) is control of body, speech, and mind with utmost faith and without selfishness.

Worship of the gods, of the twice-born, of teachers
and of the wise, purity, straight-forwardness,
continence, and harmlessness, this is said to be the
tapas (austerity) of the body.

Speech that hurts no one, that is truthful, pleasant,
and beneficial, and the constant study of the sacred
books, this is said to be *tapas* (austerity) of speech.

Serenity of mind, gentleness, silence, self-restraint,
purity of thought and feeling, this is called the *tapas*
(austerity) of mind.

'This three-fold austerity is called *sattvic* (pure),
when it is performed with supreme faith by men
of balanced mind and with no desire of reward.'

XVII: 14-17

Tapas of the body also includes such qualities as purity
or cleanliness, straightforwardness, harmlessness, and
continence. Continence is *brahmacharya*, for the body
must be free from the lusts of flesh. Therefore, the
body should be disciplined, treated with hardness.
Mortify the senses, strip them of what tempts them to
go astray. Keep them away from luxury, concupiscence,
and unruly desire. The body should be chastised and
trained to obey the Divine Law.

Tapas of speech demands observance of truthfulness,
kind and helpful words, freedom from malice and
argumentativeness, and *swadhyaya* — study of the
scriptures and recitation of the Name Divine.

Tapas of mind includes the following:

- Keeping the mind cheerful and composed, in serenity and tranquillity.

- Gentleness and meekness — remember, meekness is *not* weakness.

- Silence. This does not mean absolute solitude. Silence is being still, for some time, from your thoughts and desires and imagination, and resting in the God within. Silence also means taking off, at least temporarily, the stress and strain from your soul.

- Control of mind.

- Purity of feeling.

Do not indulge in vain speculations and idle thoughts that is, thoughts other than those relating to God. Keep the mind well-controlled and unsullied. As the body is cleansed by water, so must the mind be purified by thoughts of God. The test of true *tapas* is this — does your austerity result in elimination of self-will, self-centred thinking, self-interest, selfish wishing, and selfish imagining? True *tapas* is far removed from showy acts. In true *tapas* the man never thinks of 'fruits', the man is non-attached to self-interest. Interior mortification is necessary. Refuse consent to the suggestion of the senses. Let the will grow in purity and strength so as to overcome the flesh. Resist pleasure suggestions and incentives.

True *tapas* is spiritual mortification, is inward self-denial. Not outward poverty, but the spirit of poverty is necessary. It is the spirit of simplicity. You may have abundance, but you must not desire it. Or you may have anything but abundance: you may be ill-nourished and ill-clothed. But you must not cry for possession, you must not desire it! So must you gradually learn to die to the self — to cease identification with the body.

The voice of true *tapas* is: discipline yourself until you renounce self-will, lose the ego-centric life. Let God alone be reflected in your body, your words and your mind. Therefore, be wholly empty, and the Lord will fill you.

7. *Sattvic dana* (gift) is that which expects no return, and is given at the appropriate time and place to the appropriate person. *Dana* is right giving. In this sense, to adapt the words of Prophet Mohammed, to give water to the thirsty is *dana*; to remove stones and thorns in the wayside is *dana*; to smile in the presence of a brother or sister who needs to be cheered is *dana*. So too, all that renowned kings and philanthropists of our country did in the past — digging wells, erecting drinking-water fountains, making roads, and planting trees to shade the wayfarers is *dana*. Is not *dana* then, the true wealth of a man? As Prophet Mohammed says, "When a man dies, mortals ask: What property has he left behind him?" He who gives with a glad heart in *dana*, plants a tree which sends forth branches beyond the sky, he leaves behind him the best kind of 'wealth.' *Dana* then, in its noblest form, is the pouring of your heart's sympathy upon God's creatures — man and bird and beast. *Dana* is the gift that makes some human hearts happier, more blessed, that makes a

corner of God's creation better, and more beautiful!

And so Sri Krishna says:

'The gift which is given, from a sense of duty, to one from whom nothing in return is expected, and which is given in the right place, at the right time to a deserving person, such a gift is *sattvic* (pure).'

XVII: 20

8. *Sattvic tyaga* (sacrifice) is true sacrifice. It is sacrifice of attachment and fruit. But let us remember, sacrifice of our own duty (*swadharma*) is not true *tyaga*; in fact the Lord tells us:

'Verily, renunciation of actions which are ordained is not right. Such renunciation through ignorance is declared to be *tamasic* (dark).'

XVIII: 7

In true *tyaga*, you take up what duty bids you do. You perform actions prescribed by the scriptures, but unmoved by gain: you act impersonally, without attachment. You do an act, because it is *due*. You do your duty for duty's sake: you renounce all egotism, all attachment, and all fruits.

'He who performs a prescribed action, O Arjuna, because it ought to be done, giving up attachment and also the fruit, that *tyaga* is regarded as *sattvic* (pure).'

XVIII: 9

The *sattvic* tyagi does not avoid humble or unpleasant tasks; nor is he specially attached to agreeable, pleasant, lofty tasks. He feels towards his work no emotion of repulsion and none of attachment. He does his task as a duty. Is the duty unpleasant? He does not hate it. Is the duty pleasant? He is not attached to it. He accepts life ungrudgingly. So is the teaching reaffirmed: 'Arjuna! Play your part faithfully and courageously! Neither grieve nor glory! Submit to the Will of God! For His Will alone is fulfilled, not yours!'

'The wise man who is pervaded by *sattva* (purity), whose doubts are cut asunder, such a renouncer neither hateth unpleasant action, nor is attached to agreeable action.'

XVIII: 10

The *sattvic tyagi* does his duty, disregarding fruit, knowing that duty, well discharged, paves the way for liberation and illumination. He does his duty, setting the Law, the Wheel in motion. Do your duty and the Divine Law will operate: leave the results to God's wisdom — trust in God and the Divine Law.

9. *Sattvic buddhi* (understanding, insight, conscience, or discernment) knows exactly when one must go forth in action, and when one must renounce or withdraw from action. Such a discerning intellect knows fit and unfit actions, as well as right and wrong actions; it teaches one what to fear and what not to fear; what binds and what liberates.

'The *buddhi* which knows *pravritti* (right action) and *nivritti* (right cessation of action), what ought to be done and what ought not to be done, what should be feared and what should not be feared, what work binds and what brings release, that *buddhi*, O Arjuna, is *sattvic* (pure).'

XVIII: 30

10. *Sattvic dhriti* (determination or willpower) controls the mind activity. By *sattvic* will we secure thought-control. The *sattvic* will also controls our actions so that we ask for no return: we act in sympathetic compassion. Pure will disciplines mind, breath, and the senses, and takes them in the right path. The mind does not wander: the vibrations, *prana*, are steadied: the senses are held under restraint.

'The determination which is unwavering, which, through *yoga* or concentration, controls the activities of the mind, the life-breaths and the senses, that, O Arjuna, is *sattvic* determination.'

XVIII: 33

11. *Sattvic* joy is *ananda*, pure bliss. It arises out of self-realisation or a vision of the Self. *Sattvic* joy can be attained after long experience and tremendous effort.

'Which appears like poison at first, but in the end is as nectar, and which springs from a clear understanding of the *atman* (self), that joy is said to be *sattvic* (pure).'

XVIII: 37

There are three marks of *sattvic sukha*:

- It is attained after *abhyasa* (practice) that is practice of *bhajan, dhyana,* and *puja.*

- It is difficult — bitter as poison — at the start, in the period of self-discipline; but it is sweet as nectar in the end.

- It does not spring from outer knowledge or outer objects, but out of clear and unclouded understanding; it is not born of *vishaya bhoga* (sense-pleasure) but of the inner serenity of the soul. It is wisdom which liberates.

12. *Sattvic* food is preferred by men of purity. It promotes integrity, intelligence, intellectual brilliance, strength, vigour, health, pleasure of physical and mental life, cheerfulness, delight, and the true joy of living.

> 'The foods which prolong life and promote purity, strength, health, joy and cheerfulness, which are sweet, soft, nourishing, and agreeable, are liked by *sattvic* men.'
>
> XVII: 8

Sattvic foods are palatable, savoury, sweet, juicy, and health-giving. They are agreeable to the taste, too. These are foods such as wheat, rice, green beans, dairy products, fruits, vegetables, etc. We must eat *sattvic* food, for it purifies heart, mind, and body. Remember too, *sattvic* food is the product of honest work. If you eat food purchased with ill-gotten money, or received as a gift from a person who is not honest, you are *not* eating *sattvic* food. Remember the story of the holy man, who, after great

persuasion, consented to accept *bhiksha* at the house of a
known evil-doer; when he left the man's house, he found
to his horror, that he had actually stolen some silver
articles that belonged to his host! The food that he had
accepted at the hands of the evil-doer, had actually turned
the holy man into a thief!

Man is what he eats, according to a German proverb. The
mind is also a product of the food you eat. So, you must
be careful! Eat food that is cooked by a person whose
vibrations are pure. The right persons to feed you are your
mother, wife, daughter, sister, and your guru.

Before you begin to eat, mentally offer your food as an
ahuti to the Lord; then your food will give you strength for
work and service. Also, when you are eating, make sure that
the atmosphere around you is peaceful. Do not eat in the
midst of noises.

Sattvic food not merely appeals to the tongue, it is also a
source of nutrition to mind and body. Naturally,
vegetarian foods such as fruits, milk, nuts, lentils, and
vegetables are the best kind of *sattvic* food. The Lord also
tells us, that if *sattva* prevails over the mind at the time of
death, one will be led to heaven after death. And if this
sattva is absolutely free from the influence of *rajas* and *tamas*
at the time of one's death, one attains liberation, and is
freed from the cycle of death and birth.

> 'If *sattva* prevaileth when the body of the
> embodied soul dies, then he goeth forth to the
> spotless worlds where dwell those who know the
> Highest.'
>
> XIV: 14

In the stillness of meditation and reflection, the aspirant should learn to recognise and distinguish between the *gunas* that operate on him. It is essential that he should not confuse *tamas* with *sattva*. For example, a person may be in a state of inaction due to inertia or dullness – this should not be confused with the tranquillity or stillness of mind associated with *sattva*.

We must also realise that *sattva* impels us to act in the spirit of service. Thus *sattva* is not meant to be practised upon oneself, alone, behind the closed doors of one's own home. Otherwise, it becomes no better than *tamasic* inertia. A *sattvic* doer promotes harmony in his life. He has a definite goal – spiritual evolution and enlightenment.

Sattva is light. But even light binds the *jiva* to the body, when it causes attachment. For example, there are scholars eager for knowledge; their joy is in study and scholarship. But they develop an attachment to knowledge and will not easily renounce the scholar's way. And they do not cease to be ego-centred. Though they have tendency towards introversion, self-analysis, scholarship, and deep thought, these become ends in themselves to these people – not means to the ultimate transcendence of thought and scholarship. They may be *sattvic* by temperament, but they are not God-centred.

Think of Nietzsche! What a great intellect he had! In his private life, he was pure as a maiden. His admirers described him as a "saint." He protested against vulgar money-making. Lonely was his soul, but it was not in communion with God. He too, was ego-centred, not God-centred. His thought eclipsed the spirit. He despised the common people. He misunderstood Christ. He asked for leaders who would 'deduce their rights' not from God, nor even from the people, but who would 'boldly rule in their own right, because they are stronger' in mind and willpower.

Here, we see the difference between the scholar's knowledge and true Enlightenment. In the West too, as Sadhu Vaswani pointed out, there are very many scholars of *sattvic* temperament, but their concern is less with Eternity than with the future and the present: they are concerned with plans and programmes of reform and progress. In India, even after centuries of anglicization, we have not forgotten that the goal of life is enlightenment, *mukti*, emancipation from bondage. This is why we still find men, even in middle life, who give up position and power, wealth and academic pursuit, to become *jignasus*, seekers after enlightenment, seekers after God. Their endeavour is to transcend the *sattvic* life to a life of contemplation and one-pointed devotion to the Divine Reality.

In the state of enlightenment, even *sattva* is transcended. A true saint has no need of *sattva* to elevate his mind, because he is no longer bound, confined by his mind and its moods. Such a man has transcended the three *gunas*.

The story is told to us of a king who was attacked by three thieves, while he was passing through a forest. One of them beat him up severely and looted him of his possessions; the second tied up his hands and feet and pushed him into a deep pit, and both of them departed. However, the third one took pity on the king. Escaping the notice of the other two, he came back, untied the king, led him out of the forest and bid him escape. The king thanked him profusely and begged him to accompany him to the palace so that he could be rewarded. But the thief declined, and went back to join his companions.

In the same way, the three *gunas* possess our soul, and deprive us of our spiritual treasure. We are tied by the bonds of *karma*, and thrown into the pit of the world process. *Sattva* can help to free us — it can even point to us the path of liberation, but it cannot take us to our ultimate goal. Therefore, as true seekers and aspirants, we must transmute *tamas* into *rajas* and *rajas* into *sattva*, and ultimately transcend *sattva* and become established in the Divine Self.

Appendix 2

Conquering the Three Gunas

Sri Krishna tells us in the *Gita*:

> 'When the embodied soul hath crossed over the three *gunas*, whence all bodies have been produced, then, indeed, freed from birth and death, from old age and sorrow, he drinketh the waters of immortality.'

XIV: 20

The Lord's message to His dear, devoted disciple is: "Conquer the three *gunas*, Arjuna!" The one who transcends the *gunas* becomes a seer. He realises:

- that liberation is won by him who knows that all work, all action, arise out of the three *gunas*.

- that there is One beyond the *gunas*, One who is Supreme. He is higher than the *gunas*.

- *gunas* are the seeds in *prakriti* : out of this seed, the body grows. So, out of *prakriti* are produced the *gunas*.

The wise man is one who crosses over the three *gunas*, controls them, conquers them, so that they move in rhythm and harmony with the wisdom of Krishna. Such a man is truly liberated. His marks are as follows:

1. He is indifferent to the three *gunas* when they are in action, as also when they cease to act.

2. He is undisturbed by the results of action. He realizes that all activity belongs to the *gunas*. He sees the *gunas* at work in himself and others, and is seated in their midst, indifferent, unconcerned. He is unshaken by the *gunas*. He is a pilgrim. As dreams do not disturb the wakened one, so *gunas* do not bind him.

3. All things and beings are states to him. Indifferent is he to *dwandas* (pairs of opposites). Therefore is he the same to friend or foe, the same in love or dislike, in censure and praise, in misery and prosperity. To him, a clod and a pebble are alike.

4. He does all his work without desire. He hath abandoned all ambition, undertaking, and enterprise. What is the way that a man must tread in order to cross the *gunas* and become one with the Eternal? It is the way of exclusive, unswerving devotion, and loving service to Sri Krishna. In love, he annihilates himself and enters into union with the Lord. He becomes nothing, a zero, and is united with the Self Supreme. Such a man realizes the *atmasvarupa*. He enters into Krishna, the Eternal, he becomes the Eternal.

'He who serveth Me with unswerving devotion, passes beyond the *gunas* and becomes one with the *Brahman*.

> 'For I am the abode of *Brahman*, the inexhaustible nectar of immortality: (I am the ground) of Eternal Righteousness and (the source) of unending Bliss.
>
> XIV: 26-27

Glossary

Aascharya	Wonder
Abhaya	Fearlessness
Abhinivesha	Clinging attachment
Abhyasa	Constant practice
Acharya	A holy teacher, a spiritual master who has not only mastered the philosophical systems but also realised the Truths they contain
Adharma	Lack of righteousness and virtue; injustice
Adhibuta	All the five elements of perishable nature
Adhidaiva	The Cosmic Soul, the Gods
Adhiyagna	All sacrifice
Adhyaya	Chapter
Advaita	Non-duality – a school of philosophy declaring the Oneness of God, the Soul, and the Universe
Agni	God of Fire
Ahuti	The offering of oblations
Ahankara	Ego

Ahimsa	Non-violence
Akarma	Inaction
Alasya	Laziness
Ananda	Bliss
Ananta gita	The Song of the Infinite
Anavasada	Freedom from depression
Angavastra	A piece of cloth worn over the shoulder
Antahkarna	The Inner Instrument
Antakala	The hour of death
Archana	The offering of flowers
Arjavam	Honesty, straightforwardness
Asat	Untrue
Ashrama	Hermitage; a centre for religious study and meditation
Ashvatta	Not stable, in a flux, that which is subject to change
Asmita	Egoism
Asti	Existence
Atmanivedana	Absolute surrender
Atmashakti	Spiritual strength
Atman	The Immortal Self
Avatara	An incarnation of Divine Consciousness who has descended upon earth
Avibhaktam	Entire, inseparable
Avidya	Ignorance which is responsible for the non-perception of reality
Avyakta	Not manifested
Avyayam	Imperishable, deathless

Be-anta	The One without end
Bhakta	Devotee
Bhakti	Love of God: single-minded devotion to one chosen ideal
Bhakti Marga	Path of love and devotion
Bhakti Yoga	The *yoga* of devotion
Bharat varsha	The continent of Bharata, ancient India
Bhashya	Commentary
Bhathi	Recognizability
Bhava	Conscious feeling, awareness
Bhavana	Feeling of devotion
Bhikku	Buddhist monk
Brahmagnani	A wise sage who has realised the Divine Truth
Brahmacharya	Walking with God: continence, practice of purity in thought, word, and deed
Brahman	The Absolute; the Supreme Reality of the Vedanta philosophy
Brahmanirvana	Bliss of God
Brahmisthithi	The Divine State
Buddhi	Intellect, reason
Chatraka	Rainbird
Chitta	A storage of impressions
Daana	Charity
Dama	Control of the senses
Darbar	A royal court
Daya	Compassion
Deha	Body

Deva	Divinity; God
Dharma	Righteousness, virtue, law
Dharmakshetra	Holy battlefield
Dharmayuddha	The battle for righteousness, a righteous war
Dheera	Sage
Dhriti	Fortitude
Dhyana	Meditation
Digvijaya yatra	Successful, country-wide campaign
Dina Bandhu	Brother of the weak
Dwandas	Pairs of opposites, binary contradictions
Dwaparayuga	One of the ancient epochs — an era in which righteousness is reduced by one-half
Dwesha	Hatred
Ekagritha	One-pointedness
Ekatvam	Oneness
Gita amritashtam	The nectar of the Gita in eight *slokas*
Gitasaran	The Essence of the Gita
Gitopanishd	The milk of the Scriptures, the Essence of the *shastras*
Gnana	Knowledge of God arrived at through discrimination and reasoning
Gnana Marga	Path of knowledge
Gopa	Cowherd
Gopi	Milkmaid
Goshala	Cowshed
Gunas	The three fundamental qualities — *sattva, rajas, tamas*

Gunatita	One who has conquered the three *gunas*
Gurubhakti	Devotion to the teacher
Gurukul	Abode of the *guru*, where students congregate in pursuit of knowledge
Gwala	Cowherd
Indriyas	The five senses and their domains
Janma	Birth
Japa	Prayer
Jignasu	The seeker
Jiva	The embodied soul; a living being; an ordinary man
Jivan shakti	Strength for life
Jivatma	The embodied Soul
Kalyana	Virtuous conduct
Kama	Lust, sensual desire
Karma	Mental or physical action
Karma kshetra	Plane of action
Karma Marga	Path or way of action
Karma sanyasa	Renunciation of action
Karma Yoga	The right performance of action, the way of action
Karmi	Man of activity
Kirtan	Group singing; communal chanting; devotional music
Klesha	Affliction
Koel	A member of the cuckoo order of birds, also called the Indian nightingale because of its melodious call

Krishna arpanam	Offering to Lord Krishna
Kriya	Daily activity
Krodha	Anger, wrath
Kshatriya	Belonging to the warrior class
Kshetra	The body
Kshetragna	Consciousness
Kshitta	Distracted
Leela	The Lord's Divine Sport
Lobha	Greed, covetousness
Lokasangraha	Welfare of the world
Madbhavam	My (the Lord's) State
Mahavakya	Great statement
Mamata	Possession
Manas	Mind
Mantra	Sacred utterance
Maryada purushottam	The ideal man
Mauna	Silence
Maya	Illusion; ignorance obscuring the vision of God
Moha	Attachment
Mudha	Dull
Mukti Marga	Path of liberation
Mumukshatwa	Desire for liberation
Muni	Sage; a pious person, a scholar, a saint
Murkha	Stupid
Namajapa	Utterance of the Name of God
Narayan Sena	Lord Krishna's army

Nirodha	Controlled
Nirvana	The state of being free from both suffering and the cycle of rebirth
Nishkama karma	Action without desire, action as worship of God
Nityayuktah	Ever-harmonized, ever-attuned
Nivritti	Right cessation of action
Om tat sat	The triple designation indicative of *Brahman*
Padasevana	Serving at the Feet (of the Lord)
Paradharma	Another's duty
Parabhakti	Highest form of devotion
Paramatma	The Supreme Soul
Parthasarathi	Arjuna's charioteer (here, Lord Krishna)
Parva	Chapter
Patram	Leaf
Phalam	Fruit
Pitamaha	Grandfather
Prana	The life force in the air one breathes
Puja	Ritual
Prakriti	Nature
Pramada	Inattention
Pravritti	Right action
Prema bhakti	Divine Love
Priyam	Utility
Punya Karma	Right action
Purana	Epic
Purusha	The Divine Spirit

Purushottama	The Supreme Self
Pushpam	Flower
Raga	Attachment
Rama karya	Work for Sri Rama
Rajas	One of the *gunas*— restless energy, passionate action
Rajasuya yagna	A sacrifice performed by emperors and kings to establish their sovereignty
Rajdharma	Duty as a king
Rajguru	The king's priest
Rakshasa	Demon
Rishi	A seer, a saint, an inspired poet
Rupa	Form
Sadhana	Self-discipline
Sama	Balance
Samadhana	One-pointed concentration
Samadhi	State of profound communication with the Divine
Samadrishti	Unified view
Samattva	Equanimity
Samsara	Creation
Samvada	Dialogue; conversation
Sanatana dharma	The Eternal religion - Hinduism
Sankhya yoga	The *yoga* of knowledge
Santosha	Contentment
Sanyasa	Renunciation
Saptah	Week
Saranagati	Surrender to the Lord

Sat chit ananda	True, Eternal Bliss
Satguru	The Supreme Teacher
Satasaharsri	Of ten thousand stanzas
Satpurkha	The pure-hearted one
Satsang	Association with the holy; a gathering of the devout
Sattva	The noblest of the three *gunas*, characterised by purity, harmony, uprightness, and composure
Satyam	Truthfulness
Seva	Service
Shabda	Sound
Shakti	Force, power, energy
Shama	Calmness of mind
Shraddha	Intense faith
Shishya	Disciple
Sloka	Stanza, verse
Smarana	Constant remembrance
Smashan	Burning ghats
Sravana	Listening
Srimad Bhagavat Purana	The most famous of the eighteen *puranas*
Sthithaprajna	The man of steady wisdom
Sukha	Pleasure
Surya	The Sun God
Swadharma	One's own duty
Swadhyaya	Study of Scriptures
Tamas	One of the *gunas* – darkness, blindness, ignorance; slothful inaction

Tapas	Austerity
Tapasya	Self-discipline
Tapasvi	Ascetic
Taposhakti	Power of penance and austerity
Tapovana	Forest of meditation
Taraka mantra	The Name of God by which one is initiated into spiritual Life
Tarka	Debate
Titiksha	Power of endurance
Trishna	Desire
Toyam	Water
Tyaga	Sacrifice
Upanishad	An assembly of pupils sitting down near their teacher to listen to his instruction (original meaning); Hindu Scriptures constituting the core teachings of Vedanta
Uparati	Contentment of mind
Vairagya	Dispassion, absence of desire
Vanara	The missing link between monkey and man
Vandana	Bowing down
Vasana	Subtle desires
Vastraharan	Disrobing
Veda	Sacred teachings taken collectively, to which Hinduism ascribes Divine Authority
Vedanta	The essence of the Vedas
Vibhuti	Glory, sovereignty; also sacred ashes
Vichara	Reflection, enquiry

Vignana	Knowledge
Vikara	Modification
Vikarma	Wrong action
Vikshipta	Partially distracted
Vimoka	Freedom of mind; rejection of gross desires
Vishada	Depression, darkness of the Soul
Vishaya	Object
Vishaya bhoga	Sensual pleasure
Vishwarupa	The Cosmic Divine Form
Vishwarupa	Vision of the Cosmic Form darshana
Viveka	Discrimination, abstention
Vyadha	Butcher
Yagna	Offering, sacrifice
Yagneshwara	The Lord of all sacrifices; the Eternal
Yaksha	Demi-god
Yoga	Union with the Divine
Yuga	A cycle or world-period according to Hindu mythology

JAICO PUBLISHING HOUSE
Elevate Your Life. Transform Your World.

ESTABLISHED IN 1946, Jaico Publishing House is home to world-transforming authors such as Sri Sri Paramahansa Yogananda, Osho, The Dalai Lama, Sri Sri Ravi Shankar, Robin Sharma, Deepak Chopra, Jack Canfield, Eknath Easwaran, Devdutt Pattanaik, Khushwant Singh, John Maxwell, Brian Tracy and Stephen Hawking.

Our late founder Mr. Jaman Shah first established Jaico as a book distribution company. Sensing that independence was around the corner, he aptly named his company Jaico ('Jai' means victory in Hindi). In order to service the significant demand for affordable books in a developing nation, Mr. Shah initiated Jaico's own publications. Jaico was India's first publisher of paperback books in the English language.

While self-help, religion and philosophy, mind/body/spirit, and business titles form the cornerstone of our non-fiction list, we publish an exciting range of travel, current affairs, biography, and popular science books as well. Our renewed focus on popular fiction is evident in our new titles by a host of fresh young talent from India and abroad. Jaico's recently established Translations Division translates selected English content into nine regional languages.

Jaico's Higher Education Division (HED) is recognized for its student-friendly textbooks in Business Management and Engineering which are in use countrywide.

In addition to being a publisher and distributor of its own titles, Jaico is a major national distributor of books of leading international and Indian publishers. With its headquarters in Mumbai, Jaico has branches and sales offices in Ahmedabad, Bangalore, Bhopal, Bhubaneswar, Chennai, Delhi, Hyderabad, Kolkata and Lucknow.

SINCE 1946